Konrad Morgen

Konrad Morgen SS Nazi Party identification card, Estate of Konrad Morgen, courtesy of Fritz Bauer Institut

Konrad Morgen

The Conscience of a Nazi Judge

Herlinde Pauer-Studer
University of Vienna, Austria

J. David Velleman
New York University, USA

First published 2015 by
PALGRAVE MACMILLAN

Palgrave Macmillan in the UK is an imprint of Macmillan Publishers Limited, registered in England, company number 785998, of Houndmills, Basingstoke, Hampshire RG21 6XS.

Palgrave Macmillan in the US is a division of St Martin's Press LLC, 175 Fifth Avenue, New York, NY 10010.

Palgrave Macmillan is the global academic imprint of the above companies and has companies and representatives throughout the world.

Palgrave® and Macmillan® are registered trademarks in the United States, the United Kingdom, Europe and other countries.

ISBN 978–1–137–49694–2

This book is printed on paper suitable for recycling and made from fully managed and sustained forest sources. Logging, pulping and manufacturing processes are expected to conform to the environmental regulations of the country of origin.

A catalogue record for this book is available from the British Library.

Library of Congress Cataloging-in-Publication Data

Pauer-Studer, Herlinde, author.

Konrad Morgen : the conscience of a Nazi judge / HerlindePauer-Studer, University of Vienna, Austria; J. David Velleman, New York University, USA.

pages cm

ISBN 978–1–137–49694–2 (hardback)

1. Morgen, Georg Konrad, 1909–1982. 2. Judges—Germany—Biography. 3. Germany. GeheimeStaatspolizei—Biography.
4. Nazis—Germany.—Biography. 5. World War, 1939–1945—Law and legislation—Germany. I. Velleman, James David, author. II. Title.

KK185.M667P38 2015

347.43'0234—dc23   2014049915

[B]

Typeset by MPS Limited, Chennai, India.

*For Torsten
and for Leah and Evan*

CONTENTS

LIST OF
ILLUSTRATIONS

PREFACE

STERN (voice over)
The SS auditors keep coming around, looking over the books—Goeth knows this—
EXTERIOR. CRACOW—DAY
The trucks at the loading dock of Goeth's private warehouse. Polish workers, under Hujar's supervision, throwing down the "surplus" bags of flour and rice—the supplies for the phantom 10,000 prisoners.
STERN (voice over)
You'd think he'd have the common sense to see what's coming.

In this scene from *Schindler's List*, workers are unloading provisions intended for 10,000 prisoners of the concentration camp Cracow-Plaszow—non-existent prisoners invented by the commandant, Amon Göth, so that he could requisition extra provisions to sell on the black market. The narrator says that Göth is being audited by the SS.

The men described here as SS auditors were actually criminal investigators for the SS, and the man who sent them was an SS judge, Georg Konrad Morgen (1909–82). Morgen also investigated corruption and other crimes at Buchenwald, Dachau, and Auschwitz, among other camps. He eventually pursued not just Göth but major perpetrators of Hitler's "Final Solution."

This is the little-known story of how an SS judge came face-to-face with the Nazi killing machine and, within the limits of his powers, tried to do something about it.

Morgen was a judge in the SS Judiciary, a system of courts that tried cases against members of the Nazi Waffen-SS, much as military courts try cases against members of the military. In 1941 and the first half of 1942 he investigated cases of financial corruption by members of the SS in occupied Poland. In July 1943 he was delegated by Heinrich Himmler, Reichsführer of the SS, to investigate SS corruption in the concentration camps.

Morgen did not confine his investigations to corruption. Exceeding his brief, he brought charges of murder against the commandant of Buchenwald and the chief of the Gestapo at Auschwitz. He even sought a warrant to arrest Adolf Eichmann. Eventually, five concentration-camp commandants were charged, at least one of whom was eventually executed for his crimes.[1]

After the war, Morgen was taken into custody and extensively interrogated by the American Counterintelligence Corps (CIC). He testified at numerous war-crimes trials—first at the Trial of Major War Criminals at Nuremberg, then at several lesser trials in the immediate post-war period, and finally, after establishing himself as a lawyer in Frankfurt, at the later wave of trials that began in the 1960s. He gave his last deposition in 1980, two years before his death.

Morgen explained after the war that although he could charge the chief of the Auschwitz Gestapo with 2,000 murders, he could not have charged anyone with the extermination of millions in the gas chambers of Auschwitz-Birkenau, because the person responsible was Hitler, whose will was literally law in the Führer-State. Morgen asserted that prosecuting ordinary murders was his means of impeding the program of extermination, given that he had no means of stopping it.

Morgen once described himself as a *Gerechtigkeitsfanatiker*—a fanatic for justice. This self-description is true in a sense, but that sense is neither as clear nor as favorable as he thought. Morgen was indeed fanatical about justice as he conceived it, but his conception of justice was inadequate to the systematic inhumanity that surrounded him. And his fanaticism was too single-minded to allow for self-critical reflection. It led him aright in some instances and grossly astray in others. He was therefore an equivocal figure, and his case is a study in moral complexity. Our aim is to understand both the positive and negative aspects of Morgen's *Gerechtigkeitsfanatismus*, by examining how he felt, thought, and deliberated about the events in which he took part.

Morgen's story is also of independent historical interest. As an experienced lawyer and judge, he witnessed the Holocaust through a moral lens, however flawed. He was also a dogged and, one might even say, brilliant investigator who never flinched from the sight of monstrous crimes. A record of his investigations survives both in his contemporaneous reports to superiors and in his post-war testimony to interrogators and war-crimes tribunals. Finally, he was not himself accused of war crimes, and so he was a far less defensive witness than the perpetrators about whom he testified.

We have found Morgen to be a largely reliable reporter of his wartime activities. With a few notable exceptions, which we will examine,[2] his postwar testimony squares with the documentary record, including not only his own papers but also, for example, the personnel files of those with whom he dealt during the war. His most improbable claim—that he

sought to arrest Adolf Eichmann—was confirmed by Eichmann himself
on the stand in Jerusalem. Morgen could be a selective and even insensitive observer of his surroundings, but he later passed up opportunities
to tailor his observations to what postwar audiences knew or wanted to
hear. Whether out of honesty or mere naiveté, then, he was a remarkably
ingenuous witness.

We think of this book as a moral biography, a case study of how one
man's moral consciousness coped or failed to cope with an immoral
world. Our account covers only Morgen's career as an active and former
member of the SS, and so it is less extensive than a cradle-to-grave biography; it is also less dependent on speculation. We avoid reconstructing
scenes and events for literary purposes, though when Morgen narrates
them, we give him the floor, so that readers can hear his voice. Finally,
we try to maintain a dispassionate tone despite the pathos of our topic.
In our view, it would be hubris to think that readers need protestations
from us to rouse their passions about the Holocaust.

Attempting a nuanced portrait of an SS officer raises a sensitive question: Doesn't it commit us to share a perspective that is morally unacceptable? Doesn't it amount to playing in the Devil's playground? In our view,
whether agents of evil systems must themselves be evil is a question that
cannot be decided a priori, nor should it be ruled inadmissible on moral
grounds. These agents are real individuals whose characters are available
for study, and we think it morally important to study them.

One further note on our methodology. In calling this book a moral biography, we may seem to invite comparison with that famous and controver-
sial moral biography, Hannah Arendt's *Eichmann in Jerusalem*. Although
there are some similarities, there are many more differences, and not just
because we lack Arendt's towering intellect and biting style.

For one thing, our moral themes, though no less significant than
Arendt's, revolve around a character of a different kind. Morgen's story
raises a variety of moral issues, but unlike Eichmann, he was not an exem-
plar of evil; he was rather, as we have said, a case of moral ambiguity and
complexity.

Another difference between our book and Arendt's is that, whereas
she used Eichmann to illustrate a provocative thesis—"the banality of
evil"—we have no equally sweeping thesis to present. Our view is that a
detailed look at a case such as Morgen's can illuminate how a person's
moral thinking works, and fails to work, under extreme conditions.
We interpret Morgen's actions and intentions, especially as they bear

on moral issues, but we would not do justice to our project—namely, to explore the nuances of Morgen's case—by using it to support a bold thesis. Looking at moral thought as it plays out in the mind of an individual caught up in catastrophes such as the Holocaust yields insights that cannot easily be captured in grand generalizations.

Having recounted Morgen's career, we will offer some concluding reflections on his character and some implications of his story for legal and moral philosophy. But these reflections will not exhaust the insights that, we hope, the reader will have gained. An exhaustive theoretical discussion would be a project for a different book.

ACKNOWLEDGMENTS

We thank Raphael Gross and Werner Konitzer, of the Fritz Bauer Institut in Frankfurt am Main, for drawing our attention to the case of Konrad Morgen. Raphael Gross's own essay on Konrad Morgen stimulated our first reflections on the case; Werner Konitzer offered advice during the many stages of the project and gave us comments on the complete draft of the manuscript. Other historians who offered guidance include Norbert Frei, Ian Kershaw, Barbara Schwindt, Sybille Steinbacher, and Rebecca Wittmann.

For comments on the manuscript, we thank Don Herzog, David Owens, Nishi Shah, Sharon Street, David Dyzenhaus, Veronika Hofer, Christopher Theel, Renate Zoitl-Wolfsgruber, Martin Kusch, Werner Konitzer, Christoph Hanisch, Sarah Buss, Brian Slattery, and Hans Petter Graver.

We owe special thanks to Christopher Theel. We have benefited from his profound historical knowledge of the SS jurisdiction and his help in finding archival sources at the Bundesarchiv Berlin-Lichterfelde, the Bundesarchiv Ludwigsburg, and the Staatsarchiv Ludwigsburg.

Thanks to David Dyzenhaus for organizing a discussion of the book manuscript in October 2013 with his NYU Law School reading group, and to all the participants for most helpful responses. We also presented material about Konrad Morgen to a conference on "Authority, Legality, and Legitimacy" at the University of Vienna in May 2011, where we received many helpful comments.

We also thank the following persons for generous help in archives: Kirsten Carter, FDR Library in Hyde Park, NY; Laura Joy, Hartley Library, University of Southampton; Teresa Gray, Jean and Alexander Heard Library of Vanderbilt University; Andreas Grunwald, Bundesarchiv Berlin-Lichterfelde; Petra Mörtl and Dr. Klaus A. Lankheit, Institut für Zeitgeschichte Munich; Dr. Peter Klefisch, Landesarchiv Nordrhein-Westfalen, Düsseldorf; Dr. Johann Zilien, Hessisches Hauptstaatsarchiv Wiesbaden; Rebecca L. Collier, US National Archives at College Park, MD; and last but not least, Werner Renz from the Fritz Bauer Institut, where the Nachlass of Morgen is kept.

We thank Isabelle Lewis for drawing the map of the German Reich and Polish Territories. Thanks to Michael Gartler for editorial help, to Steven B. Rogers for research assistance, and to Alexander Seifert for help with the archival material.

The book is part of the ERC-Advanced Research Grant "Distortions of Normativity." We thank the European Research Council and New York University for funding in support of the project.

TIMELINE

1930–33	Morgen studies law.
March 1, 1933	Morgen joins the SS.
April 1, 1933	Morgen enters the Nazi Party.
August 1934	Morgen refuses to vote in election of Hitler as *Reichspräsident*.
	Morgen passes first state exam in law (*erste juristische Staatsprüfung*).
1934–38	Morgen is in legal training to prepare for his second state exam.
1936	Morgen earns a doctorate in law and publishes his dissertation, a book on war prevention and war propaganda.
1938	Morgen passes second state exam (*zweite juristische Staatsprüfung*).
1939	Morgen joins the district court in Stettin.
April 1939	Morgen is dismissed as judge by order of the Reich Ministry of Justice; he begins work for the German Labor Front.
September 1, 1939	Germany invades Poland, Morgen is inducted into Waffen-SS (Reserve Unit).
Spring and Fall 1940	Morgen is demobilized and enters the SS Judiciary.
January 1941	Morgen is assigned to the SS court in Cracow.
June 22, 1941	Germany invades the Soviet Union.
September 1941	Morgen writes up his account of the Fegelein case.
March 27, 1942	Morgen requests reassignment out of the General Gouvernement.
March 1942	First transport of Jews to Belzec.
May 1942	Morgen is dismissed and demoted to the rank of private.
July 1942	Morgen is in basic combat training.
December 1942	Morgen joins Division "Wiking" in the Soviet Union.

May 1943	Morgen is recalled from the front to the SS Judiciary in Munich.
	Morgen is transferred to the Reich Criminal Office in Berlin.
June–July 1943	Morgen begins work in Kassel investigating Buchenwald.
August 18–19, 1943	Last transport of Jews to Treblinka.
August 24, 1943	Morgen arrests Karl Otto Koch, former commandant of Buchenwald.
September (?) 1943	Morgen investigates Jewish wedding in Lublin.
October 20, 1943	Prisoner revolt at Sobibor.
November 3, 1943	The *Erntefest* Massacre in Lublin.
November 1943	Morgen visits Auschwitz.
January (?) 1944	Morgen visits Globocnik in Trieste.
April 11, 1944	Morgen files investigative report on Buchenwald.
Summer 1944	Morgen forwards evidence on Eichmann to SS court in Berlin.
August 17, 1944	Morgen files indictment of Buchenwald defendants.
September 1944	First Buchenwald trial.
October 1944	Trial of Maximilian Grabner.
November 1944	Morgen is reassigned to the SS court in Cracow.
December 1944	Second Buchenwald trial.
January 1945	Germans abandon Cracow.
September 1945	Morgen enters American custody in Mannheim.

MAIN CHARACTERS

Horst Bender (February 24, 1905–November 8, 1987): *SS-Oberführer* (senior colonel); chief lawyer on the personal staff of *Reichsführer-SS* Heinrich Himmler; worked as a lawyer after the war; investigated for war crimes in 1977, charges dismissed.

Werner Best (July 10, 1903–June 23, 1989): *SS-Obergruppenführer* (lieutenant general) and jurist; civilian administrator of occupied France and Denmark. Sentenced to death by a Danish court in 1948, sentence reduced to imprisonment.

Philipp Bouhler (September 11, 1899–May 19, 1945): *SS-Obergruppenführer* (lieutenant general); Chief of the Führer's Chancellery; responsible for the *Aktion T4* euthanasia program; committed suicide in 1945 while in American custody.

Karl Brandt (January 8, 1904–June 2, 1948): *SS-Gruppenführer* (major general) in the General SS and *SS-Brigadeführer* (brigadier general) in the Waffen-SS; headed the administration of the *Aktion T4* euthanasia program; later Reich Commissioner for Health and Sanitation; convicted in the "Doctor's Trial" at Nuremberg and executed in 1948.

Franz Breithaupt (December 8, 1880–April 29, 1945): *SS-Obergruppenführer* (lieutenant general); second Chief of the SS Judiciary Head Office, succeeding Paul Scharfe; murdered by an aide in May 1945.

Erwin Ding-Schuler (September 19, 1912–August 11, 1945): *SS-Sturmbannführer* (major); surgeon at Buchenwald; committed suicide in 1945 while in American custody.

Oskar Dirlewanger (September 26, 1895–June 7, 1945): *SS-Obersturmführer* (first lieutenant); commander of the "Dirlewanger Brigade"; died in 1945 while in French custody.

Albert Fassbender (June 30, 1897–1964): adopted child of the owners of the German chocolate firm of Fassbender; *SS-Sturmbannführer* (major); commander of an SS cavalry brigade.

Hermann Fegelein (October 30, 1906–April 28, 1945): *SS-Gruppenführer* (major general); commander of the Death's Head Horse Regiment, garrisoned in Warsaw, later of the 1st SS Cavalry Regiment; married Eva Braun's sister Greta; executed for desertion by an improvised court martial in Hitler's Berlin bunker in 1945.

Hermann Florstedt (February 18, 1895–April 15, 1945): *SS-Standartenführer* (colonel); served at Sachsenhausen and Buchenwald; promoted to 3rd commandant of Majdanek; said to have been executed by the SS for crimes committed at Majdanek.

Odilo Globocnik (April 21, 1904–May 31, 1945): Higher SS and Police Leader in the Lublin district of the General Gouvernement; oversaw the construction and operation of the *Aktion Reinhard* extermination camps; from fall 1943, Higher SS and Police Leader in the Adriatic Littoral; committed suicide in 1945 while in British custody.

Maximilian Grabner (October 2, 1905–January 28, 1948): Chief of the Gestapo at Auschwitz; tried at the Polish Auschwitz Trial and executed in 1948.

Ernst-Robert Grawitz (June 8, 1899–April 24, 1945): Chief Physician of the SS; killed by grenade wounds, perhaps self-inflicted, during the Soviet advance.

Eberhard Hinderfeld: *SS-Obersturmführer* (first lieutenant); member of the SS Judiciary Head Office department of disciplinary affairs.

Waldemar Hoven (February 10, 1903–June 2, 1948): *SS-Hauptsturmführer* (captain); physician at Buchenwald; tried at the Nuremberg "Doctor's Trial" and executed in 1948.

Rudolf Höss (25 November 1901–16 April 1947): *SS-Obersturmbannführer* (lieutenant colonel); commandant of Auschwitz from May 4, 1940 to November 1943; returned to Auschwitz in May 1944 to oversee extermination of Hungarian Jews; witness at the International Military Tribunal at Nuremberg; later tried in Poland and executed in 1947.

Ernst Kaltenbrunner (October 4, 1903–October 16, 1946): *SS-Obergruppenführer* (lieutenant general); Chief of the Head Office of Reich Security (RSHA); tried before the International Military Tribunal at Nuremberg and executed in 1946.

Ilse Koch (September 22, 1906–September 1, 1967): wife of Karl Otto Koch; tried at Dachau and sentenced to imprisonment in 1947; after sentence was reduced, retried in 1950 and sentenced to life imprisonment; committed suicide in prison in 1967.

Karl Otto Koch (August 2, 1897–April 5, 1945): *SS-Standartenführer* (colonel); commandant of Sachsenhausen (1936), Buchenwald (1937–41), and Majdanek (1941–43); executed by the SS on 5 April 1945.

Eugen Kogon (February 2, 1903–December 24, 1987): Christian opponent of the Nazi Party; imprisoned for six years at Buchenwald; author of *The Theory and Practice of Hell*.

Walter Krämer (1892–1941): Communist prisoner at Buchenwald.

Jaroslawa Mirowska: Polish spy for the SS, double agent for the Polish resistance.

Kurt Mittelstädt: *SS-Obersturmbannführer* (lieutenant colonel); SS judge; from May 1944, head of the investigative office of the Special Purpose Court (*Gericht zur besonderen Verwendung*) established by Himmler at Morgen's request.

Joachim Mrugowsky (August 15, 1905–June 2, 1948): SS physician; Chief of the Hygiene Institute of the Waffen-SS; Senior Hygienist of the Reich.

Erich Muhsfeldt (February 18, 1913–January 28, 1948): non-commissioned SS officer in Auschwitz and Majdanek extermination camps; assigned to cremating the victims of the *Erntefest* massacre; tried in Warsaw and executed in 1948.

Heinrich Müller (April 28, 1900–May 1945): *SS-Gruppenführer* (major general); Chief of the Gestapo, a unit of the Head Office of Reich Security; never captured after the war.

Arthur Nebe (November 13, 1894–March 21, 1945): *SS-Gruppenführer* (major); from 1939 Chief of the Criminal Police (Kripo) at the Head Office of Reich Security; in 1941 commanded *Einsatzgruppe B* in the Bialystok district, with an extermination center in Minsk; executed for involvement in the July 20 (1944) assassination attempt on Hitler.

Werner Paulmann: *SS-Sturmbannführer* (major); president of the SS and Police Court in Kassel.

Karl Peix (1899–1941): Communist prisoner at Buchenwald.

Hermann Pister (February 21, 1885–September 28, 1948): *SS Oberführer (senior colonel)*; in 1942 succeeded Karl Otto Koch as commandant of Buchenwald; tried by the Americans at Dachau and sentenced to death, but died of a heart attack in prison.

Norbert Pohl (1910–68): SS judge; Morgen's superior at the SS and Police Court in Cracow (1941–42).

Oswald Pohl (June 30, 1892–June 8, 1951): *SS-Obergruppenführer* (lieutenant general); chief of the SS Head Office of Economic Administration (*SS Wirtschafts verwaltungshauptamt*, or WVHA), with responsibility for concentration camps; sentenced to death by an American military tribunal in 1947, executed in 1951.

Günther Reinecke (April 18, 1908–April 24, 1972): *SS-Oberführer* (senior colonel); SS Judge and Chief of Legal Affairs at the Head Office of the SS Judiciary.

Ferdinand Roemhild: inmate and medical clerk at Buchenwald.

Ernst Röhm (November 28, 1887–July 2, 1934): co-founder of the *Sturmabteilung* (SA), the Nazi Party militia, later its commander; executed by order of Hitler in 1934 in the "Night of the Long Knives."

Georg von Sauberzweig: chief of a troop-supply depot in Warsaw.

Paul Scharfe (September 6, 1876–July 29, 1942): *SS-Obergruppenführer* (lieutenant general); first Chief of the SS Judiciary Head Office, succeeded by Franz Breithaupt.

Kurt Schmidt-Klevenow (August 19, 1906–January 30, 1980): *SS-Obersturmbannführer* (lieutenant colonel); from 1940, legal advisor to Oswald Pohl; from 1942, Chief of the Court and Welfare Office of the Economic Administration Head Office (*Wirtschafts- verwaltungshauptamt*, or WVHA); testified at the WVHA trial (USA v. Oswald Pohl).

Martin Sommer (February 8, 1915–June 7, 1988): *SS-Hauptscharführer* (first seargant); guard at Dachau and Buchenwald; tried in SS Court together with Karl Otto Koch, demoted and sent to the Eastern Front; captured by the Soviets in 1950, released to Germany in a prisoner swap in 1955; tried in West Germany in 1957, sentenced to life imprisonment; died in prison in 1988.

Jakob Sporrenberg (September 16, 1902–December 6, 1952): *SS-Gruppenführer* (major general); lieutenant general of the Police in Minsk and Lublin; tried in Poland and executed in 1952.

Otto Georg Thierack (April 19, 1889–November 22, 1946): Nazi jurist and politician; Reich Minister of Justice from 1942; committed suicide while in prison after the war.

Walter Toebbens (May 19, 1909–November 16, 1954): industrialist, owner of the *Többenswerke* in the Warsaw Ghetto, which were transferred to Poniatowa (Poland) after the suppression of the Warsaw Ghetto rising in spring 1943.

Martin Tondock: *SS-Oberführer* (senior colonel); SS judge at the Head Office of the SS Judiciary.

Maria Wachter: fiancée of Konrad Morgen, married after Morgen's release from American custody.

Josias Erbprinz zu Waldeck und Pyrmont (May 13, 1896–November 30, 1967): *SS-Obergruppenführer* (lieutenant general); heir apparent to the throne of the Principality of Waldeck and Pyrmont; Higher SS and Police Leader for Weimar, with responsibility for Buchenwald; tried by the Americans in the "Buchenwald Trial" at Dachau and sentenced to life in prison, released after three years for ill health.

Gerhard Wiebeck (1910–?): SS judge and assistant to Konrad Morgen in 1943–45.

Christian Wirth (November 24, 1885–May 26, 1944): German policeman and *SS-Sturmbannführer* (major); inspector of *Aktion T4* euthanasia facilities until 1941; then commandant of Chelmno and commandant of Belzec; appointed inspector of the *Aktion Reinhard* extermination centers by Odilo Globocnik in 1942; reassigned with Odilo Globocnik to the Adriatic Littoral in 1943; killed in May 1944 near Trieste by a Yugoslav partisan.

MAP OF THE
GERMAN REICH
AND POLISH
TERRITORIES, 1942

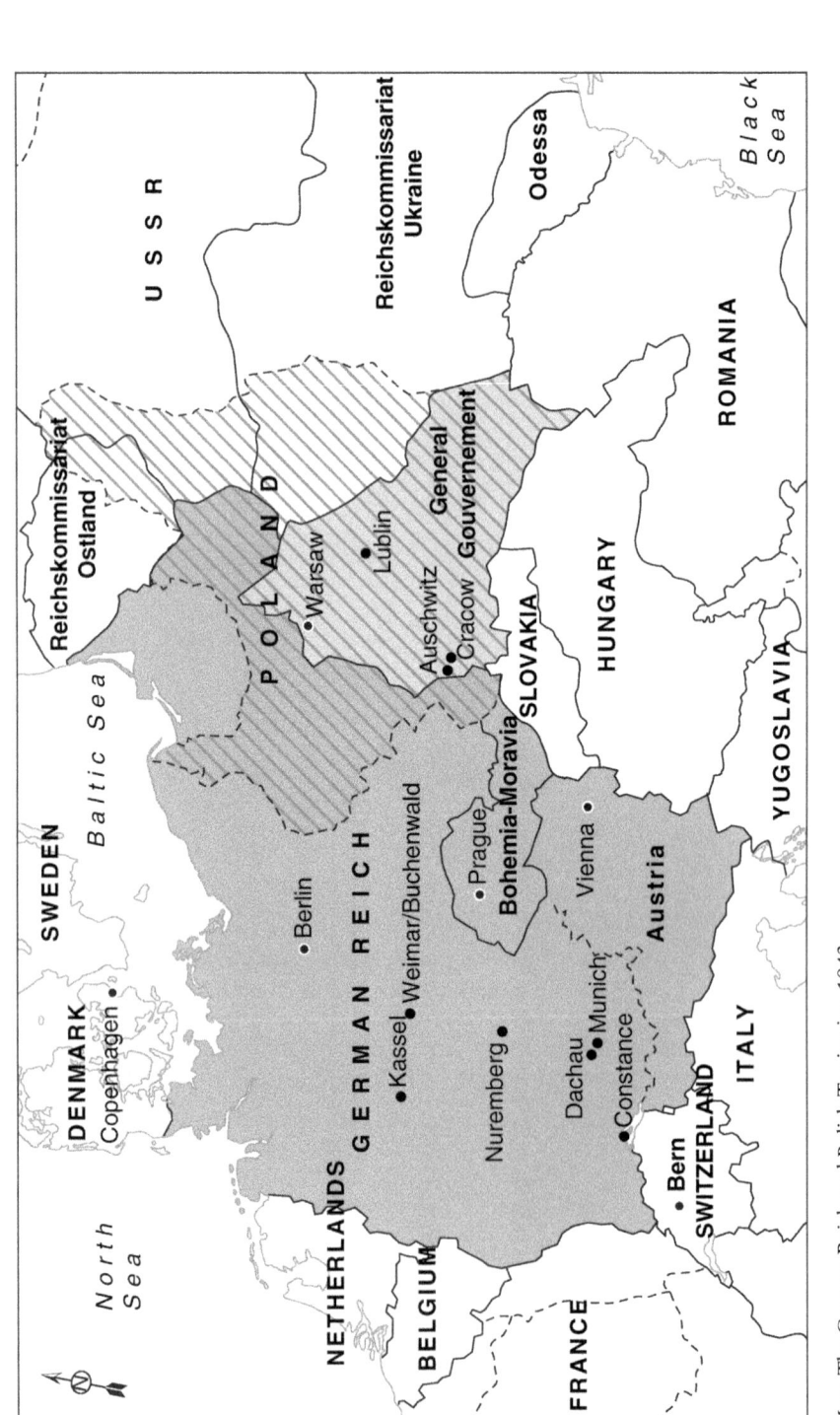

Map. The German Reich and Polish Territories, 1942

ONE

INTRODUCTION

Transcript of The Auschwitz Trial
Twenty-fifth day of the proceedings, March 9, 1964
Examination of the witness Konrad Morgen[1]

My investigations in the concentration camp of Auschwitz were triggered by a small package in the military mail. It was a somewhat small packet, long rather than short, an ordinary box, which had probably come to the attention of the postal service because of its enormous weight, and the customs investigators had confiscated it because of its contents. It contained three lumps of gold. Gold was a currency subject to inspection, and that is how it came to be confiscated by the customs investigators. The sender was an SDG—that is, a medical assistant—in the concentration camp Auschwitz, and this packet was addressed to his wife. He came under the jurisdiction of the SS Police Court, and this confiscated mailing was directed to me, with a short notation; I think it was "for further action."

As for the gold, it was high-caret dental gold that had been crudely smelted together. It was a very large lump, perhaps the size of two fists; the second was considerably smaller, the third less significant. But in any case, it was a matter of kilos. Before I dealt with it any further, I reflected on the matter. First, the audacity with which the as yet unknown perpetrator had proceeded—astounding. It seemed to be outright stupidity. But as I thought more about it, I thought that this interpretation underestimated the perpetrator. For after all, among hundreds of thousands of packages in the military post, there was a very small chance that this particular risky shipment would be confiscated and uncovered. But here it seemed to me that a refined barbarity and unscrupulous recklessness had predominated in the perpetrator— a trait that my later investigations in the concentration camp Auschwitz confirmed. That's generally how things were carried out. My further reflection, however, sent no small shudder down my spine, since a kilogram of gold is 1,000 grams.

I knew that the dental wards of the concentration camps were tasked with collecting the gold that accumulated from the burning of bodies and sending it to the Reichsbank. And a gold filling is only a few grams. One thousand grams, or several thousand grams, thus represented the death of several thousand people. But not everyone had gold fillings in that impoverished time, only a fraction. And depending on whether one estimated that one twentieth or fiftieth or hundredth had gold in their mouths, one had to multiply the number, and so this confiscated shipment represented as it were twenty- or fifty- or a hundred-thousand bodies. [Pause] A shocking thought. But the literally incomprehensible thing was, that the perpetrator could have set aside such a considerable quantity undetected. And given that little notice was taken of the suspect's exploit, I concluded, equally little notice might be taken if 50,000 or 100,000 people had disappeared and been turned to ash.

A natural cause of death wouldn't have done it: those people must have been murdered.

It was from this standpoint that I first realized that this little-known Auschwitz, whose location cost me some trouble to find on a map, must have been one of the largest human-extermination facilities that the world had ever seen. [Pause] I could have dealt with the case of this confiscated gold shipment very easily. The pieces of evidence were conclusive. I could have had the perpetrator arrested and accused, and the matter would have been taken care of. But given the reflections that I have briefly delineated for you, I absolutely had to have a look for myself. So I went as quickly as I could to Auschwitz, in order to carry out inquiries on the spot.

One morning, then, I stood at the station in Auschwitz. One instinctively expects a facility in which the monstrous, the unspeakable, the unimaginable takes place, that the traces must somehow be visible, a peculiar atmosphere. So I stayed for a little while at the station, in order to see anything there. But Auschwitz was a small city with a very large transit and transfer station, a bit like Bebra. Trains were constantly going through, troop transports to the East, transports of the wounded coming back, coal trains, trains of ore, goods, and passengers too. The people who disembarked— the young ones gay, the older ones glum, worn out, as if it was the most mundane thing in the world. I also saw prisoner transports in striped uniforms. But they were leaving Auschwitz; none arrived.

So. You couldn't miss the concentration camp, but from the outside it had the appearance that one was accustomed to from war-prisoner camps and other concentration camps: high walls, barbed wire, guard towers, guards walking back and forth. A gate, hustle and bustle of prisoners, but nothing noteworthy. I reported to the commandant, Standartenführer Höss, a somewhat stocky, taciturn, monosyllabic man with a stony face. I had already notified him by telegraph of my arrival and let him know that I had inquiries to make. He said something to the effect that they had been handed an enormously hard assignment, and not everyone had the character for it. He then asked curtly how I wanted to begin. I told him that I must first tour the whole camp. Before I began an investigation in a concentration camp, I inspected the camp overall, especially its main features. He looked quickly at the duty roster, made a phone call, and a Hauptsturmführer came. And he directed this man to drive me around the compound and show me everything I wanted to see. I started with the beginning of the end, namely, the ramp in Birkenau.

The ramp looked like any other ramp at a freight terminal. There was nothing special to discover there, no special precautions being taken. So I asked my guide how it went. He explained to me that the camp was notified by the station of a transport, usually of Jews, shortly before arrival, before it was due in Auschwitz. Then a guard unit was called out and they cordoned off the tracks and the ramp. Then the doors of the cars were opened, and the arrivees had to disembark and put down their luggage. Men and women had to form separate lines, and then, he explained, the rabbis were called for first. Rabbis and other Jewish notables were immediately separated out and brought into the camp, into a barrack that they had to themselves. I saw it later: it checked out. They were well cared-for, they didn't have to work, they were expected to write letters and postcards all over the world from Auschwitz, as many as possible, so as to allay any suspicion that anything horrible was going on there.

Then a call went out for specialists needed in the camp—the camp was connected with large industrial concerns—and these people were picked out. Then the remainder were divided into those who were fit for work and those who weren't. The ones who were fit for work marched on foot into the camp of Auschwitz, were duly recorded as prisoners, outfitted, divided into groups. The others had to take a seat in a lorry and went, without their names being taken, straight to Birkenau and into the gas chambers. My guide told me, with black humor, that if there was no time, or no doctor was present, or there were too many arrivees, they occasionally shortened the procedure by telling the arrivees in polite terms that the camp was several kilometers away, and whoever felt too sick or too weak or would find it uncomfortable to walk could make use of the transport facilities that the camp had provided. Then there was a stampede for the vehicles. And only those who didn't join in could march into the camp, while the others had unwittingly opted for death. [Pause]

From the ramp we followed the path of the death cargoes to the camp Birkenau, which lay a few kilometers away. Outwardly there was again nothing remarkable to be seen: a large mesh-wire fence, a bit warped, with a guard. Behind it lay the so-called camp "Canada," where the effects of the victims were searched, put in order, recycled. You could see a pile of burst-open suitcases from the previous transports, items of lingerie, briefcases, but also complete dentist's equipment, cobbler's equipment, medicine bags. Obviously the so-called evacuees really had the impression, as they had been told, that they were being resettled in the East and would find a new life there, and had therefore brought all the necessities with them. [Pause]

And in the back were the crematoria. They were one-story, gabled buildings that could just as well have been small workshops or work-sheds. Even the wide, massive smokestacks needn't have attracted the attention of civilians, since they were very low, ending a bit higher than the roof. On the side where the lorries drove up, the ground was sloped, about the size of a schoolyard, spread with cinders [unintelligible]. They drove in in such a way that a bystander who saw the caravan of lorries could just tell that they had disappeared into a depression in the ground, without being able to tell where the transportees had been dropped off—here again one of those subtle but fundamentally primitive precautions that one repeatedly found, like a common thread running through the whole organization. [Pause] In the courtyard was what can only be called a pack of Jewish prisoners wearing the yellow star, with their kapo,[2] who carried a long club, and they immediately surrounded us. They continually ran around in a circle, prepared for any order and snatching at every glance. And the thought ran through my mind: they acted just like a pack of sheep dogs. So I said that to my guide, who laughed and said, yes, that was their job. The condemned should at first be reassured by seeing their co-religionists. And this commando had instructions not to strike the arrivees. They should avoid anything that would cause an outbreak of panic. Rather, they should inspire a bit of anxiety and respect, but mainly just be there and lead or guide them where one wanted to have them.

In the back of the courtyard was a big gate that led into the so-called changing rooms, like the changing room of a gym. There were simple wooden benches with clothes racks, and each spot was clearly numbered and had a locker tag. And the victims were instructed to take note of their locker and hold on to their locker tag—all so as not to let them have the slightest suspicion until literally the last second, and to lead the condemned into the trap without a clue.

On the wall was a big arrow pointing to a corridor, and on it the terse words "To the showers" repeated in six or seven languages. They were told: you folks undress and you'll be showered and disinfected. And on this corridor there were various chambers with no furnishings—cold, bare, a cement floor. What was noticeable and at first inexplicable was that there was a grated duct in the middle, reaching to the ceiling. At first I could think of no explanation for it, until I was told that gas—Zyklon B in crystalline form—was poured into this death chamber through an opening the ceiling. Until that moment the prisoner was clueless, and then of course it was too late. Across from the gas chambers were the lifts for the corpses, and these led to the second story, or, viewed from the other side, the ground floor. [Pause] The actual crematorium was a vast hall in which, on one side, was a long row of crematory ovens, with flattened floors, all exuding a matter-of-fact, neutral, technical, bland atmosphere. Everything was spick-and-span, and a few prisoners in mechanic's outfits polished the armatures and contrived to look busy. Otherwise, it was completely quiet and empty.

Having seen these outer installations without any SS making an appearance, I was of course interested in meeting the SS personnel who managed the whole apparatus and kept it running. So I was allowed a brief glimpse into the so-called guardroom of the camp Birkenau, and here for the first time I received a real shock. As you know, in every army in the world a military guardroom is distinguished by a spartan simplicity. There's a desk, a few notices hung up, a few cots for those who have been relieved, a desk and a telephone. But here it was different. It was a low, rather dim room, and a few colorful couches had been thrown together. And on these couches, lying picturesquely, were a few SS men, mostly below officer grade, drowsing with glassy eyes. I had the impression that they must have drunk a fair amount of alcohol the night before.

Instead of a desk there was a giant hotel stove, on which four or five young girls were baking potato pancakes. They were obviously Jewesses, very pretty, oriental beauties, full-busted, fiery eyes, wearing not prisoner's uniforms but normal, even coquettish dresses. And they brought the potato pancakes to their pashas, who lay around on the couches and dozed, and asked them anxiously whether there was enough sugar on them, and fed them. [Pause] No one took any notice of me and my guide, though he was an officer. No one saluted, no one stirred. And I couldn't believe my ears: These female prisoners and the SS, they called each other "du." I could only give my guide a dumbfounded look. He just shrugged and said, "The men have a hard night behind them. They had to dispatch several transports." I think he put it that way. That meant that during the night, while I stood riding on the train to Auschwitz, several thousand people, several trains' full, had been gassed and turned to ash. And of these thousands of people, not the slightest bit of dust remained on the oven fittings. [Pause]

After I had seen everything there was to see in Birkenau, I made a tour of the camp. In quick succession: some well-chosen prisoners' rooms or barracks, the cultural amenities that the camp even had, [pause] the sickbay. And then I of course had them bring me to the so-called bunker, and there I was shown—openly and most willingly—the so-called Black Wall, where the shootings took place. [Pause]

After I had looked over the camp—it had meanwhile become late afternoon—I went into action and had the whole SS crematorium commando fall in before their lockers, in their quarters, and I made a search. And as I had thought, various things came to light: gold rings, coins, chains, pearls, pretty much all the currencies of the world. Here small "souvenirs," as the owner called them; there a small fortune. What I hadn't expected, though, was, that out of one or two lockers the genitals of freshly slaughtered bulls fell at my feet. I was at first completely flabbergasted and couldn't imagine their purpose. Until the owner of the relevant locker—blushing, believe it or not—confessed to me that one got them to revive one's sexual powers. [Pause] After I had made this search, and pretty well nailed down, questioned the whole crematorium commando, the day was over. And I went to my quarters.

Understandably, I couldn't sleep a wink that night. I had already seen some things in concentration camps, but never anything like that. And I considered what could be done about it.

The speaker is Georg Konrad Morgen, former SS judge and criminal investigator, testifying for the prosecution on March 9, 1964, the 25th day of the *Auschwitz-Prozess* in Frankfurt am Main, where 22 defendants were tried for crimes committed in the combined camps of Auschwitz and Birkenau. Many of the senior officers of Auschwitz, including the former commandant, Rudolf Höss, had been tried and executed in Poland shortly after the war, in what is sometimes known as the first *Auschwitz-Prozess*. The second Auschwitz trial dealt with lower-level perpetrators. At trial's end, six of the defendants were sentenced to life imprisonment, five released, and the rest imprisoned for terms as short as three-and-a-half years and as long as 14.

Morgen was a star witness in Frankfurt, having seen all there was to see at Auschwitz-Birkenau. He spoke in a ponderous drawl, punctuated by throat-clearings and dramatic pauses. The judge let him go on uninterrupted for over an hour, despite the sometimes questionable relevance of his narrative to the guilt or innocence of the defendants. Perhaps because Morgen was neither perpetrator nor victim at Auschwitz, he was considered to be a somewhat disinterested witness to its role in implementing the "Final Solution."

The "Final Solution" was meant to be the solution to a supposed problem, the answer to a particular question, namely, the "Jewish question," or *Judenfrage*.[3] The notion of a *Judenfrage* first arose in the wake of the Enlightenment and French Revolution, when the Jews were granted civil rights, or "emancipated." The supposed question was whether their newly accorded status as fellow citizens of Christians could be reconciled with their religious commitment to "chosenness" and to their future reunion from the diaspora in a restored kingdom of Israel. Posed thus dispassionately, the question was entertained by the Jews themselves, who sometimes wondered to what extent they wished to be assimilated as Frenchmen, Germans, or Austrians. But the question also became a lightning rod for all sorts of anti-Semitism,under the influence of which it mutated into the question of "what to do about" the Jews, or how to reverse their perceived encroachments. The tragically ironic result is that the phrase "a solution of the Jewish question" (*eine Lösung der Judenfrage*), which appeared in the subtitle of Theodor Herzl's Zionist manifesto, *Der Judenstaat*, subsequently littered the correspondence and memoranda of Nazi leaders.[4]

The Nazi regime initially addressed the "Jewish question" by trying to remove the Jews from public and economic life—boycotting and then confiscating Jewish businesses, gradually excluding Jews from the professions, and greatly restricting personal contacts between Jews and non-Jews. They also began to pursue their goal of redefining the state itself in racial terms. The "Law for the Restoration of a Professional Civil Service," excluding the Jews from public employment, was enacted on April 7, 1933, slightly more than two months after Hitler's accession to power.[5] This process was to culminate in the Nuremberg Laws of 1935, stripping German Jews of their citizenship in the Reich.

The Nuremberg Laws enshrined the racial line between Aryans and non-Aryans in legal terms. Prominent legal theorists sympathetic to the Nazi regime emphasized that the Nuremberg Laws had constitutional status, thus belonging to the legal foundations of National Socialist Germany.[6] The state thus came to embody a racial ideology, which permeated all state functions, even down to the level of the police. Such instruments of state coercion were guided by an ideology whose core elements were stated by Werner Best in an essay on the Gestapo Law in 1936:[7]

[The Political Police is] an institution which carefully supervises the political sanitary state of the German body of people, an institution which recognizes in a timely manner each symptom of disease and identifies the germs of destruction—whether they developed due to inner corrosion or were imported externally due to willful poisoning—and extinguishes them by any sort of appropriate means. This is the idea and the ethos of the Political Police in the racial Führerstaat of our time.

How these ideological commitments were to be implemented became clearer after the annexation of Austria in March 1938, when the Nazis initiated a program, managed by Adolf Eichmann, of forcing the Jews of Vienna to emigrate. In November of that year, the nationwide *Kristallnacht* pogrom raised the pressure and the rate of emigration. By May 1939, Eichmann claimed to have forced 100,000 Jews out of Austria by "legal" means.[8]

The "Jewish question" took on a new complexion with the invasion of Poland in September 1939. The outbreak of the war narrowed and finally closed the avenues of forced emigration, while the incorporation of previously Polish territories added millions of Jews to the population of the Reich. The troops of the *Wehrmacht* were followed by police forces and *SS Einsatzgruppen* ("task forces"), whose ostensible mission was to secure civil order by executing local officials, members of the intelligentsia, criminals, suspected partisans, and others deemed to be security risks. Jews were included in these executions on the pretext of their belonging to any and all of these suspect groups, as natural resisters, criminals, and vectors of disease or subversive ideology. These operations quickly expanded into spontaneous mass shootings of Jews and Poles during the first weeks of the war.[9]

At this time, however, official Nazi policy for the Jews had the final goal of expulsion.[10] Jews were to be concentrated in ghettoes for the purposes of "control and later deportation."[11] Ethnic Germans living outside the newly expanded Reich were to be repatriated and settled on land confiscated from Poles and Jews, the latter of whom were to be expelled to a "Jewish reservation" in unincorporated Polish territory.[12] An eastern wall (*Ostwall*) would separate this territory from Germany, and Hitler anticipated moving the line of demarcation further to the east only "after decades."[13] This vast shuffling of populations quickly encountered serious bottlenecks, however, raising an especially pointed version of the question of what to do with the Jews.

Attempts to overcome these bottlenecks became embroiled in various controversies among Nazi leaders and local officials, as a result of which the expulsions stalled.[14] Contention also arose over whether the Jews were to be used—indeed, imported—as laborers in support of the war effort, or simply isolated and expelled,[15] and whether the ghettoes were to be deathtraps or self-supporting enclaves.[16]

The "Jewish Question" mutated once again with the German invasion of Western Europe in May 1940. The invasion added hundreds of thousands of Jews to German control, and it raised the prospect of access to the sea and to Western European colonies abroad.[17] The destination envisioned for the Jews therefore shifted.

In May 1940, Himmler wrote a memorandum expressing the "hope completely to erase the concept of Jews through the possibility of a great emigration of all Jews to a colony in Africa or elsewhere."[18] At the same time, alien populations in the East were to be screened for the purpose of "fish[ing] out of this mush the racially valuable, in order to bring them to Germany for assimilation."[19] These plans still extended no further than the resettlement of populations: "However cruel and tragic each individual case may be," Himmler wrote, "this method is still the mildest and best, if one rejects the Bolshevik method of physical extermination of people, out of inner conviction [that it is] un-German and impossible."[20] The following fall, Reinhard Heydrich, Chief of the Reich Security Head Office (*Reichssicherheitshauptamt*), still wrote about the "settlement of the Jewish question" as being achieved through "evacuation overseas."[21] But as the prospect of victory against Britain dimmed, and with it the hope of controlling the seas, the idea of shipping Jews abroad became unrealistic. Even so, the notion of expelling the Jews to some destination or other stayed alive.[22] In February 1941, Heydrich wrote of achieving a "total solution to the Jewish question" by "sending them off to the country that will be chosen later."[23] The notion that resettlement would provide the solution to the "Jewish question" persisted among the Nazi leadership until at least June of 1941.[24]

This view began to change with the "war of destruction" against the Soviet Union, which would add more Jews to the sphere of German control while pushing further east the boundaries beyond which they would have to be expelled.[25] As in Poland, executions of supposedly dangerous elements were carried out in the wake of the invading forces, and Jewish men were targeted on the pretext that they were bolshevists ("commissars") and *Weltanschauungsträger*—carriers of a worldview inimical to the Reich.[26]

When the invasion did not succeed as quickly as planned, even Jewish women and children, who had been excluded from the initial executions, were slated to be shot.[27] Thus began, in August 1941, the first use of mass murder to render areas completely *judenrein*. By the end of the summer, however, an obstacle to large-scale executions was becoming clear. Frontline members of the firing squads, who had been shooting their victims individually, were suffering psychological trauma from the rigors of this grisly work.[28] More "humane" methods of eliminating unwanted populations were needed—methods that would be more humane for the victims, perhaps, but whose real purpose was to spare German troops the onerous task of murdering them one-by-one. The idea of such methods was already in the air. In July, Rolf Heinz Höppner had written the following to Eichmann about the possibility of interning the Jews of the Warthe region:

> There exists this winter the danger that all the Jews can no longer be fed. It should be seriously considered if it would not be the most humane solution to dispose of the Jews, insofar as they are not capable of work, through a quick-acting agent. In any case it would be more pleasant than to let them starve.[29]

Such a "quick-acting agent" already existed—a preexisting hammer to which these developments served up the Jews as an exposed nail. Gas chambers such as those eventually used to murder Jews at the notorious death camps had first been developed in the winter of 1939–40 for the purpose of "euthanizing" large numbers of mentally and physically handicapped adults,[30] a program that appears to have been envisioned by Hitler as early as 1935.[31] Six medical killing centers, under the supervision of resident physicians, received transports of handicapped patients from all over the Reich.

The first gassings of Jews as such—that is, simply because they were Jews—were carried out on German soil in 1940 as a relatively small part of this "euthanasia" program.[32] Whereas non-Jewish patients were selected for "euthanasia" after a cursory medical evaluation, Jewish patients were sent to the medical killing centers in exclusively Jewish transports on no medical pretext whatsoever. These Jews, along with roughly 70,000 ill and handicapped,[33] were killed in gas chambers disguised as shower rooms. Hitler ordered a stop to the "euthanasia" program in the summer of 1941, but all that changed was the source of victims. Physicians previously involved in "euthanasia" had begun to make periodic visits to concentration camps, where they selected inmates to be transported to the medical killing centers, for the purpose of reducing the number of potential troublemakers and inmates unable to work.[34] Here again, the selections included Jews as such,[35] but only as one group among many who were selected for this "special treatment."

It remains a matter of debate among historians exactly when a decision was reached to apply this technology to solving the "Jewish question" once and for all. At some point in the summer or fall of 1941, the techniques that had been developed for large-scale "euthanasia" were married to the policy of wholesale extermination that had developed on the Soviet front, begetting what is now known as the "Final Solution."

Consultants from T4, as the "euthanasia" program was known, visited Lublin for the construction of extermination centers,[36] which belonged to what was later to be called "Operation Reinhard" (in honor of its architect, Reinhard Heydrich, who had been assassinated).[37] Almost all of the staff in these killing centers were then recruited from T4.[38] They brought their methods and procedures with them:[39] gas chambers camouflaged as showers, lockers where the victims deposited their valuables for "safe-keeping," and so on.

Auschwitz had been built in 1940 as a concentration camp, that is, a prison camp; extermination centers did not yet exist. The prison camps called *Konzentrationslager* (abbreviated *KZ*) did not generally become involved in the "Final Solution": they had no gas chambers, and their crematoria handled far fewer dead. The distinction is not generally understood today, largely because Auschwitz acquired an extermination center with the construction of Auschwitz-Birkenau, where gas chambers went into operation early in 1942.[40] Those gas chambers were still in service when Morgen arrived at Auschwitz, in November 1943, but the extermination centers of Aktion Reinhard had been dismantled.

Morgen says that having confronted industrialized mass murder at Auschwitz-Birkenau, "I thought to myself, what could be done about it." His professional position gave him the means to do *something*—something ultimately ineffectual but no less courageous for that. The deliberation behind his choice was not as straightforward as his Frankfurt testimony makes it sound. He was, after all, an SS man, and he arrived at his choice from different premises than would naturally occur to his courtroom audience in 1964. How he arrived at it can be understood only in light of his remarkable career as an SS judge.

TWO

THE SS MAN

In September 1945, Morgen surrendered himself to the Army Counter-Intelligence Corps in Mannheim Seckenheim, Germany.[1] He told the Americans that he was a witness to war crimes; they suspected that he might be a war criminal himself.

Morgen brought with him a number of documents from his service as an SS investigator, including investigative reports and criminal indictments that he had filed against members of the SS.[2] During his three years in American custody, he was extensively interrogated and deposed, and more documents from his wartime career were uncovered.

The American CIC began interrogating Morgen on August 30, 1946. The interrogation opens with Morgen's account of his education and entry into the SS:[3]

I was born on the 8th of June, 1909, in Frankfurt am Main. My father drives a train. I went to school in Frankfurt. Before college I was employed for half a year as an intern in a bank. Then I studied in Frankfurt, Rome, Berlin, the Hague, and Kiel. Before that, while in school, I had already been an exchange student in France. From that you can see that from my earliest childhood onwards I was already interested in international relations. During college I was also a member of the Pan-European Union. And I belonged to the brotherhood of the German People's Party. In May 1933, on the advice of my parents, I entered the [Nazi] Party, though I had no function in it. In the same year I joined the SS. At the time I was a student, in my last semester, and we were accepted into the SS without much question.

Q. Accepted as what? Were you in some organization?

A. It was the so-called Reich Board for Youth Fitness. At that time people said that for academics in particular, books were too one-sided and so on, some physical counterpart had to be arranged. [...] There were exercises. Then they said, You need a pair of boots. You have to show a sense of belonging. And you need a brown shirt. And it went on like that. And before you knew it, you were involved. That period gave me no qualms or doubts. For Hitler emphasized that he wanted to dedicate all his power and policy to peace. Time and again he said: "I myself fought at the front [in World War I]. I know the horrors of war. What the people need, what the world needs, is peace." [...] It was all so convincing that one couldn't imagine that this man would lead the world into a new catastrophe.

Morgen points out that he wrote a book on the topic "war propaganda and the prevention of war." The book analyzed propaganda as a cause of war, ending with a naïve paean to National Socialism as dedicated to the cause of peace.[4]

In short, Morgen tries to convince his interrogators that he joined the Nazi movement without knowing where it would lead, deceived, like so many other Germans, by Hitler's pretense of peaceable intentions. His reasons for joining the Party, he says, were purely opportunistic:[5]

> I entered the Party on May 1, 1933. At the fervent request of my mother. She said: "You won't get a position if you want to go into the civil service. We have made so many sacrifices for your studies." I already mentioned that my father drove a train. In order to put up the funds for my training, my parents often had to go without. So I thought to myself, "OK, it's just a formality," and I joined.

The photo on Morgen's Nazi Party ID (see frontispiece) shows an earnest 27 year old with a high, narrow forehead topped with a high brush of hair, and a short chin that is already slightly doubled. He stares out at the camera through round wire rims, quietly alert.

In fact, Morgen joined the Party on April 1, not May; and he had already joined the SS on March 1.[6] In any case, he came in with a flood of new recruits. Between January and May 1933, the SS doubled in size, from 50,000 to more than 100,000,[7] and the Party added 1.6 million members.[8] The fact that Morgen joined the SS before the Party tends to support his claim that he was drawn in through a student organization, interested more in belonging to an elite fraternity than in politics or ideology. The claim is further supported by an affidavit submitted to Morgen's postwar denazification trial by one of his student friends, stating that the organization he joined was incorporated into the SS only later, at the initiative of its leader.[9]

Founded in 1925, the SS—*Schutzstaffel*, or "security squadron"—was originally a praetorian guard for Hitler and other high officials of the Nazi Party. When Himmler took command of the SS in 1929, his plan was to form it into an elite, close-knit brotherhood committed to the ideals of National Socialism.[10] A mystic and romantic, Himmler cultivated a myth of the SS as a knightly order in the tradition of the *Deutscher Ritterorden*,[11] with a mission of promoting the Aryan race. Like knights of old, SS men were bound by a code of personal virtue and unquestioning obedience. This moralized ideology was reiterated by Himmler over the years, notwithstanding the growing record of crimes committed by members of the SS.

By the spring of 1933, the SS had become (in the words of the historian Hans Buchheim) "a slightly more prestigious version" of the para-military "storm troopers" (SA)—more prestigious in the sense of eschewing the rampant thuggery of the latter, plebeian organization, sharing with it only the outward form of military uniforms and drills.[12] Men applied for membership in the SS if they wanted to join one of the National Socialist organizations without committing too much time to political activity.

The SS came into its own in the Röhm putsch of June 1934. The SA had become a threat to Hitler's authority, and Hitler sent SS men to kill its leader, Ernst Röhm, and more than 100 of his lieutenants. From then on the SS was a force to be reckoned with in the Nazi state. In the fall of 1934, Hitler created armed SS regiments to serve as a military branch of the Nazi Party. With the outbreak of war in 1939, these regiments became the core of the Waffen (militarized) SS, into which almost all SS members, including Morgen, were automatically inducted. Men who had joined a political fraternity with para-military trappings thus found themselves in a military organization.

The depiction of SS members in historical literature has changed since the immediate postwar period.[13] At the Nuremberg trials, the entire SS was indicted as a criminal organization. But historians have debunked the picture of the SS as a band of brutes from the dregs of German society—a picture made famous by former Buchenwald inmate Eugen Kogon in his book *The Theory and Practice of Hell*.[14] Kogon's characterization fits many of the SS guards he knew in Buchenwald, but it cannot be applied to the members of administrative and political arms of the SS, such as the Reich Security Head Office (RSHA), where those involved in genocide were "desk murderers," many with academic degrees.[15] The SS was a diverse organization, and Morgen would find his way into its more refined precincts.

The killings of SA members and political opponents in the Röhm purge shocked many Germans by revealing the ruthless extremes to which the Nazi regime would go in securing the Führer's sole authority. The incident was also remarkable from a juridical perspective. The Justice Minister Franz Gürtner was forced to countenance the murders by retroactive legislation, the Law Relating to the National Emergency Defence Measures of 3rd July 1934. The crown jurist of the Third Reich, Carl Schmitt, published an article titled "The Führer Protects the Law," in which he not only defended the murders but declared them to be legal. He argued that Hitler, acting as the "Supreme Justiciar" (*oberster Gerichtsherr*), had "protected law against the worst kind of misuse" by creating law on his own "in the moment of peril."[16]

The next step in consolidating Hitler's power was to unify the offices of Reich Chancellor and Reich President in the person of the Führer.[17] Again, the regime was eager to give the march toward absolute rule a veneer of legality. The Law concerning the Highest State Office of the Reich was passed on August 1, 1934,[18] and on August 19th a plebiscite was held to ratify this step.

Morgen refused to vote. "I [. . .] didn't think it was a good idea for all of the power of the state to pass into one hand," he says.[19] He would have been expelled from the Party had it not been for the intercession of the SS: "They said, 'This man belongs to us.'"[20] It might also have helped that his father made a large contribution to the *Nationalsozialische Wohlfahrt*, the Party's welfare organization.[21]

Whatever Morgen may have thought when refusing to vote in 1934, he seems to have reconciled himself to one-man rule by 1936, when he wrote in his book on war propaganda, "The first accomplishment of the new Germany consists in abolishing the liberal democratic system and replacing it with the Führer Principle."[22] Maybe his abstention from the plebiscite had not been as principled as he later claimed; or maybe the concluding passages of his book were designed to appease the Party. If the latter, they were a failure, since his book was condemned: "I was reproached with not having pointed out that the Jews were [. . .] actually instigators of the wars."[23]

There is no evidence of any activities by Morgen in the SS or the Nazi Party between 1933 and 1938. He held no office in either organization and, he later claimed, hardly engaged in Party or SS life. Were there evidence to the contrary, this claim would have been challenged at his first public denazification trial, in 1948, where he declared that he had no time for politics in 1933, because he was focused on finishing his studies.[24] We have no contemporary evidence about his reaction to Röhm's murder or the militarization of the SS later the same year.[25] As we will see, however, he was generally oblivious to social and political developments, sometimes for better but more often for worse. The justice for which he was fanatical did not include social or political justice.

From 1934 to 1938 Morgen was in legal training, serving as a junior lawyer (*Referendar*) at several courts in Frankfurt am Main. In October

1937 Morgen was sent for further training to the camp Jüterbog in New Brandenburg. Jüterbog was "the symbol of judicial education in the Third Reich."[26] Founded in July 1933 by the Prussian Minister of Justice, Hanns Kerrl, it was devoted to educating future generations of Prussian lawyers, judges, and state prosecutors in the spirit of National Socialism.[27] From 1936 on, all German junior lawyers were required to complete a six-week course. By the time of Morgen's stay, the training focused on law, geopolitics, economics, and racial doctrine—plus athletics. The goal was to cultivate a sense of community and group morality in the National Socialist sense.

The atmosphere in Jüterbog was highly repressive. The main instrument of control was the trainees' need for a "camp certificate," a written evaluation that was indispensable for admission to the judiciary. Relations among the trainees were poisoned by mistrust and suspicion, sometimes culminating in denunciations.

Morgen did not do well in Jüterbog. For one thing, he failed the sports exam. More serious was that he showed a lack of interest and bonhomie. "In week 5 and 6," reported his evaluator,

> Morgen became lazy and sleepy. In posture and attitude he was offhand; even his expression in discussion became significantly clumsier. One could almost believe that he was too lazy to utter a word. Because of this behavior—and because he tried to evade unpleasant group tasks with lame excuses—his comrades did not appreciate him.[28]

Morgen's unwillingness to participate seems to have exceeded the general caution of his comrades, who avoided speaking up on sensitive topics for fear of ruining their careers.[29] His recalcitrance may be an indication of his resistance to the ideological drill.

Morgen contested his evaluation. In a letter to the Reich Minister of Justice, he defends his record in sports ("I only failed in the 3,000 meter run") and attributes his silence in discussion to illness. With respect to his lack of sociability, he adds,[30]

> A community never spares its sensitive members! Soft natures, the ones who are easily hurt, become the targets of general ridicule and teasing. Such characters have never been handled with care by their comrades. It is no different in Jüterbog. My evaluator would have hit on the truth if he had spoken of a certain reluctance on my part.

In 1938 Morgen completed his legal training and passed the examination to qualify as a judge. Before taking up his first position, however, he became embroiled in defending his honor as an SS man against what he perceived as an affront.[31]

At the home of a friend, Morgen met Karl Julius Speck, who advertised himself as a tax counselor and economist, although he had not passed exams in either economics or law. More importantly, Speck was not a member of the SS and had lost his membership in the Nazi Party because of nonpayment of dues. Perhaps out of a feeling of inferiority, perhaps out of disdain for the SS, Speck took offense at an innocent reference to his profession, and he retorted with ironic condolences for Morgen's having "too few groats in his head"—which is apparently akin to playing with half a deck.

Speck escaped a duel only by managing to be unavailable on both occasions when Morgen's seconds arrived at his house. A lawsuit before an SS court of honor proved difficult to arrange because Speck did not belong to an honor society—that is, an organization accredited to represent him by virtue of having an honor code. Morgen finally deigned to settle for a written apology on the condition that the SS would regard Speck as enough of a gentleman to make such an apology—"a gentleman in the National Socialist sense."

This episode, trivial as it is, shows Morgen subscribing to the code of personal honor that characterized the SS. He had clearly internalized the fraternal values of the organization, if not its political ideology.

Morgen's first post was in the district court in Stettin, but he was soon dismissed from the Reich Judiciary.[32] He had run afoul of the Party again, this time in the trial of a teacher accused of exceeding the legal limits on corporal punishment. Morgen suspected that the Hitler Youth were behind the prosecution—the defendant did not belong to the Party—and a look at the files revealed that the senior judge was suppressing exculpatory evidence. Several confrontations ensued, whereupon disciplinary procedures were initiated against Morgen and he was dismissed. After his dismissal from the district court, Morgen became a legal advisor to the German Labor Front, which represented workers in disputes over salary and benefits.

In September 1939, Germany invaded Poland and war was declared. Morgen was drafted into the Waffen-SS, but he was not involved in combat. He first served in the Reserve Unit East.[33] Stationed in Stolp in Pommern, he sent his parents an emotional letter anticipating the hardships to come:[34]

How much worry it cost you to raise me, dear Mommy! How lovingly you watched over me. How diligently you cared for my clothes and how you sacrificed to satisfy my wishes, large and small. And you, dear Father, how frugal you were. How you always provided for us! Now in wartime, when everything will become so scarce, one realizes all the more what it meant in the last war to feed a family and keep them from going hungry. My current department head, a former lawyer, has told me how hard his wartime youth was and how they had to go hungry. He has never recovered from it, and he is still a delicate, worn-out guy, so that the military sent him straight home after a few days—and these days that's saying something. You, dear Father, protected us from all those hardships. I've become a fellow who won't be so easily knocked down, come what may. For this, I now give my thanks!

Morgen repeats what he has heard from soldiers stationed in Poland: "One hears over and over that every day in Poland our people are being shot, stabbed, and massacred in other insidious ways. The population there is so devious, hate-filled, and dumb that pacification seems out of the question." Here Morgen buys into German war propaganda emanating from Poland. There is no reason to believe that he had yet heard of the mass executions being carried out behind the lines. Morgen himself was *hors de combat* in Stolp in Pommern, which was then in Germany.

After the invasion of France, in May 1940, Morgen was demobilized and reported back to Berlin:

I said to the man in the personnel office that I would like to resume employment in my profession, since if one has just passed one's exams and then leaves the profession for more than a year, it is very hard to work one's way back in. He said, "OK, the Head Office of the SS Judiciary is looking for judges. So you'll get a job there."

Morgen had good reason for thinking that a career in the Civil Judiciary was closed to him after the incident in Stettin. He now entered training for the SS Judiciary and was assigned to the SS court in Cracow.[35]

THREE
THE SS JUDICIARY

The SS and Police Judiciary (*SS- und Polizeigerichtsbarkeit*) was not an arm of the Reich Judiciary but a special judicial system set up within the SS to try criminal offences by members of the Waffen-SS, of police task forces (the *Einsatzgruppen*), and of the Security Police. It was established in October 1939,[1] ostensibly on the grounds that civil or military courts could not understand the mentality and worldview of the SS man. Its true purpose may have been to prevent members of the Waffen-SS and *Einsatzgruppen* from being tried by military courts for war crimes committed in Poland.[2]

Several SS courts were established in the major cities of the Third Reich and the annexed territories. The courts were located at the headquarters of the Higher SS and Police Leaders. The highest court of the jurisdiction was the Head Office of the SS Judiciary (*Hauptamt SS-Gericht*) in Munich, but the highest judicial authority was Hitler himself.

There was no penal code specifically for the SS.[3] Formally, the SS Judiciary resembled the military court system and relied on the civil and military criminal codes. Materially, however, the SS Judiciary was heavily influenced by the values prevailing in the SS. The duties of an SS man were interpreted as requiring "ethical fulfillment," that is, obedience motivated internally rather than by external sanctions.[4] And when external sanctions were required, SS judges were expected to make rulings that conformed to the SS ethos, which the SS Judiciary fixed in explicit guidelines, published in regular memoranda (*Mitteilungen*) by the Head Office. The notion of a "higher law" expressing "the right and the just" served as a handy means of reinterpreting statutes of military law to suit SS ideology. Criminal offenses were redefined accordingly.[5]

One conduit by which SS ideology found its way into the criminal law for SS members was §92 of the military penal code, which regulated the offence of military disobedience.[6] The SS Judiciary interpreted military disobedience so broadly that practically every violation of Himmler's orders could be classified as disobedience, and Himmler held the SS to a stricter ideological standard than ordinary citizens. For example, whereas the first of the Nuremberg Laws forbade citizens of "German or related blood" to have sexual relations with Jews,[7] members of the SS were forbidden to have relations with members of any other races—including, for example, non-Jewish Poles. This restriction was spelled out in Himmler's "Order concerning *völkisch* Self-respect" (*Befehl über völkische Selbstachtung*), violation of which counted as military disobedience under §92.[8] And whereas the penalty for sexual relations with Jews was imprisonment, violators of §92 could be sentenced to death.

The chief of the SS Judiciary's Head Office in Munich, Franz Breithaupt—himself not a lawyer—declared that "SS judges are not 'jurists' but SS leaders familiar with law."[9] The SS Judiciary should be in the hands of "young, fresh SS leaders" and not "over-aged and senile jurists."[10] As the historian James Weingartner puts it, the SS judge was "expected to conduct himself in a manner fundamentally different from that of the traditional judge. No slave to the letter of the law, he was, ideally, a political fighter and educator to whom principle took precedence over paragraph."[11]

De facto, however, most of the SS judges were jurists who had worked before the war in the legal profession as attorneys or public prosecutors.[12] They consequently faced conflicting demands. On the one hand, they were expected to affirm the SS ethos, which granted them a high degree of discretion. On the other hand, they still had to follow the rule of law by hewing to existing statutes. The commitment to legal statutes, on the one hand, and the SS ethos, on the other, produced considerable tension.

The rules for sexual relations again provide an illustration. Morgen says that SS members were resistant to Himmler's order on *völkisch* self-respect, and that SS judges took no pleasure in enforcing it. Morgen says,[13]

> Sexual intercourse with other races was forbidden for the whole sphere of the SS by an internal service-order by the Reichsführer [Himmler] and that had to be enforced via paragraph 92, which says that military disobedience will be punished. [...] We had many such proceedings in the General Gouvernement. The troops were very resistant and we took no pleasure [in enforcing it]. To me it seemed crazy. I thought the racial thing was something else.

In other words, Morgen was uncomfortable regulating sexual relations with other races under §92.

For long periods, Morgen managed to harmonize his two roles, as a judge and as an SS officer, by giving them intersecting interpretations. But this reconciliation was severely tested by his discovery of the "Final Solution." And as we will see, he could maintain it only by transcending his former conceptions of corruption and the task of a judge.

FOUR

CRIMINALS AND SPIES

At the end of December 1940, the Head Office of the SS Judiciary assigned Morgen to its court in Cracow, the seat of German administration in the General Gouvernement, which comprised the portion of Poland that was not incorporated into the Reich. The General Gouvernement was initially slated to be a source of slave labor. Later it was designated for German settlement: Poles were to be driven further eastward or reduced to serfdom. The administration, under Hans Frank, occupied Wawel Castle, former residence of the Polish kings.[1]

By the time Morgen arrived in Cracow, its German occupiers had expelled two-thirds of its 60,000 Jewish inhabitants and herded the remainder into a ghetto, where they lived eight to a room. The Jagiellonian University was closed, the National Museum turned into a casino and restaurant for members of the Nazi regime. Citizens were regularly rounded up and shipped to concentration camps; others fell victim to mass shootings. The Security Police were known to operate a torture cellar in their headquarters on Pomorska Street.[2]

Morgen arrived in January 1941. "I wasn't there long," he says, "before I was overcome with astonishment at what I saw." What astonished him, however, was not the viciousness of the occupation:[3]

> You have to imagine: I had studied law and also become somewhat familiar with the German civil service tradition during my three or four years of legal practicum. What one saw there made one's hair stand on end. It was as if a swarm of locusts had descended to devour the land. [...] In every agency one met with the most incompetent officials who couldn't be of use in the Reich. And everyone had landed there who didn't want to be a soldier in the war and saw an opportunity to feather his nest. On the one hand was the poverty of the populace, which was obvious; on the other was the carousing and extravagance and—corruption.

Crimes of corruption—embezzlement, double-bookkeeping, black-marketeering—would become the main focus of Morgen's career, until he could no longer ignore the far greater crimes of the regime. In his eyes, SS

20

men guilty of corruption were a blot on the escutcheon of an honorable fraternity. His almost obsessive focus on corruption would lead him into the concentration camps of Buchenwald, Dachau, and Auschwitz, where he would finally look into the abyss.

Morgen's first major suspect was Georg von Sauberzweig, son of a famous World War I general.[4] In 1941 Sauberzweig was serving as chief of a troop-supply depot in Warsaw. Sauberzweig was embezzling provisions and selling them on the black market. Morgen arrested him, and he was tried, convicted, and shot. An appeal for clemency had gone all the way up to Hitler in his capacity as highest judicial authority. Hitler rejected the appeal. His rejection is preserved in Sauberzweig's SS personnel file, along with Morgen's arrest warrant, the court's judgment, naming Morgen as prosecutor, and a confirmation of Sauberzweig's execution.[5] Sauberzweig's cronies were sentenced to only a few years in prison, but Himmler voided the sentence as being too lenient, and several of those men were shot as well.[6]

Note the harshness of these sentences. Sauberzweig had not committed murder or treason; he was guilty of no more than theft and fraud. Death was an extreme punishment for such pedestrian crimes, but death sentences were not uncommon in the SS Judiciary. Morgen could be shockingly strict. In the run-up to Christmas 1941, he handed down five death sentences in the space of ten days.[7] But he could also be surprisingly lenient—an inconsistency traceable to the prevailing theory of adjudication, which we will examine shortly.

When Sauberzweig was arrested, in March 1941, he turned to his wife and said, "Call Fegelein."[8] This Fegelein became Morgen's next major suspect.[9] Hermann Fegelein was a horseman whose father owned a private riding school in Munich.[10] In 1936 he was in charge of the main riding school (*Hauptreitschule*) of the SS, while also pursuing a successful career as a competitive equestrian. In the fall of 1939, Himmler assigned him to assemble and lead a mounted regiment of the SS, with the *Hauptreitschule* as its supply depot.

In a photo from the period, Fegelein poses for the camera with a dashing sideways glance, a full, almost pouting mouth, a weak chin, and a high sweep of fair hair. He was a favorite of Himmler's and later became his liaison to Hitler, thereby gaining entry into Hitler's inner circle. From that advantageous position, Fegelein courted and married Eva Braun's sister, Greta. Albert Speer listed him as among the most repulsive people in Hitler's entourage. Hans Baur, Hitler's personal pilot, added another 'l' to his name and called him "Flegelein"—"Little Lout."[11]

Fegelein was present in the famous bunker during Hitler's last days. Hitler biographer Ian Kershaw describes the scene:[12]

> Not everyone was willing to join a suicide pact. Hermann Fegelein, the swash-buckling, womanizing, cynical opportunist who had risen to high position in the SS through Himmler's favour then sealed his bonds to Hitler's "court" through marry-ing Eva Braun's sister, had disappeared from the bunker. His absence was noted on 27 April. And that evening he was discovered in civilian clothes in his apartment in Charlottenburg, allegedly with a woman friend, worse for wear from drink, and with a good deal of money in bags packed for departure.

Fegelein was brought back to the bunker, put before an impromptu court martial, and shot.

Even before crossing paths with Morgen in 1941, Fegelein had come under investigation for corruption. In March of 1940, he was accused of having trucked booty from Poland to his *Hauptreitschule* in Munich.[13] A search of the school uncovered goods of questionable provenance. Fegelein wrote a letter to Himmler contesting the charges. The goods and trucks were of legitimate origin, he claimed, and his accusers were acting from malice. Himmler wrote to Reinhard Heydrich, Chief of the Reich Security Head Office, affirming Fegelein's version of events, and the inves-tigation was quickly brought to a close.

Morgen was led to Fegelein, as we have seen, by his investigation of Sauberzweig. Sauberzweig was a Warsaw city councilman, and in that capacity he had confiscated the Jewish fur company of Nathan and Apfelbaum—"Aryanized" it, in the parlance of the time—appointing a cavalryman named Albert Fassbender as its liquidator.[14] Fassbender had come to Warsaw with Fegelein's cavalry regiment. Fegelein and Fassbender took two Apfelbaum employees as mistresses, who then helped them to loot the firm and sell off the carcass for a fraction of its original value.[15] Fassbender's mistress, Jaroslawa Mirowska by name, was especially well placed for this exploit, since her previous lover had been Apfelbaum him-self, who had fled from the German invasion and left her in charge of the firm.

When Morgen suspected that the firm's assets were being dissipated—in some cases, as gifts to powerful members of the SS—he interrogated Fassbender and later searched his apartment.[16] According to Morgen's postwar account of the case, he conducted this search *auf eigene Kappe*, "on his own cap," or in other words, his own initiative.[17] When Morgen arrived, Fassbender was with a reconnaissance party at the Russian front, Fegelein off in East Prussia with a mounted brigade. Morgen found

Mirowska at home. She immediately called their garrison in Warsaw, which radioed to Fassbender and Fegelein in the field. Fassbender raced home by motorcycle. Fegelein hopped a courier plane to headquarters, where he spoke to Himmler.

Himmler once again came to Fegelein's defense. Responding to the allegations, Himmler wrote that he knew and approved of the suspects' plan for the firm. The ostensible plan was to turn the firm, with its international connections, into a contact point for German agents.[18] Himmler said that it was thanks to Fegelein, Fassbender, and Mirowska that the value of the firm had been salvaged—meaning, presumably, converted into an intelligence asset.

Himmler had met Mirowska. With her open face and sweet smile, she easily disarmed him. Morgen says that she was treated as the "first lady" of the SS.[19] In Himmler's memo excusing Fegelein, he went on to sing Mirowska's praises:[20]

> This lady has some German ancestry, and having once seen her in person, I agreed and arranged for her to be recognized as *volksdeutsch*. As reported to me by SS-Standartenführer Meisinger, former commander of the Security Police, she has performed incredibly good and faithful services for us.

From now on, Himmler ordered, he himself should be consulted before any SS officers were arrested or subjected to judicial procedures.[21]

This first lady of the SS was not as sweet as she looked—witness the farewell that she bid to her husband. She and Fassbender wanted to get him out of the way so that they could marry. While he was away from home, Sauberzweig showed up and hid a pistol in the oven. When the husband got home, the Gestapo arrived, found the pistol, and arrested him. Weapons possession by a Pole was a crime that the Gestapo could try on its own in a summary court martial. After the husband was sentenced, Mirowska appeared in his cell carrying a financial power of attorney for him to sign. An hour later he was shot.[22]

In September, Morgen wrote a summary of the Fegelein case for Martin Tondock, who was taking it over from him, and a memo memorializing a conversation between them.[23] Morgen reveals that Mirowska is a fraud. She is not, as advertised, the daughter of a Russian father and German mother: she is *rein polnisch*.[24] She claims to be working with the Security Service, but they deny it.[25] The supposed purpose of taking over the Apfelbaum firm was to incorporate its international network into the Intelligence Service, "but this idea has so much going for it that I can't imagine the Polish regime had not already made use of the possibility."[26]

Morgen therefore suspects that Mirowska is a spy for the Polish underground. He backs up his suspicion with several pages of circumstantial evidence leading to this conclusion: "[A] woman as beautiful and charming as she is intelligent and unscrupulous, expert in languages, known internationally, a leader in society and fashion—she would be an excellent tool for espionage."[27]

Nine days later, Tondock sent Himmler a memo marked "Urgent," "Secret," and "To the Reichsführer personally."[28] He writes that the purported half-Russian has made misleading representations about her past and she appears to have "dangerous contacts." Morgen's suspicions were borne out: "One year later the whole Polish underground was rolled up and Frau Mirowskaja, the first lady of the SS, was their head agent."[29] Mirowska had sold Himmler on the idea of using Nathan and Apfelbaum to gather intelligence, but she was working as a double agent for the Poles.

In the end, Himmler let her off the hook. "A call came from the Reichsführer. The message was: Yes, Mirowskaja is a spy." But when the question was raised where she should be tried, "he said, 'No, no—that isn't going to happen,' and he snatched her from the jaws of the Gestapo."[30]

The *affaire Mirowska* is significant for our understanding of Morgen and his role in the SS. The documents in the case include a letter written in September 1941 by his superior in Cracow, Norbert Pohl, to the SS Judiciary Head Office in Munich. In this letter Pohl protests "the endless opposition from the highest offices in the SS" to Morgen's investigation.[31] Pohl mentions the significant detail that Mirowska had been introduced to Himmler. He complains that Fegelein had issued a threat against Morgen.[32] And he alludes to other cases in which Fegelein "time and again brought investigations in his own case to a halt through personal pleading with the Reichsführer."[33] A year and a half later, Pohl's successor as chief of the SS court in Cracow is still complaining to the Chief of the SS Judiciary Head Office that Fegelein and others in his regiment have been allowed to do with impunity things that have "broken the necks" of lesser SS men.[34] Clearly, then, the SS Judiciary expected to be free of outside interference. Their expectation was dashed but it was genuine.

This case also exposed Morgen to a criminal type that he may not have expected to meet in the SS. We have already noted Albert Speer's description of Fegelein as one of the most repulsive characters in Hitler's entourage, and Hans Baur's nickname for him, "Little Lout." A similar portrait of Fegelein's sidekick Fassbender appears in Eugen Kogon's report on the concentration camps, *The Theory and Practice of Hell*. Kogon was imprisoned for six years in Buchenwald, he served as clerk to a camp doctor, and he was then instrumental in helping the American liberators collect testimony about the camp from its survivors. In his chapter on the psychology of the SS, Kogon describes a few case studies, including this:[35]

> SS Major Albert Fassbender: Origins unknown, adopted child of the owners of the famous German chocolate firm of Fassbender. A ne'er-do-well, drunkard, and wastrel. Married to a Countess Stollberg. Made the acquaintance of the head of the so-called Mounted SS, SS Major General Fegelein, whom he financed, becoming battalion commander in the First SS Mounted Regiment, and together with Fegelein one of the worst SS criminals in Warsaw. Among other things, he "aryanized" the worldwide fur company of Apfelbaum, in concert with Slawa Mirowska, secretary to the owner, who had fled. Fassbender marked down the value of the firm from around 40,000,000 to 50,000 marks. Responsible for the pregnancy of his mistress, he had Fegelein and the Gestapo arrest her husband, a Polish officer, and a few days later, again in concert with the Polish she-devil who obtained a general power of attorney to his fortune at the last moment, shot him down in his cell.

Kogon could not have learned this story from any source other than Morgen, whom he knew at Buchenwald. So this case study reflects Morgen's perceptions.

Finally, the Mirowska case is significant for its scope and visibility. Morgen was not content to prosecute just any Kurt or Heinz for drunkenness or absence without leave. He went after a large conspiracy involving personal favorites of Himmler. But then, his chosen target was corruption, and unlike drunkenness or dereliction of duty, corruption is a crime for which opportunities and temptations are greatest in the regions of power. As late as the end of 1944, Morgen was still saying, in letters to his fiancée, that it was his "fate" to carry investigations into "the highest ranks."[36] In carrying his investigations into the highest ranks, he showed the courage of moral conviction, but in the case of Fegelein, who belonged to the Nazi inner circle, Morgen may also have been politically naïve.

FIVE

THE CRIMINAL
CHARACTER

Morgen's experience with Fegelein, Fassbender, and Sauberzweig turned him into a specialist in corruption, a category of crime whose name also stands for a deficiency of moral character.[1] These particular criminals exemplified corruption in both senses of the word. By specializing in corruption as a crime that manifests bad character, Morgen was initially able to combine his roles as judge and as upholder of moral virtue in the SS. This combination of roles was facilitated by National Socialist legal theory.

Immediately after the Nazi's rise to power in 1933, leading theorists began to discuss which kind of criminal law would best meet the requirements of National Socialism. The main impetus for criminal law reform was a 1933 order from Hitler establishing a commission chaired by Reich Minister of Justice Franz Gürtner.[2] The commission issued a two-volume report,[3] and a revised criminal code was drafted, but in December 1939, Hitler refused to sign it, being less and less willing to submit himself to legal norms under the circumstances of war.[4] Nevertheless, the commission's work and the scholarly work of its members, among others, continued to influence judicial practice in the Third Reich.

Nazi jurists rejected the liberal principle *nullum crimen, nulla poena sine lege*—"no crime or punishment without a law." The principle was represented in German criminal law by §2, which stated, "An action can be punished only if that punishment is legally set before the action was performed."[5] Designed to protect citizens against the arbitrariness of judges, this provision was condemned by Nazi jurists as the "Magna Carta of the criminal,"[6] because it enabled a wrongdoer to avoid punishment by exploiting loopholes in poorly drafted statutes.[7] Because the liberal principle required the facts of a case to be subsumed under written statutes, the legal theorist Karl Schäfer claimed that it reduced the judge to a mere "subsumption machine" and should be replaced by the principle *nullum crimen sine poena*—"no crime without punishment."[8]

Paragraph 2 of the penal code was therefore replaced in 1935 with the following:[9]

> Whoever commits an act [*Tat*] which is declared punishable by law, or which deserves to be punished according to the fundamental idea of a penal law and the sound perception of the *Volk*, will be punished. If no particular penal law is directly applicable to an act, then the act is punished according to that statute the fundamental idea of which fits it best.

The last sentence of this paragraph allowed for the use of analogy in adjudication—that is, the punishment of acts that were not explicitly outlawed but merely similar to acts that were. Although this sentence allows specifically for the use of "statutory analogy"—the application of particular statutes to analogous cases—several Nazi jurists argued that it should be broadened to include "analogy of law" as well. Analogy of law extended to "the application of an idea (of law) inherent in the whole legal order to a legally unregulated matter of fact which may count as a particular instance of that idea."[10]

Analogy of law was thus far-reaching indeed, since "the idea of the whole legal order," in the eyes of Nazi jurists, was nothing less than the protection of the *Volks*-community.[11] Loyalty to that community was regarded as both an ethical and a legal duty,[12] so that the fight against crime became a fight against betrayal of the community, and atonement for such betrayal became one goal of punishment. Criminals were portrayed as *Volksschädlinge*[13]—parasites on the *Volk*—and judges were granted wide discretion to punish them for acts not envisioned by lawmakers.

Note that the new version of §2 also ties the use of analogy to "the sound perception of the *Volk*." In the words of the legal theorist Georg Dahm, "The legal statute [. . .] contains merely the general guidelines according to which the judge exerts the perception of the *Volk*."[14]

The perception of the *Volk* came into play via the fusion of law and morality.[15] The connection was explained by Roland Freisler, State Secretary of the Ministry of Justice and later President of the People's Court:[16]

> There can be no gap between a legal imperative and an ethical imperative. This is so because imperatives of law are imperatives of decency [*Anständigkeit*]; however, what is decent is determined by the conscience of the *Volk* and the individual member of the *Volk*.

Dahm and Freisler do not cast morality merely as a guide to interpreting statutes; they cast it instead as constituting the law, with the statutes reduced to the status of "guidelines." Because, as Freisler says, moral imperatives are delivered by the conscience of the *Volk*, the *Volk*'s moral perceptions articulate the law itself. And the most authoritative expression of those perceptions, of course, was to be found in the will of the Führer, who was the people's "true representative."[17]

In practice, the interpretation of this standard was up to the judge, whose discretion was thus substantially expanded. As long as the judge claimed to be implementing the ethical order and the sound perception of the *Volk*, he was relatively autonomous in determining whether an act fell within legal jurisdiction. What's more, the objective elements of a crime were no longer the sole basis of adjudication.[18] The will and character of the criminal were now taken into account as well.[19] The commission established by Hitler and chaired by Gürtner endorsed what was called will-based criminal law.

Directing punishment at the perpetrator's will served both purposes adumbrated in the new version of §2. First, it safeguarded the *Volk* by deterring crime before the act, at the stage of its planning and preparation.[20] According to Freisler, who was a main advocate of will-based criminal law, the state should react to crime "as early as possible and with all available power!"[21] Thus, for example, Nazi legal theorists rejected differential sentencing for attempted and completed crimes, arguing that both expressed a criminal will that had to be thwarted.[22] The second purpose of focusing on the criminal's will was to express the moral view of the *Volk* that it was the site of evil. As such, it could be treated as a constitutive element of the crime, not just as an aggravating circumstance in sentencing, as in liberal criminal law:[23]

> Just as in Kantian and Fichtian ethics nothing is good but the good will, so the core of crime lies in the evil will. [. . .] This connection between crime and moral badness could only be obscured when an exaggerated liberal conception drew a sharp line between law and morality, as well as between the will and external behavior.

Consideration of the perpetrator's will then led to consideration of his character. According to the legal theorist Edmund Mezger, will and character were connected because "the particular crimes are due to a typical resolution of the will which allows us to characterize specific types of perpetrators."[24] Mezger therefore developed the notion of "conduct-of-life-guilt" (*Lebensführungs-Schuld*), which inhered in the perpetrator's character as manifested in his life overall: "Guilt is offense-guilt, but also conduct-of-life-guilt, and therefore punishment is directed not only at the particular offense, but also at the personality of the perpetrator."[25]

These innovations in legal theory were incorporated into the practices of the SS Judiciary. One illustration of their influence is a long letter from Morgen's superior at the SS court in Cracow, Norbert Pohl, to the SS Judiciary Head Office protesting its repeal of sentences handed down by trial judges.[26] Pohl objects that when repealing a sentence, the Head Office relies on experts who have merely studied the facts as depicted in the files of the case. Pohl argues that a sentence sometimes seems too mild to a judicial expert studying the files but was justified in the eyes of the judge because the defendant displayed a positive character and a firm demeanor. Sometimes a mild sentence was justified because the defendant, being uneducated, had no insight into the nature of his offense. Although such considerations are used as mitigating factors in liberal legal systems as well, Pohl goes so far as to place them above the letter of the law. He says that "the personality of the defendant, not first and foremost the legal statute, dictates the finding of justice."[27]

Pohl describes his own practice of adjudication as follows:[28]

> In deliberating about the sentence I start with the question: What punishment must the perpetrator get for the offense whose occurrence has been established at trial? Only if clarity has been attained on this point are legal statues consulted, which are then subsumed under the decision reached.

Here Pohl turns the liberal principle on its head, subsuming the statute under the sentence rather than vice versa: if the judge

> falls back on the facts of the case as set out in the records, subsumes them neatly under the legal statute, and then reaches the result that a man who has violated the law so much can be penalized with only the harshest punishment [. . .] this way of proceeding is nothing but a regression to law-bound, liberal adjudication.[29]

Pohl even echoes Karl Schäfer's remark that liberal adjudication reduces the judge to a "subsumption machine." Law and statute, he writes, "remain bloodless [*blutleer*] and degrade the judge to a mechanical instrument if in addition the personality of the defendant and his community-relatedness [. . .] are not also consulted as sources of legal knowledge."[30]

Morgen finished his legal studies and passed his first *Staatsexamen* in 1934, submitted his dissertation in 1936, and passed his second *Staatsexamen* in 1938, qualifying to serve as a judge in the German judiciary. It was during this period that the commission established by Hitler and chaired by Gürtner endorsed will-based criminal law and, in 1935, revised §2 of the criminal code. Thus, Morgen's education as a jurist coincided with and must have been shaped by the transformations in legal theory underway in the Third Reich.

Morgen later articulated the new conception of law in an article on "The Corruption Criminal" published in December 1943.[31] The notion of a corruption criminal belonged to a typology by which perpetrators could be classified in accordance with the new emphasis on their characters. Perpetrator typologies also included such characters as the "habitual criminal [*Gewohnheitsverbrecher*]," the "sexual criminal," the "cheater and defrauder," "the traitor," and so on.

Characteristic of the corruption criminal, Morgen writes, is

> a broken career marked by disloyalty to his milieu, a striving for recognition, social dysfunction [. . .] His inner structure is hubristic, self-seeking to the highest degree, unscrupulous, cold, calculating, without ties to people or moral ideals. He is lacking in depth, in inner conflict and fundamental poise.[32]

Here Morgen portrays the corruption criminal as constitutionally inimical to the *Volks*-community: disloyal to his milieu, socially dysfunctional and disconnected. Morgen also compares penal sanctions to sanitary measures such as eugenics or medicine:[33]

> No regime in the world has ever taken up so total and radical a struggle against corruption in all its manifestations as the National Socialist regime. First, the biological-eugenic preventive measures, then the actual political measures of education, selection, and monitoring, and then penal sanctions of draconian harshness. Taking part in this struggle is the physician as well as the educator, the editor as well as the professional and business organizations, not to mention the Party and the apparatus of officialdom [. . .].

Criminal corruption is thus one among many forms of corruption that weaken the *Volks*-community, and penal law is like a sanitary measure for dealing with the corruption criminal as if he were indeed a parasite or pest. Conversely, Pohl argued that a perpetrator whose character was not pestilential deserved more lenient treatment than one who was by nature inimical to the *Volks*-community.

The new approach to adjudication is already evident in a memo that Morgen wrote in February 1942, during his time in Cracow. The memo was written about the case of Paul Kleesattel, who was accused of abusing civilians in occupied Galicia. Morgen recommends that he be given a lenient punishment, for reasons of the sort that had been summarized by Norbert Pohl:[34]

During the operation in Galicia, Hauptmann of the *Schutzpolizei* Paul Kleesattel was guilty of continually assaulting Poles, Jews, and Ukrainians of both sexes. He used his riding crop and his hand, and instructed his subordinates to strike them. The reason for these assaults was generally minor, and they were occasionally also due to excessive drinking by the accused.

Nevertheless, I consider it inappropriate to submit the indictment for the Court Master's signature. First, let me note that in the eastern territories generally it is necessary to rule with a stronger and rougher hand. Thus—when the end calls for it—the criminal law in force is not taken into account.

Disobedience and disrespect are mainly punished with corporal penalties by uniformed personnel on the spot. Public prosecutors, police, and security officers cannot handle native populations of foreign races without the application of the utmost force, including as a means of extracting confessions. However regrettable this may be, it is a procedure to which the native peoples have been accustomed for centuries and without which German rule at the moment would probably be endangered.

So much for the purely factual situation.

In addition, there is among our men a widespread mental attitude to the effect that the eastern region, as an area for future German immigration, is to be freed up for the Germans through the extirpation [*Ausrottung*] and annihilation [*Vernichtung*] of the native population, and that the population is therefore to be tolerated as a currently necessary evil and treated as such.

Given this situation and this mental attitude, transgressions and excesses in the use of bodily force are quite understandable. The view that generally predominates is that it is better to beat someone too much than too little. Combatting this with penal provisions is pointless and would on no account be understood by the troops.

For this reason, the SS- and Police Judiciary in adjudicating cases of this kind has taken the approach of intervening in a legal way against such misdemeanors and crimes only when the accused manifests by his act severe character flaws that make him intolerable to the German *Volksgemeinschaft*. Thus, for example, if assaults degenerate into sadistic tortures, or sexual motives play a role or—and here the law is to be applied ruthlessly—when the victim is German by nationality or race, or has citizenship in an allied state.

The SS- and Police Judiciary is there to preserve the purity of our own ranks, not to protect the rights [*Rechtsgüter*] of an enemy people. Carrying out this principle is occasionally made more difficult for the local court in cases of the former kind; for example, just recently SS-members in Debica trampled a Jew literally to death without good reason. After this incident, the accused were transferred to Berlin, so that they were no longer subject to the local court, and the Head Office [of the SS Judiciary] informed us here that the matter should not be pursued further.

In view of this situation, I think it is unreasonable to make an exception in the case of former Hauptmann Paul Kleesattel. Though Kleesattel might have made a serious mistake, it should not be forgotten that at the time of his act (September 1941) the situation in Galicia was extremely difficult. As is well known, after the failure to establish a Ukrainian national state, the population became far more recalcitrant than even the Poles. Gun fights, acts of sabotage, and resistance were the order of the day. Naturally, this situation makes troops insecure and fosters excesses, as in the present case. From a political point-of-view, it strikes me as debatable whether, in such a transitional period, measures of terror, even if they were clearly arbitrary in a particular case, might nevertheless be for the time being politically proper in the end. Nevertheless, instituting legal investigations into them strikes me as unwise. There is too great a danger that the troops will become confused.

Judging the *curriculum vitae* of the accused [. . .] this is in the end a case of an officer who gave a good account of himself in the [First] World War and until now has conducted himself with irreproachable character. Considering the particular combat circumstances and the situation in the East, I am of the opinion that a sufficient punishment for Hauptmann Kleesattel will be dismissal from the police.

I ask for consent to adjourn the procedure until the end of the war, and recommend that this warhorse be given the opportunity to prove himself at the front.

The SS Judiciary brings the law to bear, Morgen writes, "only when the accused manifests by his act severe character flaws that make him intolerable to the German *Volksgemeinschaft*"—precisely the grounds envisioned in will-based criminal law. By this standard, according to Morgen, Kleesattel qualifies for leniency, because his conduct thus far—his *Lebensführung*, in Mezger's phrase—has been irreproachable. Even in the present case, Morgen argues, his motives were not sadistic or sexual but perfectly understandable responses to the circumstances—the prevailing lawlessness in Galicia; the need to enforce German rule; the distinction between Germans and other races or nationalities; and the "mental attitude" among the troops that such people were to be eliminated to make room for German immigration and settlement. Given that these motives are not indicative of character flaws, Morgen says, Kleesattel's actions should be viewed not as a crime but merely as a mistake for which he should be dismissed from the police.

Many postwar theorists thought that the experience of the Third Reich had taught us that a tighter connection had to be drawn between law and morality. One example of this view can be found in Ronald Dworkin's theory of adjudication. According to Dworkin, adjudication depends not only on legal rules but also on general principles derived from and supported by moral considerations.[35] When legal rules do not clearly settle a case, the judge should reach his verdict in light of principles that provide the best moral justification for the relevant precedents, statutes, and regulations. In the case of thoroughly wicked legal systems, Dworkin thought, this method of adjudication should lead the judge to ignore the existing body of law altogether, since no moral principles can justify it. The judge must therefore look to morality alone.

As we have seen, however, Morgen's practice of adjudication hardly divorced the law from morality. On the contrary, his practice illustrates how Nazi jurisprudence erased the distinction between law and morality. It was, after all, the Nazi State Secretary of Justice who said, "There can be no gap between a legal imperative and an ethical imperative."[36] Of course, postwar theorists who argue for infusing the law with morality assume that the operative conception of morality will be sound. In Dworkin's theory of adjudication, for example, there is the implicit assumption that judges know the true morality. Yet in the legal system of the Third Reich, the true morality was taken to flow from "the sound perception of the *Volk*," and it was this *völkisch* morality that was incorporated into the law.

SIX

THE ISSUE OF RACE

Morgen's memo on the Kleesattel case raises the issue of race, when he speaks of the SS officers in Debica who "trampled a Jew literally to death without good reason." Morgen argues that the officers should have been prosecuted, but only "to preserve the purity of our own ranks, not to protect the rights of an enemy people." The murderers of a Jew should be punished, in other words, but not for violating the victim's right to life; they should be punished for polluting the ranks of the SS.

Such reasoning will reappear in Morgen's submissions to superiors, but never in the harsh terms used here. Combatting crime to protect SS virtue becomes a familiar theme with Morgen, but dismissing the rights of "enemy people" is uncharacteristic of him. Before leaving the memo, then, we should carefully examine its racially charged tone.

Why, to begin with, does Morgen say that the troops have a "mental attitude" to the effect that the native population is to be eradicated? He must have known that Jews were being massacred in large numbers. When he arrived in Cracow, in January 1941, there had already been large-scale shootings in the General Gouvernement. And that summer, while in Morgen's sights, Fegelein participated in the "cleansing" of the Pripyat marshes in the Soviet Union, where his cavalry regiment executed 14,000 Jews.[1] Walther Funk reportedly told Albert Speer, when both were in Spandau Prison, that there was a saying about Fegelein: "Where Fegelein goes, there are no more villages, no more people, no more life."[2] By February 1942, the date of Morgen's Kleesattel memo, the gas chambers of Belzec were almost complete; transports of Galician Jews began arriving in March.[3] There were also plans, drawn up by academic demographers, to depopulate the region to make room for a modernized German economy.[4]

Yet if Morgen knew of a plan to eradicate the local population to make way for German resettlement, he could simply have said that Kleesattel's actions were understandable given the operation in which he was engaged. If Morgen thought that such an operation was unmentionable, then he could have made an indirect allusion to the "historic mission" in the East, or he could simply have avoided the subject altogether. To project it onto a "mental attitude" of the troops was to say too much for the observance of secrecy and too little for the expression of credence. Apparently, then, Morgen thought that the matter was relevant, but not because he himself believed, much less endorsed, that the troops were implementing a policy of systematic ethnic cleansing; he thought it was relevant only because their motives included a belief to that effect.

Morgen's emphasis on the absence of sexual or sadistic motives in this case is a different matter, since it is in line with Nazi racial ideology. Later in the year, Himmler's legal adviser, Horst Bender, would write a memo to the SS Judiciary Head Office conveying Himmler's instructions for dealing with "shootings of Jews without orders or authorization" (*Judenerschiessungen ohne Befehl und Befugnis*). Bender divided these cases into two categories:[5]

1. In cases of purely political motives, no punishment ensues, unless the maintenance of order requires it. In the latter case, depending on the circumstances of the case, a sentence based on §92 or §149 of the military penal code or a disciplinary action may take place.[6]
2. In cases of self-seeking or sadistic or sexual motives, judicial action ensues—where applicable, even charges of murder or manslaughter.

The Nazi racial mindset is already evident in Bender's premise that *Judenerschiessung* is a distinct category of killing. And since the only such killings regularly subject to punishment are those committed from self-seeking, sadistic, or sexual motives, shootings on racial grounds are implicitly exempted as "political." Morgen's reference to sexual and sadistic motives chimes in with this ideology, though he doesn't apply the euphemism "political" to the racially motivated killing of Jews.

Like all Germans, Morgen had been exposed to public threats against the Jews by Hitler and other leading Nazis. In a notorious speech to the Reichstag in January 1939, Hitler declared that "if international finance-Jewry inside and outside Europe should succeed in plunging the nations once more into a world war, the result will be not the Bolshevization of the earth and thereby the victory of Jewry, but the annihilation [*Vernichtung*] of the Jewish race in Europe." Hitler reiterated this "prophecy," as he called it, at least four times in subsequent years.[7] In February of 1942, he addressed an audience at the Berlin Sportpalast as follows:[8]

On September 1, 1939, in the meeting of the Reichstag I said two things. First, after we were forced into this war, neither the power of weapons nor the factor of time would defeat us; second, if Jewry unleashed an international world war in order to bring about the extermination [*Ausrottung*] of the Aryan peoples of Europe, then it will be not the Aryan people, but rather Jewry, that will be exterminated.

Noting that these words elicited long applause from the audience, the historian Jeffrey Herf remarks that "The audience reaction in the Sportpalast suggests that the Nazi faithful understood that Hitler was telling them in language by then familiar that the Nazi regime was at that moment murdering the Jews." Even if the audience's understanding of Hitler's words could be discerned from their applause at language that was familiar precisely because Hitler had used it years before the murder of Jews had begun, there is ample evidence, as we will see, that Morgen himself was not prepared for his discovery, in 1943, of industrialized mass murder at Auschwitz-Birkenau.

The fact remains, however, that Morgen must have known by 1942 about atrocities on the Eastern Front. We cannot say that he turned a blind eye, since he prosecuted the worst perpetrator within his reach, Hermann Fegelein. But he prosecuted Fegelein only for corruption, and there is no evidence that he was motivated by Fegelein's record of leaving in his wake "no more villages, no more people, no more life." We will come in due course to Morgen's response to the culmination of the "Final Solution." Our question for the moment is whether his apparent indifference to the earlier phases of anti-Semitic violence was due to racial animus on his part.

The complexity of Morgen's attitude toward matters of race is evident in his dealings with another abuser of civilians, Oskar Dirlewanger. Dirlewanger led a commando assigned to guard road-construction crews in the area of Lublin. In November 1941, Morgen sent a telegram to Norbert Pohl reporting that Dirlewanger and his men had established a "despotic rule" (*Willkürherrschaft*) in the region, carrying out nightly raids to rob and round up Jews.[9] The telegram deplores the "seizure, extortion, and plundering of Jews under cover of night"—hardly an expression of contempt for the rights of a targeted population.

As Morgen describes to the CIC after the war, Dirlewanger arrested Jews for the crime of kosher slaughtering, released those who could pay a large ransom, and then shot the rest.[10] He performed "experiments" on Jewish men and women, having them killed by injection, their flesh mixed with horseflesh, and the mixture turned into soap. Morgen even has a sample, so he tells his interrogators.

Morgen says that when he tried to have Dirlewanger arrested, he was told that Dirlewanger was under the protection of the SS Chief of Staff, Gottlob Berger. The commando was merely transferred out of the General Gouvernement, and the case was eventually dismissed by order of Himmler.[11] Morgen was outraged by this disposition of the case.

Morgen adds a telling anecdote:[12]

> It was striking that, although on the one hand [Dirlewanger] operated against the Jews, he himself had a female Jewish servant. A 16-year-old child, fresh as a daisy, who slept next to his bedroom and was with him all day. [. . .] An SS officer came to me and said that he had visited Dirlewanger and was introduced to a young girl. They had drunk Schnapps or some liquor together and he was pressured in jest to drink out of the girl's glass. He found it unseemly to drink from the glass of a lady whom he hardly knew, but he finally did it—and subsequently learned that the girl was a Jewess. His racial pride was terribly injured and he said, "What sort of business is that, to put me in such a position?" He looked on it as an insult.

Morgen adds, "That's just by the way, about the bizarre personality of Dirlewanger." Morgen doesn't himself call Dirlewanger's trick an insult; he says only that the officer looked on it as such. The "racial pride" of which he speaks is the officer's, not his own. What he finds bizarre, however, is not that the officer felt insulted by having been offered the glass of a Jew but that Dirlewanger went in for racial practical jokes. The attitudes on which the joke relied are not a matter for comment. Similarly, what Morgen finds striking is not that Direlwanger "operated against the Jews"; it's that he consorted with a Jewish girl while doing so.

Thus, Morgen acquiesces in the officer's anti-Semitism, but he doesn't partake of it. When a postwar interrogator refers to one of his earlier remarks by saying, "You were speaking of so-called racially inferior peoples," Morgen objects, "I didn't speak of racial inferiors, but only of Jews and Poles."[13] In this respect Morgen differs from the legal scholars of his time, whose work was shot through with racial ideology. These jurists, almost all of them university professors, based their racial jurisprudence on a definition of race enunciated by Hans F. K. Günther, Germany's leading racial anthropologist: "a group of human beings that differs from any other [. . .] human group by a specific union of bodily and mental attributes, and that procreates only its own kind."[14]

Race so defined figured, for example, in the writings of Ernst Rudolf Huber, the preeminent constitutional expert of the Third Reich. Arguing that the constitution of the Nazi state must be a *völkisch* constitution, he asserted[15] that "The political *Volk* is formed by the unity of the kind [*Art*]. Race is the natural foundation of the *Volk*. Race is a community of ancestry marked out by specific bodily and mental traits." The same conception of race was combined with vulgar anti-Semitism by the legal academic Ernst Forsthoff:[16]

> A *Volk* is a community that rests on an ontological sameness of kind [*eine seinsmäßige, artmäßige Gleichartigkeit* . . .]. The awareness of sameness of kind [*Artgleichheit*] and *völkisch* togetherness actualizes itself in the capacity to recognize differences of kind [*Artverschiedenheit*] and to distinguish between friend and foe. It is indeed essential to recognize differences of kind where it is not immediately apparent from someone's belonging to an alien nation—for example, in the Jew, who sought to create the illusion of sameness of kind and membership in the *Volk* by actively participating in cultural and economic life [. . .]. The renaissance of a German political *Volk* necessarily put an end to that deception and destroyed the last hope of the Jew to live in Germany otherwise than in the awareness of being a Jew.

The full implications of such racial thinking were articulated by Wilhelm Stuckart and Hans Globke in their commentary on the Nuremberg Laws of September 1935: "Over against the doctrines of the equality of all human beings and the fundamentally unrestricted freedom of the individual *vis-à-vis* the state, National Socialism sets the harsh but necessary recognition of the natural inequality and differentiation in kind [*Verschiedenartigkeit*] among humans."[17]

One year after the Nuremberg laws, Morgen published his book *War Propaganda and War Prevention*,[18] a scholarly analysis of how propaganda contributes to the instigation and conduct of wars. "When war propaganda arouses hatred, fear, anger, avarice, envy, thirst for glory, and the like," he writes, "then it evokes the destructive forces of war against peace."[19] Morgen speaks as a student of international law, not as an advocate of National Socialism. He does pay lip service to Hitler's peaceable intentions.[20] In what amounts to a remarkable, almost grotesque political misjudgment, he says, "Germany wants peace, an honest peace which is to the benefit of all peoples."[21] But at a time when Nazi legal theorists are defending the Nuremberg racial laws, Morgen laments the divisive effects of race. "After the [First World] War," he writes "Germany opened wide its heart to the world," expecting sympathy but meeting instead with triumphalist gloating. He draws a bitter moral:

> The world seems to have a law that aims at strictly maintaining the natural separation of peoples by race, language, and culture; that doesn't allow rapprochement or

assimilation; and that hits with clenched fist the nation that makes a conciliatory approach to others, while it smiles with lavish favor on those who stay within their borders and distance themselves from others.[22]

Thus, the separation of peoples by race is part of the problem, in Morgen's view, not part of the solution.

We will find, in studying Morgen's subsequent cases, that unlike the leading Nazi jurists, he never makes derogatory remarks about Jews. Indeed, he denounces the mistreatment of Jews and even prosecutes the killing of a Jew on the grounds that it violates his right to life. Apparently, then, his indifference to violence against the Jews was not due to race-hatred.

SEVEN

FROM CRACOW TO BUCHENWALD

In March 1942, Morgen reached a crisis. Invited to lead a new court in Lemberg (Lvov), he writes to the personnel department of the SS Judiciary Head Office in Munich asking to be spared the assignment. He asks instead to be transferred out of the General Gouvernement, preferably to Norway or the Balkans.[1] In support of this request, he recites the record of his accomplishments in the region: the number of the indictments he has filed, the number of defendants he has tried, and the travels he logged in the Sauberzweig case, which he calls a *Korruptionsherd*—a "focus of corruption," on the analogy of a *Krankheitsherd*, a focus of disease. In closing, he offers a further argument:

> The corruption in the General Gouvernement is so great, and the number of capital crimes and noxious offenses so high, that I am utterly convinced that any judge would in time become jaded and therefore run the risk of injury to his natural sense of justice. So you will understand, Obersturmbannführer, if I have the urgent wish to go back now to live once again in a different, healthier atmosphere than that of the General Gouvernement.

Morgen had been struggling to sweep the General Gouvernement with the broom of the law and getting nowhere. Fegelein, Fassbender, Dirlewanger—all of his primary targets had eluded his grasp under the protection of higher-ups. His powers as jurist had thus proved ineffectual against corruption in the SS, and so his role as an SS judge had become untenable: he could no longer see himself as a judge upholding standards of justice and SS honor as he interpreted them. So he looked for an exit, preferably to the cleaner atmosphere of Norway.

Morgen's wish to be transferred would be granted, but not as he envisioned. His transfer, when it came, was the lesser of two evils, the greater being three years in concentration camp:[2]

> It was Pentecost 1942. For the holiday I had gone to Dresden [...]. On the first evening, I was called back immediately to Cracow. I go, and there was a letter from the

chief of SS Judiciary Head Office. "The Reichsführer [Himmler] has ordered that you be removed from your duties, effective immediately, are to abstain from any official activity, and are to report forthwith to the Head Office of the SS Judiciary in Munich." What had happened is the following. [...] I had acquitted a man of a racial crime even though he had confessed. I had simply flouted the established policies. But I believed not only that it was just in this case but also that nothing more would come of it, since the acquittals were hardly ever reviewed. But because so many people were carefully monitoring my every step, they had fished out this decision. Obergruppenführer Koppe, apparently stirred up by [Oswald] Pohl, had nothing more urgent to do than to get into a plane and fly to the SS Head Office [SS-Hauptamt] and bring them the decision and say, "Here, his real attitude finally comes out: he is sabotaging orders!" In Munich I heard from the judge who succeeded me [in Cracow], Sturmbannführer Sachs, a very reputable man, that there was a secret order of the Reichsführer aimed at having me committed to a concentration camp for two or three years. But in the SS Judiciary Head Office there were very reputable people, and they said: "No way. What would happen to judicial independence? In general, not just in the case of Morgen. Something fundamental is being infringed. A decision can be appealed, but the judge can't be punished for it."

When this message reached Himmler, he said, "OK, the man disappears from the judiciary and is sent to the front." Morgen was demoted and sent off to boot camp in Stralsund. After strenuous training, he joined the panzer division "Wiking" in the Soviet Union.[3]

The "racial crime" whose confessed perpetrator Morgen had acquitted was the crime of sexual relations with a Polish woman. Morgen says that this charge was typically invoked only as an aggravating circumstance to some other crime.[4] Since there was no other crime in the present case, his handling of it would not ordinarily have attracted notice. But there were people who had it in for him, presumably because of his aggressive investigations into influential figures. They "fished out" this case as a pretext for getting him out of the way, and he avoided concentration camp only through the intervention of the SS Judiciary Head Office.

Little is known about Morgen's activities with Division Wiking. The division had committed atrocities earlier in the eastern campaign,[5] but those had ended by the time of Morgen's service, during which the division was under pressure from Soviet forces freed up by the German surrender at Stalingrad. What Morgen mainly remembered were the severe losses suffered by the division and, especially, the barbaric behavior of the Russian soldiers—memories that entered into his legal reasoning later on.[6]

In May 1943, Morgen was suddenly called back from the front to Munich. Himmler then ordered him transferred to the Reichskriminalamt—the office of the Reich Criminal Police in Berlin—to investigate corruption, which had become extreme at this point, forcing Himmler to take action. Himmler's commitment to this campaign can be seen in this passage from his infamous Posen speech to SS officers on October 4, 1943. Speaking of the victims of the gas chambers, he said,[7]

> We have taken from them what wealth they had. I have issued a strict order, which SS-Obergruppenführer [Oswald] Pohl has carried out, that this wealth should, as a matter of course, be handed over to the Reich without reserve. We have taken none of it for ourselves. Individual men who have lapsed will be punished in accordance with an order I issued at the beginning, which gave this warning; Whoever takes so much as a mark of it, is a dead man. A number of SS men—there are not very many of them—have fallen short, and they will die, without mercy. We had the moral right, we had the duty to our people, to destroy this people which wanted to destroy us. But we have not the right to enrich ourselves with so much as a fur, a watch, a mark, or a cigarette or anything else.

The implied contrast between the last two sentences is ridiculous, of course, since it suggests that the obligation not to steal is like the right to kill in that it holds vis-à-vis the Jews. In fact, no obligation to the Jews was envisioned. The obligation that Himmler had in mind was vis-à-vis the Reich, to which wealth taken from Jews was payable.

Violation of this obligation, through the misappropriation of confiscated property, was the crime with which Morgen had charged Fassbender and Fegelein in their dissolution of the "Aryanized" firm Nathan and Apfelbaum. Since then, he had written his article on the corruption criminal. He was therefore a natural choice for service in the anti-corruption campaign. He owed this second chance at a judicial career to the specialty that he had chosen the first time around, namely, crimes of corruption.

Morgen was still an SS judge; he now became an officer of the police as well. One of his first assignments in this new capacity, in late June or early July 1943, was to investigate the chief procurement officer (*Hauptlieferant*) in the concentration camp Buchenwald, a man by the name of Bornschein.[8] Bornschein was suspected of embezzling foodstuffs from the camp and selling them on the black market. The Criminal Police were asked to send an investigator with expertise in corruption, and Morgen was the one they sent.[9]

The suspicions against Bornschein turned out to be groundless.[10] But now that Morgen was in Buchenwald, he decided to have a look around. It was his first time inside a concentration camp. Here is how he describes the camp to his US interrogators in 1946:[11]

My first impression was strikingly good. The prisoners were decently housed, were well nourished. I occasionally tried the food myself. The working conditions were good. And in general, so much was done for the prisoners to ease their lot that I was really amazed. Back then I got the impression that concentration camps were a major advance on institutions in the justice system. People are out in nature, almost at liberty. They work happily and have much more freedom. What's more, the commandant, Standartenführer Pister, made an excellent impression on me.

Buchenwald was built in 1937, on a wooded hill eight or nine kilometers outside the city of Weimar, originally for the purpose of holding political dissidents, "habitual criminals," and "indolents," that is, people judged unwilling to work. Internees passed through a two-story gatehouse with a metal gate bearing the words *Jedem das Seine*, which can mean "To each his own" but in this case meant "To each what he deserves."[12]

Buchenwald was the first camp to be liberated by the Western Allies, in April 1945.[13] Images of the emaciated prisoners and stacked corpses are now familiar from photographs by Margaret Bourke-White.[14] The liberators forced the citizens of Weimar to view the camp. A silent film shows them walking to the camp as if on a jolly weekend outing, then staring ashen-faced at the scenes of death and torture.[15]

Hermann Pister, the commandant whom Morgen met on his first visit, was sentenced to death in a trial held by the Americans at Dachau in 1947. Morgen was called to testify for the defense at that trial, and he repeated his favorable description of Buchenwald under Pister.[16] Pister himself suggested that the conditions found by the Allies were due to overcrowding and shortages during the collapse of Germany at the end of the war.[17] Morgen elsewhere made the same assertion about concentration camps in general.[18]

Morgen's description of Buchenwald in 1943 is obviously false. To cite only the most glaring example, never in all his testimony about Buchenwald does Morgen mention the "Little Camp," a sector built early in the year.[19] Barracks in the Little Camp consisted of windowless horse stables in which prisoners slept on bare shelves, four rows high, as seen in one of Bourke-White's iconic photographs.[20] A prisoner who arrived in the Little Camp in January 1944 later reported gross overcrowding and primitive sanitation.[21]

In March 1944, a survey of all 20,000 inmates in Buchenwald found that over 80 percent of them were undernourished.[22] At this very time, Morgen was comfortably ensconced in the camp:[23]

Yes, I was sitting in Buchenwald the whole time. I had them give me a room with a telegraph. It was all very comfortable. The concentration camp got various news broadcasts. A sort of courier service was also part of the deal. So I sat like a spider in its web. Drove here and there. Saw what people were doing. Or had them come to me.

A survivor of the camp tells the Americans that he gave Morgen a massage every day.[24]

Morgen claims that he went over Buchenwald carefully:[25]

Before beginning an investigation, I examined the concentration camp in question in all its details very closely, inspecting especially those arrangements which seemed particularly important to me. I visited them repeatedly and without notice. I was working mostly in Buchenwald itself for 8 months [...].

He adds, "It is almost impossible to be deceived for such a long time."

Although Morgen draws a distorted picture of the camps, he was not insensible of the horrors. In a report written for the Americans in January 1946, he writes,[26]

The devilish side of the KZ system [...] lay in the cancers of the system itself, against which no reforms could avail. The system could have been operated humanely only by ideal people. That's exactly what was missing in a concentration camp. A portion of the inmates—around 40% on average—were serious criminals. Because of their egoistic mindset, their brutality and recklessness, they poisoned the environment in unimaginable ways with their criminal cunning and behavior. Because self-administration gave them power over the rest of the prisoners, they abused it recklessly. They thereby forced the "politicals" to take similar measures in self-defense. So a situation developed that is rightly described by the saying that in a KZ you could have anyone's life for a cigarette.

Although the commandant's power was curtailed *de jure*, in fact he could do what he liked.

Starting with the organization of the daily routine. He could have the prisoners stand for hours after work at roll-call. Even in ringing frost without gloves. He could harass them in every way. As is known from the military, there are countless legal means of tormenting people mercilessly.

Under normal circumstances people would raise objections against such a despotic regime. Fine, but how would the prisoner do that? He couldn't get out of the camp. He could only denounce his tormentors to themselves—precisely the men whose good will he must strive to get, so as not to lose every hope of regaining his freedom at some point. And if he got free, he couldn't open his mouth unless he wanted to risk being immediately locked up again. So the prisoners themselves did everything to help turn their life into a hell. The SS members in the camp took note of that. The commandants locked the prisoners up, tortured them, the doctors treated them badly and killed them, the guards mistreated them and engaged in "shooting while trying to escape," the capos never let their truncheons rest and, to increase their authority, often made a sport of driving their fellow prisoners to suicide. [...]

In this system everything depended on the people in charge. If the commandant was bad, the camp was hell. If the commandant was humane and kept after his staff, it was bearable. That's why reports coming out of concentration camps are so variable. Mostly the personnel of the camps were bad. Bad from the start, since one didn't deploy the most capable and unobjectionable characters there—one couldn't, given the shortage of leadership material. Only the slag that was of no use anywhere found its way there. With very few exceptions, such creatures reported there happily. Himmler well understood the corrosive, corrupting environment of the concentration camps. He had given an order that no SS member should serve in a KZ for more than 2 years. This order was never carried out—at least not consistently.

Prisoners without rights, bad human material, omnipotent police, a lack of effective controls, these are the main causes of the conditions in the concentration camps.

Here Morgen perceptively analyzes the poisonous dynamics of a concentration camp, in apparent contradiction to his sunny descriptions elsewhere. And his American captors are not the only ones to whom he describes the camps as hell when their commanders were bad. As we will see, he said the same to the SS Judiciary during the war.

In trying to understand the discrepancies among Morgen's depictions of the camps, we must keep three facts in mind. First, Morgen distinguishes the period of his investigations at Buchenwald from both the preceding and succeeding periods, when Pister had not yet arrived at Buchenwald or when Germany was in a state of collapse.[27] There is some reason to believe that conditions at Buchenwald were marginally better during Morgen's sojourn there than before or afterwards, though they were never half as good as he would later describe. Morgen worked at Buchenwald from the summer of 1943 to the spring of 1944; Pister had taken command of Buchenwald in January of 1942; and according to long-time inmate Eugen Kogon, conditions in the camp improved markedly after 1941—that is, under Pister's regime.[28]

Second, Morgen tended to be defensive on behalf of the SS, though not necessarily of its individual members. An example of this defensiveness comes in his testimony at the war-crimes trial of Oswald Pohl, who as Head of the Economic Administrative Head Office (*Wirtschaftsverwaltungshauptampt*) had responsibility for the camps. There Morgen inventories causes of death that cannot be blamed on the camps' administration.[29] These include: executions of those brought into the camp solely for that purpose ("Since these executions did not apply to concentration camp inmates, then you cannot charge the concentration camp or the concentration camp administration with such crimes"); the extermination of Jews ("those extermination installations had nothing to do with the concentration camps"); the normal death rate among the population ("people in civilian life also would have died in that same time anyhow"); epidemics ("the administration in the concentration camps did whatever was humanly possible in order to prevent the breakout of such epidemics"); infighting among the inmates ("death cases which occurred, due to the fault of the inmates"); and even the presence of intellectuals ("they, of course, possibly die faster than other people"). This inventory is almost comically defensive, but then, Morgen has been called as a witness for the defense, and he explains that he is merely trying to place the blame where it belongs—namely, on the people who instituted the system of concentration camps in the first place. "[C]oming back to the actual reasons," he says, "we will find that the establishment of concentration camps, as such, was responsible. [. . .] I shall repeat again and again that those authorities are guilty which carried out this mad policy."[30] Of course, this statement implicitly exculpates the SS.

Third and finally, Morgen was sensitive to cruelty but insensitive to generalized suffering. What inflamed his moral sentiments was harm deliberately inflicted on innocent victims by men of bad character. He thought that the concentration camp system was evil because it gave evil men free rein to commit evil deeds. That such men made life hell for the inmates outraged him; that its conditions were already hell did not much concern him, since those conditions were not the doing of particular malefactors. In 1945, with the Third Reich crumbling around him, refugees fleeing from invasion on every front, we will find Morgen rededicating himself to the war on crime in the SS, as if oblivious to the miseries of real war. This obliviousness to suffering, as opposed to crime, may account for the discrepancy between his contempt for the specimens of human "slag" who tormented the prisoners and his complacency about the conditions in which the prisoners lived.

EIGHT

KARL OTTO KOCH

Buchenwald, July 1943.[1] Morgen's examination of Buchenwald soon focused on the previous commandant, Karl-Otto Koch, the commandant under whom conditions had been "entirely different," according to Pister. By the time of Morgen's visit, Koch had moved on to command the camp Majdanek, in Lublin—a post from which he was subsequently dismissed—and much of his senior staff had been scattered to other assignments as well.[2]

A few years earlier, while Koch was still at Buchenwald, he had come under suspicion for pecuniary offenses. The President of the SS and Police Court in Kassel, the Hereditary Prince of Waldeck and Pyrmont,[3] had thrown Koch in jail during the investigation, but Himmler had ordered his release and issued a decree, known thereafter as the *lex Waldeck*, forbidding the arrest of any commandant without permission from Himmler himself.[4] Ultimately, the investigation had been suspended for lack of evidence (Koch had suborned the witnesses).[5]

Morgen decided to restart the investigation of Koch "off my own bat [*auf eigene Faust*—literally, "on my own fist"], because I'm a fanatic for justice."[6] He searched the homes of Koch's former Buchenwald staff—men who had now moved on to other posts but still kept homes in Weimar. He found large quantities of gold, plus a lifestyle incompatible with the men's pay grade, and so he had the men interrogated and he examined their bank accounts. What he found was that the accounts had suddenly swollen after the "Jewish action" of 1938. (With this anodyne phrase, Morgen is referring to the vicious pogrom known as *Kristallnacht*.)

Morgen brought all of this evidence to Himmler's legal advisor, Horst Bender, in Berlin. Bender responded that Morgen had shown up at the right moment, since Himmler had just signed the suspension of the earlier proceedings that Prince Waldeck had instituted against Koch.[7]

But Morgen's investigation of Koch and his former Buchenwald staff had led him to their subsequent post in Lublin, where clues to even greater malfeasance had emerged. So Morgen painted a picture of wider corruption in multiple camps, and on that basis he asked for authorization to pursue wrongdoing throughout the system. Faced with Morgen's evidence as presented by Bender, Himmler could not shut down this new investigation and still maintain his commitment to keeping the SS clean. As Morgen says,[8]

> I had to proceed by revealing these crimes in their full extent, so that the abundance of material would bring Himmler to see for himself that [. . .] it was inherent in the system for such crimes to take place and remain undetected. I always countered the resistance I met from the central offices with SS ideology—"You want the SS to be absolutely clean," etc. Then they were of course beaten and had to say "Yes." I considered this course to be the most effective, since I was concerned with helping people, not just making a gesture.

So Himmler gave Morgen a free hand and ordered the relevant offices to assist him. Morgen now had carte blanche to enter any concentration camp in pursuit of corruption, and he was given a small staff, which he sent to pursue the trail of evidence in Lublin.

Morgen now tried to have Koch brought back to Buchenwald. When Koch failed to appear on the appointed train, Morgen thought, "The guy has made a run for it [*Der Kerl ist getürmt*]." Sure enough, Koch's car was sighted traveling at high speed from Berlin in the direction of Buchenwald, headed for his own house. Morgen rushed there, accompanied by Chief SS Judge Werner Paulmann:[9]

> We went to his villa. It had turned midnight. Pitch black. Not a sound. Nothing. His car was nowhere to be seen. I rang the bell. All was still. Nothing moved. I took the heel of my boot and banged on the door. Nothing! Suddenly we heard a shuffling of feet. A storm had come up. Lightning flashed. Very dramatic. Paulmann said, "Get your pistol ready, there's going to be shooting." And then he appeared. In a housecoat, cool and calm. He asked, "What do you want?" Paulmann said, "We have to question you. Best get dressed." "Yes," he said, "I just got home and wanted to freshen up." He had driven there and wanted first to hear from his wife what was up in Buchenwald. [. . .] And then I questioned him all night. The slyest fox I've ever seen—and ice-cold! Without any human feeling. You had the sense that the man is nothing but a brain. He answered very, very cautiously and had an explanation for everything. I didn't believe him much. So I arrested him.

The arrest took place on August 24th, 1943; Frau Koch was arrested later the same day.[10]

Morgen's investigation of Koch and his associates continued into 1944. The inmates of Buchenwald soon became aware of his activities, and they knew that their SS guards were afraid of where his investigation might lead:[11]

Numerous witnesses out of the ranks of the SS and prisoners were deposed. The presiding SS judge, Dr. Morgen, was extraordinarily feared and hated by all SS officers in Buchenwald. They breathed easier when Morgen moved back to Berlin because they feared that the investigation could also bring to light incriminating material about themselves.

In April 1944, Morgen summarized the results of his investigation in an 87-page report, which was in his possession when he surrendered to the American CIC in 1945. Also in his possession was the bill of indictment charging Commandant Koch with embezzlement, military insubordination, and premeditated murder of prisoners. Two of Koch's subordinates were indicted along with him, also on charges of murder. Frau Koch was indicted for trafficking in stolen goods.

These charges went well beyond Morgen's assignment to investigate crimes of corruption, and Morgen's investigative report goes far beyond the charges, into a psychological analysis of the perpetrators and a portrait of life in the camp—all written during the war for submission to the SS Judiciary. It repays detailed study.

After summarizing Koch's early career, the report turns to a minute audit of his financial records. The discrepancies amount to 94,000 Reichsmarks in embezzled funds and 105,000 Reichsmarks in misappropriated goods and services—over $6 million in present-day purchasing power. There follows an enumeration of the means by which Koch accumulated these riches.

First on the list is the mishandling of valuables brought to the camp by Jewish internees:[12]

> After the assassination of the embassy secretary von [*sic*] Rath, almost all the Jews in Germany were rounded up and transferred to concentration camps. The arrests fell upon them suddenly. The Jews involved arrived mostly without luggage or food but, by the same token, with all of the valuables that they had on them or could gather in their haste. Irregularities already began with their admission. [. . .] According to strict camp regulations, all of a prisoner's effects were to be taken away. The valuables were to be surrendered in the presence of witnesses and stored in containers. The prisoner had to confirm on a card the things he had surrendered. This regulation was not obeyed.

Valuables were simply piled up; no records were kept. Moreover, when Jewish war veterans and Jewish husbands of Aryan women were later released, they were forced to sign a waiver stating that they had no claim against the camp because nothing of value had been taken. Morgen coolly remarks, "Given the political situation at the time [i.e., 1938], it is understandable that the released Jews would raise no objections."[13]

Obviously, Morgen could not protest "the political situation" in a report to the SS Judiciary. Yet even in his postwar statements, Morgen made no comment on the political situation of the Jews in the Third Reich—the process of exclusion, disenfranchisement, and oppression. When Morgen spoke of justice, he meant criminal justice, not political or social justice. He therefore had nothing to say about the "Jewish action" that sent a flood of new internees into the concentration camps.

Interned Jews managed to hold on to some of their valuables, Morgen says, which were quickly stolen by other inmates. There was a rumor that SS men looked out for rich Jews and shot them for their money. Money thus attracted predators:[14]

> Many Jews therefore just threw their money and valuables away. [. . .] Some of the Jews are said to have become so indifferent to their money that they wiped their asses with 50- and 100-mark notes. This has been confirmed by eyewitnesses. Because of this development, there came to be specialists who would use a bar or a board with a nail driven through its end to fish the bills out of the latrines, wash them, dry them, smooth them out, and press them.

Now, Morgen knows that conditions in the camp latrines were not within his brief, and hence not a matter requiring eyewitnesses. The only criminal charge in the offing here is the violation of camp regulations.

Morgen's report next enumerates forms of exploitation and extortion that were practiced on all inmates, not only Jews. These include profiteering on goods sold within the camp; requiring "contributions" for camp amenities; rescinding corporal punishment in return for "fines"; taking bribes for early release; and collecting dental gold from corpses without forwarding it to Berlin. The whole operation amounted to "an unscrupulous system of exploiting the prisoners."[15]

The camp also had various economic enterprises that profited the administration. Among these was a complicated purchasing scheme run by one of the favored prisoners, a career thief named Meiners. Meiners managed the kitchen of the *Führerheim*, the officers' mess. Morgen describes this establishment in great detail, despite having no evidence of its harboring criminal activity:[16]

> The officers' mess was a lavish restaurant, in which there were opulent meals and, between meals, bouillon with egg and roast chicken every day. For beverages, there were large quantities of real coffee, good wines, and the best imported liquors in stock at the bar and available for purchase at moderate prices. [. . .] When SS-Standartenführer Pister

took over, the wives in the SS community still didn't own cookware. The reason was that the lavish meals—larger than those available before the war (soup, roast, vegetable, salad, dessert)—were provided for 60–75 cents. [. . .] Part of the peculiar character of the SS colonels' mess was that only active officers could partake of these advantages. The reservists in particular got only what was served to the troops. So it was a daily sight in the mess, for example, that an active officer polished off his super-sized Schnitzel while the reservist next to him had to spoon up a stew.

Note that Morgen's focus has now shifted from criminal corruption to corruption of moral character, the two being closely connected in his mind.

The association between criminal and moral corruption is most striking in Morgen's report on Koch's wife, Ilse, whom Morgen indicted for receiving stolen property. Morgen starts by describing how Ilse mistreated her mother;[17] he then moves on to her amorous escapades. Two of Koch's subordinates, Hermann Florstedt and Waldemar Hoven, were enamored of her and tipped her off about her husband's relationship with a dancer in Weimar.[18] Ilse then began spouting accusations against him for the crimes of which he was indeed guilty, threatening to betray him to Reichsführer Himmler. Since her beaus Florstedt and Hoven feared that their role in the matter would be discovered and their credit with Koch destroyed, they contrived for Ilse to receive an anonymous letter about her husband's affair, so that they could play the part of peacemakers. Once the Koch couple had been reconciled, Hoven induced Ilse to test Florstedt's loyalty by asking him to run away with her—a proposition at which he knew that Florstedt would balk. With Florstedt out of the picture, Hoven could make his way into Ilse's bed—and she had the best of both worlds, writes Morgen: the status and wealth of a colonel's wife plus a "suave and experienced man of the world" as a lover. Morgen tells the Americans that when he searched Hoven's home and office, he found 20 to 30 "sexual preparations" to enhance his potency. Morgen remarks dryly, "He had an enormous number of women [*Frauenverkehr*]."[19]

This melodrama takes up three pages of Morgen's investigative report. It has nothing directly to do with the crimes for which he will indict Ilse Koch, but it has everything to do with her character, which to Morgen's mind has everything to do with her crimes.

NINE

FROM CORRUPTION TO MURDER

Morgen's investigative report to the SS Judiciary now passes from crimes of corruption to murder. His account of the "murder complex" under Koch begins with a review of the legal state of play.[1] Concentration camps like Buchenwald were prison camps, not extermination centers: killing was not their purpose. The power of life or death over a concentration camp inmate lay in the hands of Reichsführer Himmler. For "members of eastern peoples"—that is, Poles and Jews—this power was delegated to the Reich Security Head Office, whose chief at the time was Ernst Kaltenbrunner. The commandant of a concentration camp was permitted to kill an inmate only if Himmler or Kaltenbrunner ordered his execution, whereupon the carrying out of that order had to be documented and reported.

All deaths from unnatural causes required an autopsy by the camp physician. The local SS court would then decide whether to initiate an investigation: the corpse could not be cremated until the court gave permission. Every death in the camp, natural or unnatural, had to be reported immediately to the Security Service and to the staff of the Reichsführer. "The result," Morgen tells the CIC, "was that the life of prisoners in a concentration camp was thoroughly protected by special control mechanisms."[2]

Morgen explains that some killings were "legally insignificant"—that is, permitted. These included cases in which a doctor administered euthanasia to an incurably ill prisoner, as well as cases in which he tried to prevent the spread of an epidemic by painlessly killing those sick or suspected of being sick. We will examine Morgen's attitude to these practices shortly. In any case, he found that they could not account for many of the deaths at Buchenwald.

Morgen uncovered the murders at Buchenwald through careful detective work.[3] While investigating the crimes of corruption, he found that prisoners who had witnessed them were dead. He looked up the records of these prisoners and found that they had been in the hospital or in detention shortly before they died. After weeks of scrutinizing these records, he noticed discrepancies: prisoners appeared in hospital records as having died of natural causes before they were recorded in prison records as having been released. "I said to myself, this prisoner cannot be in the camp prison and at the same time a patient in the hospital."

Koch had developed a system for eliminating witnesses to his corruption:[4]

> The prisoners were taken to a secret place and were killed there, mostly in a cell of the camp prison, and sick reports and death certificates were prepared for the files. They were made out so cleverly that any unprejudiced reader of the documents would get the impression that the prisoner concerned had actually been treated and had died of the serious illness which was indicated.

Murders of other kinds often occurred as well.[5] Inmates were killed in the sickbay by injections of phenol.[6] Inmates were "shot while trying to escape," which usually meant that they had been forced at gunpoint to make a run for it and then shot from behind.[7] All of these deaths were covered up with fictitious medical certificates.

This investigation tested the limits of Morgen's remit from Himmler, which was confined to crimes of corruption. But testing limits was Morgen's way, as he often boasted after the war. Already quoted earlier are his claims to have pursued matters "on my own cap" and "on my own fist."[8] He even claims to have taken a step that the Security Service could not, namely, secret surveillance of the Kochs' mail. Asked how he could have done it, he replies, "I just did. I went to the chief inspector of the mails and gave him the order."[9] He was equally peremptory about the arrest of witnesses:[10]

> I sent a telegram to the court masters, "So-and-so is to be immediately arrested and transferred to Buchenwald," so that he came within my jurisdiction. [...] I already had such a reputation that they complied without checking up. They said to themselves, If Morgen is doing it, there must be something big.

Despite his imperious tone, Morgen knew that he was always subject to Himmler's authority—which is why he had brought his evidence of Koch's corruption to Berlin, for authorization to range across the concentration camp system. He was now testing the limits of even that authorization by investigating murder.

Morgen's report to the SS Judiciary details Koch's personal involvement in these killings, but first it digresses into "the general atmosphere in the Koch era." Morgen explains: "The prosecution is of the opinion that the extent of the unlawful killings of prisoners was caused by the unjustifiable, inexcusable arbitrariness of SS Standartenführer Koch."[11] Koch himself gave something like this explanation when he finally confessed:[12]

> I can't find an explanation for my behavior. It could be that I was spoiled by my superiors. Everything I suggested and did was OK'd. I got only praise and laurels. No one examined me critically. That went to my head. I became a megalomaniac.

Morgen offers several examples of behavior that was capricious, sometimes comically so. Koch once denied a subordinate the use of the *Führerheim* for his daughter's wedding only two hours before the ceremony was to begin. To another officer, he sent mocking letters as a joke. During the wee hours in the *Führerheim*, Koch would pelt the officers with teaspoons. Later on someone gave him wooden tomahawks for this purpose.

As for Ilse, Morgen says that she tried to attract the sex-starved prisoners by wearing revealing clothes, and if a prisoner looked her way, she took down his number and had her husband sentence him to 25 lashes "as a down-payment." She was so haughty that she didn't return the greetings of the other wives.

Suddenly Morgen turns to serious matters:[13]

> This feeling by which Koch was ruled—of arrogant superiority, of self-indulgence and brutal arbitrariness—worked itself out in the most tragic way in the treatment of the prisoners. Prisoners were strictly forbidden to move about the streets of the camp at anything but a trot. They had to stand at roll-call for hours, often even day- and night-long, in every rigor of weather. It made no difference that many fell dead of exhaustion or were carried ill to the sick-bay *en masse*. Blows, kicks, siccing of dogs were the order of the day. In severe frost the prisoners sometimes had to take off their gloves, so that there were countless cases of frostbite. [...]
>
> One of the worst hell-holes in the concentration camp was the stone quarry. As the prisoners marched off it was already clear "who was in for it today." These prisoners, designated by the camp administration, had to carry the stones at a trot. They were constantly goaded by kapos with truncheons. Their caps were continually knocked off their heads, which were buffeted with blows. Witnesses observed prisoners beaten to a pulp and then placed before a red-hot oven, so that their wounded flesh would swell and become terribly inflamed. SS members also observed water being poured by the bucketful through a tube into the mouths of prisoners, whose stomachs were then trampled on. Prisoners thus tortured would then run through the security perimeter and were shot. The shootings always took place between outposts 59 and 61, which the prisoners preferred because there was a clear shot and they could hope for a swift death.

Frau Koch expressed the hope that her husband's name would gain such notoriety abroad that no one at home would dare prosecute him, lest they lend credibility to enemy propaganda.

Morgen does not make these abuses the basis for any charges against Koch—he has more serious crimes in view—but he does show genuine sympathy for the victims, all of whom were prisoners and many of whom were Jews. Taken together with his earlier account of how Jews were mistreated upon entering Buchenwald, these passages show sensitivity to the rights of other "races," far from the attitude expressed in the memo recommending leniency for Paul Kleesattel, where he aimed only "to preserve the purity of our own ranks, not to protect the rights of an enemy people."[14] Keep in mind that these expressions of sympathy are contained, not in postwar testimony, but in an investigative report written for the SS Judiciary.

As Koch confessed to Morgen, he marked some prisoners for death upon their arrival in the camp. Looking over their files, he considered whether they deserved to live. The word Morgen uses here—which Koch himself probably used in his confession—is *lebenswert*, a word that had a notorious career in the Third Reich, since its opposite, *lebensunwert*, was used to label the mentally ill and handicapped patients who were killed in the "euthanasia" program that Hitler instituted in 1939. The life of these patients was labeled *lebensunwertes Leben*, which might be translated "life not worth living" but also meant "life not *worthy* of living," which was of course the sense in which Koch judged his prisoners.

Koch chose some of his victims on no more than a whim:[15]

> [He] once had a prisoner killed simply because this prisoner had the misfortune of running into Koch in no fewer than three separate camps. After the killing was reported to him, Koch said with satisfaction, "That bird won't follow me around any more."

In general, however, Koch focused on thugs and incurable criminals. Some were sent directly to solitary confinement, others were rounded up later. Koch would write a name or number on a slip of paper and hand it to his underling Martin Sommer, who would place the prisoner in detention. After a few days, the prisoner would be killed. The camp physician would then write up a fictitious history of illness, hospitalization, and death, so that everything looked legal. Some of the victims were even dissected so that the real cause of death was undetectable.

Although Morgen's report describes the full extent of Koch's murders, his indictment confines itself to three cases. In testimony at a war-crimes trial in 1947, he explains, "I confined myself to proving only so much against Koch and Hoven as was sufficient to cause a death sentence to be passed against the two with certainty."[16] Among the murders for which Morgen indicted Koch were the shootings of prisoners named Peix and Krämer. Krämer was a well-known figure in Germany, a Socialist member of the Reichstag.[17] He had probably been interned in Buchenwald as a political prisoner. He became an orderly in the camp hospital, where he made himself indispensable as a self-taught physician and administrator. He once treated the Prince of Waldeck and Pyrmont, who was visiting Buchenwald in his capacity as Higher SS and Police Leader in the region.[18]

Waldeck ordered that Krämer and his co-worker Peix be released.[19] Before his order could be carried out, however, word came that Krämer and Peix had instead been "shot while trying to escape." Waldeck knew that this explanation was false: for one thing, Krämer was lame and couldn't have fled if he wanted to. So Waldeck instituted an investigation.

Morgen took up the investigation upon his arrival at Buchenwald and found that Koch had sent Krämer and Peix to an external work detail with instructions that they be shot.[20] The job was given to a Hauptscharführer Blank, who was notorious among the prisoners for shooting supposed "escapees."[21] Morgen never discovered Koch's motive, but his report suggests that Krämer and Peix were witnesses to Koch's misappropriation of funds "contributed" by wealthy prisoners to the inmates' hospital.[22] A survivor of the camp says otherwise. In his recollection, Krämer's guilty knowledge was not of Koch's peculations but rather of the syphilis that Koch had contracted on a trip to Norway.[23]

Morgen's inventory of Koch's victims includes a group of Jews. The context is significant:[24]

> [...] at the time of the assassination attempt on the Führer in Munich [in November 1939] Koch, acting on his own initiative, had 18–20 prominent Jews shot in reprisal. It was arranged in advance with the participating officers and junior officers that these shootings would be presented to the local authorities, especially the police, as having been occasioned by a mass escape. [...] But afterwards some of the officers had second thoughts and didn't present themselves to make a statement. Given this new development, other junior officers had to claim that they had shot several of those fleeing, with the result that the [confessed] shootings outnumbered the corpses actually on hand. Because of this lapse, SS-Gruppenführer [Theodor] Eicke [Commander of the SS Totenkopf Units] told Standartenführer Koch that one is entitled to feel the people's anger within oneself, but not to show it.

Morgen mentions the murder of these Jews only in his depiction of the "general atmosphere in the Koch era," not in his formal indictment. His point, in the context, is that Koch did not have the authorization he claimed for killing prisoners on his own initiative, not even for killing Jews.

Morgen did indict one of the accused for killing a Jew:[25]

> The Jew Goldstein had inflicted several stab wounds on himself in an attempt to commit suicide, and lay there hopelessly. After he had cried out several times for an injection to release him from his suffering, he was set aside on a gurney in the washroom of the Jews' quarters. SS-Hauptscharführer Sommer came running, threw himself on the injured man and strangled him with his own hands. [...] Sommer denies it, but he is clearly guilty under §216 of the German Penal Code [Reichsstrafgesetzbuch] of killing upon request.

In other words, Sommer was guilty of assisted suicide, which was illegal under German law. Morgen elaborates on the relevant paragraph of the criminal code:[26]

> It makes no difference what value the depressed person has for society. Whoever expressly and earnestly asks to be killed without mustering the courage to carry it out himself is not as a rule to be viewed as a valuable and useful member of society. The right [Rechtsgut] protected by §216 is respect for the inviolability of another person's life in itself. The law-giver does not allow anyone to kill another person without a state order, irrespective of the grounds that can be given.

Here Morgen explicitly rejects a tenet of Nazi ideology—namely, that the life of a particular person should be valued in accordance with his value to the *Volksgemeinschaft*. Morgen suggests that under this doctrine, Goldstein's life would be devalued on the grounds that he was suicidal. But surely Goldstein's life would have been devalued in the first instance because he was a Jew. So while explicitly refusing to value human life in social terms, Morgen is implicitly refusing to value it in racial terms as well.

TEN

PARTNERS IN CRIME

The recollections of surviving prisoners make clear that Koch's subordinate Martin Sommer was not only a murderer but a sadist.[1] In addition to killing prisoners by beating, injection, and strangulation, he devised brutal tortures, such as "tree hanging," in which the victim's hands were tied behind his back and then hoisted until his feet cleared the ground, a position in which he might be left for hours or even days, often with dislocated shoulders.[2] Sommer came to be called "the Hangman of Buchenwald."[3] Morgen quotes a prisoner as saying, "Should there be a Hell for retribution in the hereafter, it could not be worse than the cell-block under Sommer."[4]

Sommer claimed that Commandant Koch had alluded to special powers granted by Reichsführer Himmler for the secret execution of particular prisoners. In his investigative report to the SS Judiciary, Morgen writes, "He [Sommer] claims to have believed this and to have carried out [Koch's] orders in good faith and, in the manner of a soldier, without asking for their justification."[5] This claim is cast into doubt, in Morgen's mind, by the secretive manner in which Sommer carried out the executions—often at night, with injections of poison, the bodies then being wrapped in a blanket.[6] On the other hand, notes Morgen, a number of physicians who took part in executions also claimed to have done so in the belief that they were authorized, and "the unsophisticated and pig-headed Sommer cannot be held to a different standard."[7]

Morgen sees a further mitigating circumstance:

In Sommer's favor, one shouldn't underestimate the fact that it was his years of work in the cell-block, with the barbaric punishments and forced confessions (by Sommer's description, sometimes over 2000 blows a day), that turned him into a monster [Unmensch] in the first place. In the investigator's [i.e., Morgen's] view, despite reservations about Sommer's personality, it can be assumed that outside of the concentration camp system and of his own free will, he won't continue to operate in that way.

Waldemar Hoven was more of a hardened case. According to a prisoner who worked as an orderly in the camp hospital, Hoven killed 90 to 100

58

prisoners a week by lethal injection.[8] Hoven was tried at Nuremberg in the "medical case," *USA v. Karl Brandt et al.* He was convicted of war crimes and crimes against humanity, sentenced to death, and hanged. But Hoven's first indictment for murder was filed during the war by Konrad Morgen.[9]

Hoven was a colorful figure.[10] In the early 1920s he went to America and got as far as Hollywood, where he worked as a movie extra for $500 a week. In the early 1930s he was in Paris, where (Morgen sees fit to mention in his report) he had an affair with an American woman who gave him a gold cigarette case worth 25,000 marks. He then returned home to Freiburg, where his parents owned a private sanatorium. Upon the death of his brother, who had served as the medical director, Hoven began medical studies at the University of Freiburg, where (Morgen sees fit to mention) it took him two tries to pass his preliminary examination.

Hoven wasn't much of a physician. According to Morgen's investigative report, "The senior physicians' opinion of his professional knowledge and abilities is devastating."[11] Hoven was therefore obliged to solicit the favor of superiors, especially Commandant Koch. "This gave him not the least difficulty, given his suave manners, his supple adaptability, and his unprincipled mindset." He managed to improve medical services at Buchenwald only by giving a free hand to the most capable doctors and nurses among the prisoners themselves. Indeed, prisoners wrote much of his doctoral dissertation.[12] Morgen remarks that this arrangement gave Hoven plenty of free time in which to involve himself in the "dark affairs" of the camp.

Morgen describes his first impressions of Hoven to the CIC:[13]

He impressed me favorably, presenting himself in a very friendly way, inviting me over. And I engaged him to deal with some physical complaints: at the time I was overworked and tense. And he was charmingly amiable and helpful, more so than I had ever found a person to be. He set everything in motion, had a great deal of grape sugar delivered for me—an article that was very hard to get at the time—and so forth. At first that puzzled me and I asked myself, "Does he want something from me?" But all I could tell at first was that he wanted to be in good standing with me, or maybe that he was just a very able and helpful physician and person. [. . .] [I asked whether] he would like to show me his hospital and operating room? He did so straightaway, and I must say that everything was perfectly in order. Along the way he led me into the kitchen and offered me some refreshment—a glass of milk, some white bread, and in addition a pound of butter. Given the circumstances in Germany during the war, that was extraordinary. So I got a very uncomfortable feeling: This guy is trying to buy me off. And so I distanced myself from him a bit and observed him even more acutely. He redoubled his efforts accordingly, and one evening he came over and suddenly, for no reason, he told me that he bumped people off with phenol. [. . .]

At first I stared at him speechless and didn't believe my ears, but I also stayed neutral, and he told me how he did it. With injections. The people were unsuspecting, felt no pain.

Naturally, I asked myself silently, "Why is he telling me this?"—me of all people. No criminal is so dumb as to betray himself to the judge. So at first I made no reply and considered what exactly his motives could be. To begin with, he could have been pulling my leg, on the assumption that I'd make a big fuss, and then he would reveal that there was nothing to it. Or maybe that the whole thing had been ordered, so that one couldn't do anything to him. It was totally murky. Since I was already somewhat suspicious, I was inclined to assume that there was a dangerous agenda behind it, except that I couldn't yet fathom what it was. I had already noted that the concentration camp was a dangerous place for judges.

A few days later, the Prince of Waldeck visited Buchenwald, and Morgen alerted him to the possibility that prisoners were being killed by injection. When they questioned Hoven, he claimed to know nothing about it. "I looked at Hoven wide-eyed. The guy wasn't even blushing, although he had told me flat out a couple of days before."[14]

Among Hoven's victims, according to Morgen's indictment, was a White Russian general named Kuschnir-Kuschnareff, whose case illustrates the internal politics of the camp.[15] As a White Russian, Kuschnir-Kuschnareff hated the Bolsheviks—Morgen describes him as a "communist-eater"—and he therefore served as Koch's spy on the communist faction among the prisoners, the so-called "politicals."

Hoven quarantined Kuschnir-Kuschnareff in the hospital, then killed him and sent his body to the crematorium in a sack. When questioned by Morgen, he claimed to have been ordered to kill Kuschnir-Kuschnareff for knowing too much about the mass shooting of "Russian commissars" in the camp. (We will come to this incident shortly.) In corroboration of Hoven's story, one witness claims to have heard Koch say, in reference to Kuschnir-Kuschnareff, "That bird has to go."

Morgen doesn't buy it. He argues that Kuschnir-Kuschnareff was too valuable as a spy for Koch and could have been counted on not to divulge the shootings, given that he was an anti-communist and must have been glad that Russian commissars were being shot. Even if Koch had wanted Kuschnir-Kuschnareff killed, he could have arranged it without having him quarantined and carried out in a sack. So Morgen concludes that Hoven must have acted alone and for other reasons.

According to Morgen, Kuschnir-Kuschnareff was a "thorn in the eye" of Hoven,[16] who was an ally of the politicals. Hoven's right-hand in the hospital was one of their leaders, the former socialist Krämer, and his incompetence as a physician made him utterly dependent on the assistance of prisoners such as Krämer, who were largely responsible for keeping the camp free of epidemics.[17] Being dependent on the politicals, Hoven did what he could in their cause. When Hoven was tried after the war, he tried to justify his killings—the ones to which he would admit—on the grounds that the victims were "traitors," whose betrayals of fellow inmates would have resulted in many more deaths.[18] Enemies of the politicals were traitors, according to Hoven's self-serving account, because the politicals ran the camp's underground resistance, which took itself to represent the interests of all prisoners. As an enemy of the politicals, then, Kuschnir-Kuschnareff would have qualified as a traitor, in Hoven's view. Hoven suspected that Kuschnir-Kuschnareff's treason had extended as far as complicity in the killing of Krämer and Peix. That's why Kuschnir-Kuschnareff was a thorn in Hoven's eye and ended up as a name on Hoven's indictment.

The most complex case in Morgen's report on Hoven is the killing of prisoners Freudemann and May.[19] The complexities are worth examining, because they reveal Morgen's attitude toward a notorious feature of concentration-camp administration—the use of prisoners in medical experiments.

Freudemann and May belonged to an external work detail at Quendlinburg under the command of Hauptscharführer Blank. Nearby was a chicken farm. Chickens began disappearing from the farm, and the owner alerted the Criminal Police. In the course of their investigation, they discovered Freudemann's motorcycle parked outside the home of a "female individual" (*Frauensperson*). She admitted that Freudemann often spent the night with her, bringing gifts of poultry. Before the investigation of Freudemann was completed, however, the work detail was recalled to Buchenwald.

Blank feared that the investigation of Freudemann would lead back to him. It subsequently emerged that he had allowed his favorite prisoners at Quendlinburg to consort with civilians, to steal chickens and wheat and benzene, and to join him in drinking binges and orgies. In other words, Blank had much to fear from the testimony of Freudemann and May. He therefore enlisted Hoven in a plot to eliminate them. Hoven placed Freudemann and May in Block 46, the isolation block for typhus patients and the site of medical experiments.[20]

At this point in the report, Morgen's attention is diverted to the methodology of medical experiments:[21]

> After a certain period of observation, the prisoners received an inoculation with the vaccine being studied. Then they were infected with real typhus pathogen, and the

efficacy of the inoculation was observed. The bacterial cultures, called "strains," are at different strength, called "virulence," at different times. In order to obtain a criterion for the virulence at each time, what is called a "control group experiment" goes on alongside the experiment just described. A group of prisoners doesn't receive the inoculation and are infected together with the other prisoners with the pathogen. After they fall ill, the typhus patients are given the most solicitous care. They receive all of the medications that would be used in an army hospital, especially cardiac medicine, nursing, and special diet, since the research into the efficacy of the new vaccine is valid only if the treatment plays out in the same way as in an army or SS hospital. Because the typhus and virus research institute at Buchenwald, headed by SS-Sturmbannführer Dr. Ding, produces new vaccines, or contributes significantly to their development, there is an understandable professional interest in keeping the death rate of the experimental groups as low as possible, since ascertaining the practical value of the serum depends upon it.

In an affidavit submitted to the medical trial, Morgen dilates on the compassion shown by Dr. Ding toward his subjects:[22]

Dr. Ding,—in spite of his conviction of the importance and necessity of the experiments and his usual cynical-sarcastic manner,—again and again expressed a deep, human compassion with the human sacrifices incident to them.

Even now I can see Dr. Ding sitting before me, speaking in evidently genuine sorrow of the high percentage of deaths especially among the control subjects in his experimental series.

In his CIC interrogations, Morgen defends such experiments as standard procedure in medical research:[23]

It's nothing unusual. Science has done it for centuries. [The interrogator asks, "On living subjects?"] Yes of course. For how can one test out a new drug or vaccine if not on living people? Of course one tests first on various animals, but in the end it also has to be tested on people. [. . .] You shouldn't proceed on the preconception that these experiments were devised and conducted in order to torture and ultimately kill people. Rather, the people who conducted them—they were specialists, who were striving to study epidemics for people's good. And all of these experiments were indeed in the interests of mankind and, at the end of the day, also in the interests of the prisoners themselves.

Although Morgen regarded such experiments as valuable, he was still alarmed that their conduct at Buchenwald was marred by struggles among the prisoners over the selection of subjects:

In the fight between the so-called greens and reds, that is, between the criminal and political prisoners, the strong suspicion was raised that both parties frequently instigated and achieved that hated opponents were put on the lists of persons selected for the typhus experiments in order to have them exterminated under the cover of the experiments.[24]

Morgen took corrective action by arranging for the selection of subjects to be taken over by the Criminal Police Bureau, which chose only from among serious criminals in the camp. So Morgen's "corrective action" was not aimed at preventing the selection process from being used as a means of targeting particular victims; it was aimed instead at changing which victims were targeted, so that the harms of the experiments would fall upon those who deserved them, in Morgen's eyes.

Thus, when Dr. Hoven enrolled Freudemann and May in a typhus experiment, he was following a route with which Morgen was familiar and had tried to block. Unfortunately for Hoven, the scheme fell flat. Freudemann was injected with a pathogen, but it turned out to have come from an inactive batch that made none of the patients sick. Meanwhile, Blank had come under investigation for dereliction of duty, and Freudemann's testimony was wanted in the case. When Commandant Pister learned of the situation, he ordered that Freudemann not be used in experiments, because he was needed as a witness. But Hoven advised Pister, falsely, that Freudemann could not be deposed, because he was already seriously, perhaps fatally, ill. Hoven then transferred Freudemann and May out of Block 46 and into the hospital, where he killed both with injections of phenol, the drug of choice for medical murders. When the murders were reported to Blank, he presented Hoven with a bottle of schnapps.

Morgen initially obtained evidence against Hoven from a Hauptscharführer at Buchenwald by the name of Koehler.[25] He then went off to Kassel to obtain an arrest warrant for Hoven. While he was standing in the office of Chief Judge Werner Paulmann, however, the telephone rang: Buchenwald was calling to report that Koehler had attempted suicide. Moments later the telephone rang again. Buchenwald was calling with a correction: Koehler had been poisoned. Morgen telephoned the universities of Jena and Leipzig for specialists to help him save Koehler, then headed back to Buchenwald. The patient lay there "like a shadow." Morgen asked him, "Did you try to commit suicide?" Koehler had the strength only to whisper, "The furthest thing from my mind."[26]

Unfortunately, Koehler had amnesia as to the time of his poisoning. He couldn't remember anything between Friday noon and Saturday evening, at which point he found himself tied down to a gurney. Morgen tried unsuccessfully to revive Koehler's memory, but Koehler was already dying. Morgen called the Gestapo and had Hoven arrested.

According to Eugen Kogon, the Buchenwald prisoner who served as a medical clerk, Morgen was then party to a deadly medical experiment designed to identify the poison that had killed Koehler:[27]

> The specific compound used was not established, and the members of the SS investigation commission, SS Major George Conrad Morgen and SS Captain Wehner, in the presence of the officers-in-charge, conducted a "little experiment" in Ward 46. They had four unsuspecting Russian prisoners of war fed various alkaloids in noodle soup. When the men failed to die of the consequences, they were subsequently strangled in the crematory.

Kogon testified about this experiment in the medical trial at Nuremberg. Morgen submitted an affidavit to that trial vehemently disputing Kogon's testimony. The subjects weren't prisoners of war, he says, but Russians who had volunteered for the German army and then committed serious crimes. They were in the Buchenwald arrest bunker awaiting execution, having already been tried and sentenced to death.[28] More importantly, Morgen says, "The purpose of the experiment was not to injure the experimental subjects, but was to show that this combination of drugs would *not* result in injuries."[29] Kogon retracted the most damning aspects of his accusations in a deposition to the court in Bad Homburg in August 1950.[30]

Hoven confessed to killing Freudemann and May, but he gave a long and complicated excuse. He claimed that he placed Freudemann on the list of experimental subjects in the belief that he was a dangerous criminal, without knowing that he was involved in the case against Blank. He then learned of the incredible doings in Quendlinburg. He reasoned that uncovering these incidents in court would create a scandal that would be unacceptable in this, the fourth year of the war. He felt obligated to prevent such a scandal, and the only means at his disposal was to kill Freudemann and May. Or so Hoven claimed.

In his investigative report to the SS Judiciary, Morgen says that the objective facts of the case are sufficient to convict Hoven whether or not his story is true, and at this point his report takes on a tone of high dudgeon:[31]

> To repeat: Dr. Hoven takes himself to be justified and obligated, in the interest of state security, to withhold knowledge of politically significant events from the authorized agencies. To this end he acted in violation of an explicit order of his commandant,

and killed witnesses so as to spare the main perpetrator Blank. This action constitutes military insubordination of the most serious kind, an assault on military discipline and order and due obedience [*Unterordnung*]. It is furthermore an assault on the political leadership of the Reich, through the endangerment of a governmental necessity, namely, the intelligence service, in the form of the State Security Head Office. Finally, it is an attack on the Criminal Judiciary to make it impossible to clear up and prosecute a serious crime.

The violation of life is the least of it, both objectively and considering the subjective mindset of the perpetrator. This threefold assault on the military organization, the Security Police, and the judiciary is a rebellion on the part of the perpetrator against state institutions and organs that are essential to the existence of the organized *Volksgemeinschaft*.

Morgen continues,

No state can allow one of its members to appoint himself unbidden as lord of life and death, and to arrogate to himself the absolute power and sole discretion to decide, for supposed reasons of state, what must be done and permitted. Especially not the National Socialist Führer-state, least of all with respect to a subordinate member of the military. Deigning to recognize such criminal motives in any form must lead to collapse.

Morgen concludes that Hoven must be punished because of having thus undermined the state, not because he killed sick patients.

Now, Morgen rarely invokes Nazi ideology. Phrases like "the National Socialist Führer-state" almost never appear in his surviving papers. Two other exceptions are passages in his book on war propaganda and his article on the "corruption criminal," both written for a general readership and hence required to pay obeisance to National Socialism, irrespective of what Morgen actually believed.[32] In his testimony at the Auschwitz trial in Frankfurt, Morgen suggests that he fended off interference from above by appealing to his superiors' fear of challenges to their authority.[33] And the present invocation of Hitler's authority, as expressed in the term "Führer-state," appears on the penultimate page of Morgen's report on Hoven's crimes, in what can only be described as a peroration. Perhaps, then, this passage too was tailored to the predispositions of higher-ups.

Morgen's investigative report concludes with a five-page evaluation of Hoven's personality as it bears on his accountability for his crimes. A fellow investigator, Criminal Counselor Wehner, "posed the question with respect to Dr. Hoven: dumb or criminal? He opted for the first."[34] But Morgen disagrees. Morgen thinks that Hoven feigned stupidity in order to raise doubts about his accountability. Even under the lowered standards necessitated by war, he argues, earning a medical degree and functioning as a physician required a modicum of intelligence, and so Hoven cannot be exculpated on grounds of mental incompetence, and Morgen proceeds to indict him along with Sommer and the Kochs.

The indictment manifests Morgen's dual allegiances, to the law and to uprightness in the SS. On the one hand, he indicts Koch, Sommer, and Hoven for murder under the relevant paragraphs of the civil criminal code. On the other hand, he also indicts Koch for military disobedience, and he sums up this count of the indictment by saying that Koch "directed the operation of the said concentration camps in a manner not only contrary to orders but also incompatible with all moral laws."[35] He thus uses §92 of the military criminal code to import SS standards into the law, but they are the secular moral standards to which he holds the SS, not the racial or ideological standards of Himmler.

ELEVEN

"LEGAL" KILLING

Morgen had come to Buchenwald as a specialist in crimes of corruption, delegated by Himmler to clean up rampant theft and fraud on the part of SS officers in the concentration camps. In the course of investigating Buchenwald's commandant, he was repeatedly stymied by a lack of live witnesses. Prisoners who could have testified to the commandant's crimes were dead. Further detective work revealed that they had been murdered, and so Morgen found himself with a murder investigation on his hands. And once he began to investigate the murder of witnesses, the trail of evidence led to other murders, committed for a variety of reasons and by a variety of means.

As Morgen followed this trail of evidence, he came up against a policy—carrying the force of law, by virtue of carrying Hitler's name—that limited the range of cases that he could pursue. The policy was made clear to him in 1944 by the Chief Physician of the SS, Ernst-Robert Grawitz, in reference to killings committed by Waldemar Hoven. Grawitz said that by order of Hitler, "a distinction was to be drawn between 'legal' killings—legal in the sense of the NS-system—and criminal murders":[1]

> And he [Grawitz] believed that Hoven had undertaken killings within his "competence," so to speak, such as euthanasia and executions. And he took this opportunity to tell me that there was an order from Hitler concerning the extermination of Jews, and that he [Grawitz] made these recommendations [of killings?] at the bidding and wish of the Reichsführer [Himmler].
>
> So I [Morgen] explained, to the contrary, that I hadn't arrested Hoven for the killings that he, Grawitz, had ordered, but rather for those which he had undertaken without an order or authority. And in this connection I pointed out the consequences that these mass killings have: the epidemic of corruption, the brutalization of the men, and third, that all control had completely slipped away.

It is unclear whether Morgen's use of the term "mass killings" is a reference to the extermination of the Jews or to Hoven's hundreds of unauthorized murders: both were under discussion in his conversation with Grawitz. As we will see in due course, Morgen already knew about the

"Final Solution,"[2] which Grawitz classified as "legal," and he had already decided that his only means of impeding it was to prosecute "illegal" killings like Hoven's. Before we examine Morgen's reaction to the "Final Solution," however, we must examine his approach to the other categories of killings that Grawitz classified as legal. What was Morgen's view of their supposed legality?

The first "legal" category mentioned by Grawitz was euthanasia, which had by that time been practiced in Germany for almost five years. On September 1, 1939, Hitler had secretly ordered Karl Brandt, his personal physician, and Philipp Bouhler, Chief of the Führer's Chancellery, to appoint doctors who would provide "mercy death" (*Gnadentod*) to patients who were incurably ill.[3] What they developed was a system of killing not only dying patients but also patients who were chronically ill or disabled, either mentally or physically. These victims were classified as *lebensunwertes Leben*, "life unworthy of life." They were killed by gassing in chambers just like the ones used later—by the same staff, following the same procedures—in the extermination centers of Poland. Hitler officially cancelled the euthanasia program in 1941, because it had raised public concerns, though killings continued under that rubric in the concentration camps.

In a 1971 interview with the journalist John Toland, Morgen says that young physicians and young jurists like himself were initially in favor of euthanasia.[4] It's a practice that goes back thousands of years, he says—back to the Greeks. And he speaks with feeling of his father, who "suffered like an animal" on his deathbed but was refused help in dying. Morgen claims, mistakenly, that Hitler's order required strict controls on the use of euthanasia. Nevertheless, he says that his investigations led him to the conclusion that euthanasia should not be practiced, because it is so easily abused, "And then there is no limit."

In one of Morgen's CIC interrogations, he and his interrogator engage in a long debate about the legality of the "euthanasia" program.[5] Morgen contends that Hitler's letter to Brandt and Bouhler qualified as a *Führerbefehl*—a Führer's order—which had the force of law in the Third Reich:[6]

> Law in the National Socialist state was several things. First it was, like in former times, the sum of legal norms in place, including common law, but then also the Führer's orders. The Führer in the National Socialist state united all authority in his person. He was not only head of the state, but also highest law giver and supreme judge.

In Morgen's opinion, the fact that the "euthanasia" order was secret, known at the time only to two or three people, does not undermine its status as law, despite the traditional conception of law as necessarily public. He says that Hitler's powers as supreme lawgiver included not only the power to dictate laws but also the power to set the criteria of legal validity, hence to cancel the requirement of publicity.

When the interrogator suggests that the order was tantamount to a revision of the penal code with respect to killing, Morgen replies that it merely established an exception to the code without changing it. Asked whether the term *Euthanasie* covers the elimination of *lebensunwertes Leben*, Morgen says that *Euthanasie* is not a legal but a medical term, which admittedly allows only for hastening the death of an already dying patient. But he adds that Hitler's order gave authorization, not just for euthanasia as medically defined, but for killing the incurably ill merely on the condition that "health could not be restored by human means." That was Hitler's order, Morgen insists—and with that, the discussion comes to an end.

More relevant to Morgen's work than the first "euthanasia" program was the shadow program that continued in the concentration camps after the official program was cancelled. The latter program, code-named 14f13, was instituted by Himmler for the purpose of culling prisoners unfit for work from the concentration-camp population. Starting in the spring of 1941, teams of physicians visited the camps to select the victims in cursory medical examinations, though not even cursory examinations were performed in the case of Jews.[7] These killings, also labeled euthanasia, continued after the original "euthanasia" program was halted in August.

A team of 14f13 physicians visited Buchenwald in the fall of 1941 and made a selection of several hundred Jewish prisoners. Hoven assisted in the selection and was then responsible for sending the victims to the psychiatric facility at Bernburg, where they were gassed in chambers originally built to "euthanize" patients.[8] In testimony for his postwar trial, Hoven denies having participated in the Bernberg transport.[9] In fact, he claims to have rescued hundreds of Jews by hiding them in various barracks or sending them to other camps.[10] Morgen sees it differently:[11]

> I heard that he [Hoven] was present at a euthanasia *Aktion*, and that he had committed some irregularities there. What I was able to learn about it was the following. A commission, I believe of three doctors, appeared in the concentration camp, and Hoven had prepared the documents for this commission, meaning the people to be euthanized on [his] recommendation. Then after the prisoners had been presented

and the documents handed over for inspection, the commission decided which prisoners should be killed. Afterwards Dr. Hoven had taken various people out and substituted for them others whom the commission hadn't seen—thus placing other prisoners on the list.

Morgen doesn't hesitate to use the term "euthanasia," despite the fact that such selections were intended to eliminate weaker prisoners for being unable to work and Jewish prisoners simply for being Jews. He doesn't regard the *Aktion* itself as irregular; the irregularity, in his view, was that Hoven replaced selected prisoners with others who had not been examined by the commission.

The second category of "legal" killings mentioned by Grawitz was of executions. Some 8000 Soviet prisoners of war were executed at Buchenwald. A disused horse stable was converted into a mock medical facility, where Russian prisoners were stood up against a measuring stick on the wall, as if to have their height recorded, whereupon they were shot through a slot in the stick.[12] The stable was at some distance from the main area of the camp, and its phone number, 99, became the unofficial name of the execution detail.

Morgen is asked about the legality of these executions at the Buchenwald trial held by the Americans after the war:[13]

> Q. Dr. Morgen, if a witness were to testify in this court room that an order from the Reichs Security Main Office existed ordering these executions to take place, would you then consider the executions legal?
>
> A. [. . .] If [. . .] as alleged, these executions took place of persons who were war criminals, or criminals who had violated international law, or in the form of reprisals in that form permissible under International Law, then I would be inclined to describe these executions as legal ones.
>
> Q. You used the word "reprisals." Were you in combat in Russia yourself?
>
> A. Yes.
>
> Q. Do you think or do you have reason to believe that there was occasion for the Reichs Government to use reprisals?
>
> A. I know from personal experiences that from the very beginning the war was fought in a manner of great harshness and maximum brutality on the part of the Soviet Government. During the first few days when officers and couriers who had been eye witnesses came back from the front, I received reports of the conditions in which they found Limburg. The conditions in the GPU [Soviet State Security] prison there were simply horrifying. There was rather a large number of members of the SS who were hanged up on meat hooks in the slaughter house there and thus killed. [. . .] The facts about this warfare in violation of International Law were not revealed

to the German people in many instances for reasons of propaganda, in order not to put any more moral burdens on the soldiers fighting in the East and the kin of these soldiers, but I am sure that any German soldiers who has [*sic*] ever fought on the Eastern Front must know from his own observations about these horrors. I myself was able to observe soldiers who had been slaughtered most brutally. This was common knowledge throughout the troops and particularly general within the SS, and it was also know [*sic*] that attempts were made to find the people who did these crimes, who were among the brutes of political commissars, from the various prisoner of war camps in order to bring them to justice. I can therefore well imagine that the members of such an execution detail could be convinced that they were doing the right thing if they were told that they were working on the execution of prisoners who had made themselves culpable of war crimes.

Morgen says that these killings were legal if they targeted war criminals or qualified as "reprisals in that form permissible under International Law." But of course international law does not sanction reprisal killings, and the Russian prisoners of war at Buchenwald had not been convicted of war crimes. As if sensing the weakness of his appeal to international law, Morgen fashions a fallback argument based on the executioners' subjective state of mind. And in response to a direct question about reprisals, he implicitly endorses them on the grounds of the atrocities that they requite. Here Morgen explains how reprisal killings can be consistent with sound character, and thus how they can be legal under Morgen's will-based conception of criminal law.

At the same trial, Morgen describes witnessing a public execution at Buchenwald under Pister's command.[14] Having voiced fears that Pister would continue Koch's style of rogue executions, Morgen was invited to attend an execution and vet its legality. The convicts, Morgen testifies, were eastern laborers guilty of serious crimes and sentenced to death by Heinrich Müller, the Chief of the Gestapo.

The prosecution attorney asks Morgen whether such sentences were legal. Morgen replies that the sentences were covered by the Decree for the Punishment of Jews and Poles. That decree, issued in 1942, mandated the death penalty for even minor infractions committed by Jews and Poles in the eastern territories.[15] Morgen then conflates the Decree with a different legal novelty, by which cases against Jews, Gypsies, Poles, and Russians were removed from the jurisdiction of the courts and placed in the hands of the Gestapo. He explains that the importation of eastern laborers into the General Gouvernement had caused a sharp rise in serious crimes, to which the death penalty was now applied. The resulting cases had exceeded the capacity of the courts, Morgen says, and jurisdiction over them was therefore transferred to the chief of the Gestapo. Contrary to Morgen's testimony, however, this transfer of authority was effected, not by the Decree for the Punishment of Jews and Poles, but by a personal agreement between Himmler and the Justice Minister, Otto Georg Thierack. Thierack justified giving the Gestapo jurisdiction over defendants from undesirable races "on the principle that the administration of justice can only make a small contribution to the extermination of members of these peoples."[16] Thus, when Morgen testifies that the executions he witnessed at Buchenwald were legal under a public decree, he is only half-right.[17] The substance of the sentences was covered by the Decree, but their procedure followed a racially motivated, private arrangement.

Pister's attorney then takes over, in an attempt to nail down the point that the executions witnessed by Morgen were legal in both senses. The exchange concludes:[18]

> Q. How finally then came the execution order to Buchenwald?
>
> A. Through letter.
>
> Q. In your opinion was such written execution order [*sic*] based on German law legal?
>
> A. Technically, yes.
>
> Q. What do you understand by that—technically, yes?
>
> A. That it was technically right means it doesn't have to be really right. [. . .] The same way that the court can make a mistake in its sentence, the police can make a mistake in its decision but sentences based on a mistake are still legal sentences and no matter whether the sentences were right or not they were still legal sentences.

Later Morgen tries to clarify this testimony. "Nothing is further from me than to defend this law," he says. "The only thing which I tried to point out by my testimony was that there was a legal basis for these decrees and that the executive officers of these decrees of the State Police could be convinced that they were carrying out a legal act."[19]

Morgen was often called upon in postwar testimony to explain what was legal and what was illegal in the Nazi state. The interrogators and judges were often appalled by Morgen's answers, because he contended that killing was legal if ordered from the top. But Morgen portrayed himself as a judge sworn to apply the law as he found it. He insisted that killing on higher orders—even mass murder, if ordered—had been legal in the Third Reich, because it was "legal in the sense of National Socialist law,"[20] which was the only sense of legality that was operative at the time.

Yet in appealing to the law as he found it, Morgen was availing himself of a crude legal positivism of the kind that Nazi jurists had rejected and replaced with a theory that allowed judges to go beyond written statute in order to protect the *Volks*-community and express its moral perceptions. That conception of criminal law, especially when extended by the use of analogy, could in principle have brought any morally objectionable killings within Morgen's reach, whether or not they were technically legal. When Morgen explains his inaction in positivistic terms, he seems not to abide by the conception of law that he himself espoused.

TWELVE

THE "FINAL SOLUTION": CONFLICTING STORIES

We have already seen Morgen's 1964 testimony about how he found his way to Auschwitz. Customs inspectors discovered clumps of gold that had been shipped from Auschwitz to a private address, and they suspected criminal activity.[1] It was no secret that concentration camps harvested gold from the teeth of corpses and sent it to the Reichsbank, but so far as Morgen knew, the corpses were those of inmates who had died of natural causes or legal executions. Seeing the size of the confiscated nuggets, however, Morgen inferred that they must come from 50,000 to 100,000 corpses, which could only be the product of mass murder. So he traveled to Auschwitz—"this little-known Auschwitz, whose location I had to look up with some difficulty"—where he saw the gas chambers and crematoria.

This narrative strongly suggests that Morgen knew nothing about Auschwitz before he arrived. Yet in a 1946 interrogation, Morgen says that he did not personally visit the camp at first but sent an investigative commission, himself arriving later.[2] Thus, the impression that he gives in his 1964 testimony, of finding Auschwitz on the map and then arriving at the station in a state of innocence, cannot be correct. Morgen knew about Auschwitz before he stepped off the train.[3]

This chronology may help to explain incongruities in Morgen's testimony in Frankfurt. For one thing, Morgen says that when he began his tour with the selection ramp at Birkenau, "I asked my guide how it went." But what was "it"? Or, rather, how could Morgen already have known what "it" was—that it was "the beginning of the end," as he puts it—before he saw the gas chambers? Maybe the explanation for this incongruity is that he already knew of the gas chambers when he arrived.

Morgen testifies in Frankfurt that after he toured the gas chambers and crematoria of Birkenau, he visited the guardroom. "And here for the first time," he says, "I received a real shock." His first real shock, it turns out, was the sight of drunken SS men being fed potato pancakes by Jewish courtesans, with whom they exchanged the familiar form of address, *du*, rather than the formal *Sie*. As we read this testimony, we are appalled that Morgen had not already received his first "real shock" when viewing the gas chambers. The answer, again, may be that he already knew what to expect, and so he wasn't really shocked until he reached the guardroom.

Still, an incongruity remains. By the time of the Frankfurt trial, in 1964, Morgen has had 20 years to think about his visit to Auschwitz, whose name has become a byword for inhumanity. Morgen tells the court that Auschwitz was previously unknown to him—he had trouble locating it on the map—and so his audience is expecting to hear his first reaction to the machinery of mass murder. Yet his carefully prepared narrative describes the gas chambers matter-of-factly and reaches its climax only in the guardroom. Perhaps it is evidence of Morgen's candor about his "first shock" that a more careful and politically astute narrator would have backdated this shock to the earlier scene.

Morgen says that after seeing the gas chambers and hearing how they worked, he spent a sleepless night wondering "what could be done to stop it." He had reached a turning point, a personal crisis. Before we consider how he resolved the crisis, however, we must ask why he did not arrive at it sooner. For according to the account that he gave years earlier, at the Nuremberg Trial, he had been given a detailed description of the gassing procedure even before sending his commission to Auschwitz. This account began with his investigation of a minor incident in Lublin:[4]

One day I received a report from the commander of the Security Police in Lublin. He reported that in a Jewish labor camp in his district a Jewish wedding had taken place. There had been 1100 invited guests at this wedding [. . .] What followed was described as quite extraordinary owing to the gluttonous consumption of food and alcoholic drinks. Among these Jews were members of the camp guard, that is to say some SS men, who joined in this revelry. [. . .] I went to Lublin and called at the Security Police there, but all they would tell me was that the events happened at a camp of the Deutsche Ausrüstungswerke [armament factory]. But nothing was known there. I was told it might possibly be a rather odd and shrouded (this was the actual term used) camp in the vicinity of Lublin. I found out the camp and the commander, who was Kriminalkommissar [Christian] Wirth. [. . .]

To my great astonishment, Wirth admitted it. I asked him why he permitted members of his command to do such things and Wirth then revealed to me that on the Führer's order he had to carry out the destruction of Jews.

Wirth had previously served in Hitler's "euthanasia" program, where he gained experience that would make him indispensable to the project of exterminating the Jews.[5] When Germany invaded the Soviet Union in June of 1941, special "task forces" (*Einsatzgruppen*) were detailed to shoot intellectuals, party officials (so-called commissars), and Jews. In mid-summer, executions of Jews began to include women and children as well. When the mass execution of Jews by shooting proved too slow and too stressful for the executioners, it was decided to use a method that would be more "humane" for all concerned. The staff of the "euthanasia" program was therefore transferred to Poland, where Wirth began experimenting with "gas vans" that killed Jews with carbon monoxide. Himmler then ordered the Higher SS and Police Leader of the Lublin district, Odilo Globocnik, to build a standing extermination facility at the labor camp of Belzec. Globocnik appointed Wirth as the first commandant. Wirth eventually became the inspector of three such camps—Belzec, Treblinka, and Sobibor—under the code name *Aktion Reinhard*.

Brutal in both appearance and behavior, Wirth was notorious even among his colleagues, who called him "The Wild Christian" or "Christian the Terrible."[6] He had a round, bald head and wore a Hitler-style patch on his upper lip. Franz Stangl, the commandant of Treblinka, himself notoriously pitiless, described meeting Wirth during his days in the "euthanasia" program:[7]

> Wirth was a gross and florid man. My heart sank when I met him [. . . W]hen he spoke about the necessity for this euthanasia operation he was not speaking in humane or scientific terms [. . .]. He laughed. He spoke of "doing away with useless mouths" and said that "sentimental slobber" about such people made him "puke".

The armament factory where Morgen first went to investigate the wedding was one of many that the Deutsche Ausrüstungswerke operated near concentration camps in order to exploit their inmates as slave laborers. The factory in Lublin lay within the city limits, across the road from the cemetery.[8] On the other side of town was the camp of Majdanek, which had been built primarily to house Jewish laborers. Between the two, along the rail line bisecting the city, was a disused airfield where the *Bekleidungswerke*—the "clothing works"—sorted the valuables and disinfected the clothing of victims murdered in the gas chambers of the *Aktion Reinhard* camps. The *Bekleidungswerke* turned out to have been the site of the reported wedding. There Wirth lived and kept his headquarters.

The wedding took place in June 1943.[9] Morgen says that a report of the wedding reached him "some months later."[10] It must have reached him before mid-September, since Wirth left Lublin at roughly that time. Franz Stangl told the journalist Gitta Sereny in 1971 that he left for Trieste in a "convoy" with Globocnik, Wirth, and 120 others, arriving in September.[11] *Aktion Reinhard* was winding down, and Globocnik's commando was being sent to the Adriatic Littoral. Globocnik's reassignment is dated September 13.[12] So Morgen's meeting with Wirth must have taken place in late summer.

Morgen's Nuremberg testimony continues:

> I asked Wirth what [the destruction of Jews] had to do with the Jewish wedding. Then, Wirth described the method by which he carried out the extermination of Jews, and he said something like this: "One has to fight the Jews with their own weapons, that is to say"—pardon me for using this expression—"one has to cheat them."
>
> Wirth staged an enormous deceptive maneuver. He first selected Jews who would, he thought, serve as column leaders, then these Jews brought along other Jews, who worked under them. With that smaller or medium-sized detachment of Jews, he began to build up the extermination camps. He extended this staff of Jews, and with these Jews Wirth himself carried out the extermination of the Jews.
>
> Wirth said that he had four extermination camps and that about 5000 Jews were working at the extermination of Jews and the seizure of Jewish property. In order to win Jews for this business of extermination and plundering of their brethren of race and creed, Wirth gave them every freedom and, so to speak, gave them a financial interest in the spoliation of the dead victims. As a result of this attitude, this sumptuous Jewish wedding had come about.
>
> Then I asked Wirth how he killed Jews with these Jewish agents of his. Wirth described the whole procedure, which went off like a film every time.
>
> The extermination camps were in the east of the Government General, in big forests or uninhabited wastelands. They were built up like a Potemkin village. The people arriving there had the impression of entering a city or a township. The train drove into a dummy railroad station. After the escorts and the train personnel had left the area, the cars were opened and the Jews got out. They were surrounded by these Jewish labor detachments, and Kriminalkommissar Wirth or one of his representatives made a speech. He said, "Jews, you were brought here to be resettled, but before we organize this future Jewish State, you must of course learn how to work. You must learn a new trade. You will be taught that here. Our routine here is, first, every one must take off his clothes so that your clothing can be disinfected, and you can have a bath so that no epidemics will be brought into the camp."
>
> After he had found such calming words for his victims, they started on the road to death. Men and women were separated. At the first place, one had to deliver the hat; at the next one, the coat, collar, shirt, down to the shoes and socks. These places were faked cloakrooms, and the person was given a check at each one so that the people believed that they would get their things back. The other Jews had to receive the things and hurry up the new arrivals so that they should not have time to think. The whole thing was like an assembly line. After the last stop they reached a big room,

and were told that this was the bath. When the last one was in, the doors were shut and the gas was let into the room.

   As soon as death had set in, the ventilators were started. When the air could be breathed again, the doors were opened, and the Jewish workers removed the bodies. By means of a special procedure which Wirth had invented, they were burned in the open air without the use of fuel.

Question: When Morgen tells the jury in Frankfurt about touring the gas chambers at the turn of 1943–44, why doesn't he explain that he had known about gas chambers since late summer, when he heard about them from Christian Wirth? Answer: The account that Morgen gave in Nuremberg of his meeting with Wirth was significantly embellished.

   Consider how Morgen describes his discovery of *Aktion Reinhard* to the CIC:[13]

   As far as I know, "Aktion Reinhard" encompasses the exploitation of valuables from Jews in the eastern territories. I don't know whether "Aktion Reinhard" refers only to the valuables of dead Jews, what was called "robbing the corpses," or whether it encompassed the Jews in general. I pretty much assume the latter. I wasn't officially concerned with this operation. Nor have I seen any orders about it; but the name "Aktion Reinhard" occasionally popped up during my investigations. Remember, my investigations proceeded from crimes of corruption in the concentration camps, which were the occasion for my coming upon the illegal killings. And so corruption and killing flowed together, and the "Aktion Reinhard" appeared to be one of the most fruitful offshoots.

Now, if Morgen had been directed to Wirth as the one responsible for the wild Jewish wedding, and if Wirth had inducted him into the secrets of *Aktion Reinhard* at that time, he would not have needed the name to "pop up" during his inquiries, nor would he have initially associated it with the "illegal" killing that he was already investigating, the one-off killings of witnesses. Rather, he would have realized that it represented a completely unprecedented system of mass murder, unrelated to the comparatively mundane crimes at Buchenwald.

   In fact, Morgen's Nuremberg testimony about his conversation with Wirth seems incoherent. Referring to the Jewish wedding, he says, "I asked him why he permitted members of his command to do such things, and Wirth then revealed to me that on the Führer's order he had to carry out the destruction of the Jews." This revelation would have been a non sequitur. Wirth had permitted the Jewish wedding as a means of bolstering morale at the airfield camp, which was not an extermination facility. Wirth could have explained the wedding without giving a step-by-step description of gas-chamber procedures at other camps, which were supposed to be top secret.

Morgen's Nuremberg testimony about the meeting with Wirth is not only puzzling in itself, it also conflicts with testimony he gives on subsequent occasions. In Morgen's testimony at the postwar trial of Oswald Pohl, he says that it took him four or five months to find "the first traces" of the extermination of the Jews—four or five months after he took up his assignment in Kassel, which was in late June or early July.[14] And when asked by a CIC interrogator when he learned that the term "resettlement" became a code word for extermination, he says, "Something about that first came to my attention at the turn of 1943/44."[15] And the turn of the year—specifically, the month of November—was when Morgen started his inquiries at Auschwitz.[16]

Thus, the evidence other than Morgen's Nuremberg testimony suggests that he learned the full story of mass extermination by gassing in November, from his commission at Auschwitz and his own visit, not in late summer from Wirth in Lublin. Note that the interrogation quoted here occurred after Morgen's testimony at Nuremberg—indeed, only ten days after the main war criminals had been executed—and so Morgen can be expected to have become more careful in his narrative and chronology. Morgen's Nuremberg testimony about how he learned of the "Final Solution" must therefore be taken with a grain of salt.

It seems implausible that Wirth responded to Morgen's inquiries about the wedding at the airfield camp by launching into a complete description of the "Final Solution," but it is impossible to know exactly what Morgen did learn on this visit. What we do know is that, whatever information Morgen might have received about the "Final Solution," he didn't at first believe it:[17]

> At first Wirth's description seemed completely fantastic to me, but in Lublin I saw one of his camps. It was a camp which collected the property or part of the property of his victims. From the piles of things—there were an enormous number of watches piled up—I had to realize that something monstrous[18] was going on here. I was shown the valuables. I can say that I never saw so much money at one time, especially foreign money—all kinds of coins, from all over the world. In addition, there was a gold-smelting furnace and really prodigious bars of gold.
>
> I also saw that the headquarters from which Wirth directed his operations was very small and inconspicuous. He had only three or four people working there for him. I spoke to them too.
>
> I saw and watched his couriers arrive. They actually came from Berlin, Tiergartenstrasse, the Führer's Chancellery, and went back there. I investigated Wirth's mail and I found in it confirmation of all this.
>
> Of course, I could not do or see all this on this first visit. I was there frequently. I pursued Wirth up to his death.

In fact, the visit on which Morgen saw the piles of valuables appears to have occurred significantly later than the meeting with Wirth. In the post-Nuremberg trial of Oswald Pohl, Morgen again indicates that his investigation of Wirth extended beyond Wirth's departure from Lublin. The prosecuting attorney asks him about the guilty knowledge that a defendant named Josef Vogt may or may not have received from Wirth's successor, Georg Wippern:[19]

> Q. Now, then, in connection with the case Lublin, one more question, witness. Did Wippern at any time tell you in how far he had informed Vogt about the real Reinhardt Action?
>
> A. According to my opinion, this can be seen from the connections which existed; if silver tableware, wedding rings, gold from teeth, and money and foreign exchange—and even up to eyeglass rims—were collected and made up into lists—hundreds of thousands of these items—then I don't believe that these can be normal things.
>
> Q. Did you see these things yourself, witness?
>
> A. I saw the remainder of those things myself.
>
> Q. When was it?
>
> A. Around the end of 1943 or the beginning of 1944. It could have been towards the end. I couldn't tell you exactly.

This testimony implies that Morgen saw the valuables only some months after his meeting with Wirth. The later date is consistent with Morgen's statement that he saw only the "remainder" of the valuables and that they were "made up into lists"—which indicates that attention had turned from collecting the objects to accounting for them. Globocnik filed a final accounting of the operation in early 1944, listing the values of banknotes and coins in various currencies, from dollars to yen; numbers of watches, earrings, cufflinks, and other varieties of jewelry; numbers of eyeglasses, briefcases, razors, and other personal items; and of course bars of gold, silver, and platinum, obviously smelted down from miscellaneous sources.[20] These lists must be the ones that Morgen saw being prepared. So when Morgen tells the Nuremberg court of seeing the valuables at one of Wirth's camps, he is describing a visit that took place at the turn of the year, months after the latest date on which his meeting with Wirth could have occurred.

In his testimony at the Nuremberg trial of major war criminals, Morgen appears to be summarizing what he knew by the turn of 1943–44 and placing it in the mouth of Christian Wirth several months earlier. But why?

We noted earlier that Morgen was often defensive about the SS. He was especially defensive at the Nuremberg trial, where the SS as a whole was charged with being a criminal organization and Morgen was called by the defense. Morgen was an ideal choice for a defense witness, since he could testify that, far from being a criminal organization at all, the SS had enforced German law within its own ranks, through the SS Judiciary. In his Nuremberg testimony, Morgen goes to great lengths to distance the SS from the mass murder of Jews.[21] He points out that the gas chambers at Auschwitz were operated by Jews and by volunteers or draftees from the Baltic. He even argues, lamely, that although the supervisors wore SS uniforms, they did so only for camouflage, an arrangement that he found incomprehensible, because it needlessly damaged the reputation of the SS.

Above all, Morgen emphasizes that the extermination centers reported to the Führer's Chancellery and that Christian Wirth, their architect and overseer, was not a member of the SS. He had already detailed this chain of command in a pre-trial affidavit:[22]

> Wirth was not a member of the SS. Having been known for unscrupulous investi-gative methods as a homicide detective, he was permanently transferred from the Stuttgart Criminal Police for a special assignment from the Führer. His first assign-ment was the mass extermination of the mentally ill. [. . .] The operation ran outside an SS organization or office. It had its permanent seat in the Führer's Chancellery, Berlin, Tiergartenstrasse. Wirth got his orders from there and reported there.
>
> With the extermination of the Jews, there was basically no change in the chain of command. The center continued to be the Chancellery *of the Führer*. The commando got the uniform and credentials of the Security Police only for the sake of being able to move about behind the lines. [. . .] Furthermore, the staff was improbably small. [. . .] I have reason to believe that even the local [Commandant of the Security Service] was not informed of the activities of this organization.

The defense attorney for the SS finds this affidavit so helpful that he has to be restrained by the judge from introducing it, prematurely, into his examination of a prior witness.[23] Having subsequently elicited from Morgen the claim that Wirth did not belong to the SS, the attorney ten-dentiously repeats it back to Morgen in the next session: "You spoke of Kriminalkommissar Wirth, who was not a member of the SS and whose staff did not consist of SS men."[24] Shifting responsibility from the SS onto Wirth was thus a primary motive of the defense in putting Morgen on the stand. Morgen's story of hearing all about the "Final Solution" from Wirth fits this strategy too well to be credible, given the contrary evidence of his testimony about having discovered the mass extermination at the turn of the year.

THIRTEEN
AKTION ERNTEFEST

Morgen's work in Lublin gradually divided into two distinct lines of inquiry. Looking into the Jewish wedding, he was led to Christian Wirth, from Wirth to the hoard of valuables, and from there to suspicions of "something monstrous." Looking into crimes at Buchenwald, Morgen was led to Majdanek, where Karl Otto Koch had served briefly as commandant after Buchenwald, and where the commandant was now Koch's former Buchenwald subordinate, Hermann Florstedt.

For the latter line of inquiry, Morgen was given a small investigative commission, based in Lublin. Their work led to the removal and arrest of commandant Florstedt in mid-October 1943.[1] Morgen traveled to Lublin in early November to consult with the commission; he was met at the station by its leader, Kriminalkommissar Dennerlein. Dennerlein reported that the commission's work had come to an end, because all of the prisoners in the district had been executed the day before, leaving the investigation without any witnesses.[2] This massacre, in which over 40,000 Jews were shot, one by one, at the camps Majdanek, Poniatowa, and Trawniki, took place on November 3 and 4. Cynically dubbed "Harvest Festival" (*Erntefest*) by its planners, it was the largest single mass shooting of the war.[3]

Morgen was deposed about the massacre for a trial of Majdanek war criminals that stretched from the early 1970s to the 1980s. As he recounts in 1973, he went with Dennerlein to see the new commandant of Majdanek, Martin Gottfried Weiss: "He was pale and speechless. The operation had come as a surprise to him, too." Morgen then went to meet the chief gunner: "It interested me how a person could mentally cope with such a task. The man was completely unmoved. He said, 'Someone had to do it.'"[4] Morgen then turned his attention to investigating the massacre: "I considered myself obligated as a human being to look into this monstrosity."[5]

Morgen's investigation yielded a report to the Chief of the Reich Security Head Office, Ernst Kaltenbrunner. That report was quoted back to Kaltenbrunner at his interrogation prior to the Nuremberg trials.[6] The interrogator reads from Morgen's report and asks Kaltenbrunner whether he remembers having received it:

> Q. Referring again to the Lublin murders, the result of this mass execution could not have escaped your attention, because as reported by Morgan [*sic*] after his inspection, it resulted in losing much of the available labor supply. There were no more people to work machines and in the handcraft shops. The factories were left with a tremendous stock of raw material, and the people in charge said that the order of execution came as a complete surprise.
>
> A. I never saw any such report, and I never heard about them. [. . .]
>
> Q. I will read you the description that Morgan gave as to what took place: "The proceeding was always the same. The night before the execution came the order to build very hastily shelters in zig-zag against air-raids. In the early morning came troops and the execution began in these trenches. The prisoners had to leave their work and to attend in the neighborhood of the trenches. When their time came, they had to undress and naked, pass through the trench one after one in an infinite line. Coming to the first deaths (Interrogator: I think, meaning "dead one") the victim had to lie down on the dead body and then was killed by a shot from a gun in the neck. This went on so long until the trench was filled and the last person was dead. Then the trenches were closed. The naked men had their own trenches, and the women theirs. Children were with their mothers. Nobody of the victims had been ill-treated before executions. All passed in a methodical, silent way. The troops formed only a cordon and had nothing to do with it. There had been a few German police,[7] and the most were Ukrainian. On each place there were only two or three killers who were placed above the trench. Behind them were two or three other men who spent all their time charging empty magazines. So the executions were going very quick, and the responsibility was only in the hands of very few men." Here is a second sentence: "It was the old, tried system." Do you agree that it was an old tried system?
>
> A. I am not familiar with the method. [. . .]
>
> Q. What became of all the money, jewelry and gold of the dead prisoners out of these camps?
>
> A. I don't know.
>
> Q. Didn't you ever receive any report as to what was done with these valuables?
>
> A. No.

The quoted excerpt from Morgen's report is both chilling and mystifying. Morgen himself was probably quoting a detailed description of the executions from eyewitnesses, since he had not witnessed the massacre first-hand. The comment "It was the old, tried system" would then have been Morgen's commentary on the quoted material. But why would Morgen have used that phrase? Does it indicate that he was unaware of the new system that had been tried and proved in *Aktion Reinhard*? There is no way of knowing, because his report has not survived.[8]

The victims of the massacre had been used as slave laborers at several facilities in the Lublin area, and their execution left those facilities empty. In his 1973 deposition, Morgen says, "As I remember it, all of the inmates of the camp were shot. All of the production shops were empty."[9] Again: "I still remember that an Austrian industrialist reported to me, almost in tears, that his entire operation was smashed."[10] Morgen's report focused on this effect of the massacre: "I made a broad-scale report about the events with reference to the economic effects of the loss of production. That was an argument that could still impress the SS leadership."[11]

The interrogator's questions to Kaltenbrunner suggest that Morgen's report also discussed the misappropriation of the valuables left behind by the victims.[12] Erich Muhsfeldt, who was in charge of cremating the victims of the massacre, testified at his own trial, in Poland, that he had a notebook in which to keep track of valuables and dental gold, and that he turned the notebook over to Morgen as proof that he had not pocketed anything that had passed through his hands.[13] The disposition of victims' property is thus likely to have been of concern in Morgen's report, in addition to the loss of industrial labor.

The man who directed the massacre, Jakob Sporrenberg, was arrested in Norway in 1945. From his prison cell he wrote a report in which he claimed to have seen orders to his predecessor from Himmler, empowering him to put an end to the "enormous threat" of the "Jewish problem" in the Lublin district.[14] Another postwar report, from Hans Lauffs, a former colleague of Morgen's, explains this justification as follows:[15]

> [. . .] extensive material had become available to the Security Police in Lublin, to the effect that a full-scale escape attempt by prisoners of the concentration camp was imminent. Large underground weapons caches had been prepared for this purpose well in advance. The plan was to slaughter the entire guard detail as well as all the Germans in the Lublin district, with the help of powerful gangs. [. . .] Orders of execution were issued by the highest office, since according to an evaluation of the incriminating materials, all of the Germans would have fallen victim to an inevitable bloodbath.

This rationalization reflects the Nazis' paranoid conviction that their race had to choose between exterminating every last Jew and being themselves exterminated to the very last Aryan.[16] Mass executions of civilians had been rationalized on these grounds since Germany invaded the Soviet Union in 1941.[17]

In Morgen's 1973 deposition, however, he says there had simply been an altercation among prisoners, ending in an assault on an SS officer.

The whole episode was then blown out of proportion by the leader of the Security Service.[18] Morgen adds that he accused this officer of filing a false report. As for Morgen's report to Kaltenbrunner, we know only that it detailed the method of execution and the resulting economic damage, the latter of which Morgen considered to be "an argument that could still impress the SS leadership."

The Erntefest massacre was the only mass murder that Morgen came close to witnessing. He arrived in Lublin to see the immediate aftermath, whereas he never saw even the aftermath of a gassing at Auschwitz, as he concedes in his Frankfurt testimony.[19] Nevertheless, Morgen doesn't mention the Erntefest massacre after the war, until he is directly questioned about it in 1973, as the perpetrators are coming to trial.

Morgen does tell of a similar though much smaller massacre at the end of his 1971 interview with John Toland.[20] Toland has flattered Morgen and lamented the way he was treated by American forces: "I'm amazed that the Allies would not honor you for the things you did in those camps. You risked your life."[21] Morgen has sounded somewhat embarrassed by these effusions. The interview is almost over, the closing pleasantries have begun. Morgen suddenly launches into a long story about a fellow SS judge.

While serving in the Balkans, this judge prosecuted an SS lieutenant for carrying out a summary execution. After local farmers shot and killed three members of the lieutenant's unit, he had picked out a suspect and, despite his denials, had him shot. The judge said, "He had no right to kill this man without legal process" and accused him of murder. Then in 1945, as Germany was collapsing, the same judge was in the Ruhr region, when an order was issued for the killing of foreign workers to prevent a feared revolt. This judge who had once prosecuted a single execution now had workers led into the forest and shot. Morgen's comment, though partially unintelligible, is about what extraordinary circumstances can do to the human mind.

A mass shooting to prevent a revolt behind the lines—the same rationale that was given for the massacre in Lublin. Morgen clearly thinks that the reasoning was absurd; but then, he also thinks that acting on it was, if not absurd, then at least explicable under the circumstances. And Morgen feels somehow compelled to come out with this story unprompted, out of the blue, just as a fawning interviewer is taking his leave. The Erntefest massacre has left unfinished business on his mind.

The massacre further confirmed Morgen's suspicion that murder was being committed on a monstrous scale. He then got additional evidence in the form of gold nuggets mailed from Auschwitz, to which he then turned his attention.

FOURTEEN

AUSCHWITZ

As we have seen, Morgen must have known fairly early about the mass execution of Jews on the Eastern Front. As he was investigating Hermann Fegelein in Cracow, Fegelein was involved in the execution of 14,000 Jews in the Pripyat marshes.[1] Even if Morgen believed, as was claimed, that Fegelein's victims were partisans, he certainly knew in 1942 that soldiers like Paul Kleesattel believed themselves to be systematically eliminating civilians to make room for German settlers, though Morgen seems not to have known how right they were. When Morgen was subsequently sent to the front, he joined a division that had earlier participated in atrocities, though by the time he arrived, they were in retreat from the Soviets.[2] A case involving mass executions came before the SS Judiciary in his absence.[3] So when Morgen rejoined the Judiciary, in the early summer of 1943, he could scarcely have been ignorant of the first, disorganized phases of extermination.

In late summer Morgen met the architect of the industrialized extermination centers in *Aktion Reinhard*, Christian Wirth, who may have told him about the "Final Solution," though Morgen seems to have embellished his later testimony about the meeting with information that he learned only afterwards. Then in the last quarter of 1943, he discovered the gassing of hundreds of Jews at Bernburg under the pretense of "euthanasia"; the execution of tens of thousands by the "old, tried method"; and stunning quantities of scavenged valuables, at an airfield in Lublin and in a package post-marked Auschwitz. Morgen sent a commission to investigate Auschwitz and then went to have a look for himself.

Shouldn't Morgen have known about the "Final Solution" sooner, or seen it coming, or at least taken action against atrocities on the Eastern Front, about which most Germans had some knowledge from soldiers writing home or coming home on leave?

As it happens, if only by accident, Morgen did what he could have done about the latter atrocities. For during his work in Cracow, he attempted to prosecute the perpetrator of the infamous massacre in the Pripyat marshes. There is no evidence that Morgen pursued Fegelein because of this reputation, but neither can there be evidence that he turned a blind eye.

As for the gas chambers, Morgen was not in a position to learn of them before it was almost too late. The first gas chambers in Poland started up in March 1942, and as we have seen, Morgen was dismissed from the SS Judiciary that same spring. Between July 1942 and May 1943, he was an army private,[4] at first in basic training and then on the Soviet front. When he took up his new assignment as a judge, in July 1943, the last deportations to Belzec were over and deportations to Treblinka and Sobibor were soon to end. Thus, Morgen had little access to information during the period when *Aktion Reinhard* was in full swing. And he is unlikely to have drawn conclusions from faint clues; for as an investigator, he was a stickler for solid proof.

By the time Morgen began his investigations into concentration camp corruption, in 1943, the only large extermination camp still in full operation was Auschwitz-Birkenau. Morgen went there immediately after seeing the aftermath of the massacre in Lublin.

We have now returned to the point where we began: Morgen's tour of Auschwitz-Birkenau, which he narrated in his testimony at the *Auschwitz-Prozess* in 1964. We can pick up where we left off in Morgen's testimony:[5]

Understandably, I couldn't sleep a wink that night. I had already seen some things in concentration camps, but never anything like that. And I considered what could be done about it. Given the apparent power of a judge, and a public prosecutor too, laymen tend to ask, "Why didn't you immediately arrest those responsible at the top and try them for these horrible crimes?" Let me remind the lay observer first of all that a judge has no power to make an arrest except when conducting the main trial of a criminal case. [. . .] The SS and Police Judiciary was a war judiciary, alongside the war judiciary of the army, the marines, the air force; it was the war judiciary of the fourth part of the armed services, namely, the Waffen-SS and the police on special tasks.[6] A war judiciary is an outgrowth of the military command, from which it is derived and on which it depends. All of the important functions exercised normally by a court staffed with independent judges lie in the hands of so-called Court Masters, that is, the commanding general and, over him, the general of the corps, of the army, and the Commander in Chief of the armed forces as highest Court Master, who at that time was Hitler. The Court Master prepares and signs an arrest warrant. The Court Master orders the opening of a legal process. The Court Master staffs the war court. He confirms or overturns judgments, he determines the execution of punishment.

So in order to be able to proceed against Himmler or Hitler, the initiators of these crimes—to be able to proceed against them judicially, I would have had to propose to Hitler himself or Himmler himself a warrant to arrest themselves. And even if he had opened proceedings against himself, it would have been impossible to convene a court. For the court must be composed in this manner: with a lay observer of the same rank as the accused, and with a higher official. So one would need to have brought in a Hitler as lay observer, and an über-Hitler as second observer. So you can see that it was absolutely impossible. You have to realize that Hitler moved within a legal vacuum in which all constraints of the separation of powers had been overturned, and that he embodied the Reich Chancellor, the Reich President, the Commander in Chief of the armed forces, the highest lawgiver, the chief executive, and the highest Court Master—all in a single person. [. . .] And what went for the ultimately responsible parties—namely, Hitler and Himmler—obviously went as well for those directly employed by them, Standartenführer Höss [Commandant of Auschwitz] and his subordinates. For if the former had brought accusations against these men, they would likewise have had to prosecute and judge their own deeds. The prosecutor, the judge can only apply the law as he finds it, and can't make up his own. If he steps outside the constraints of the law, then he becomes a criminal himself.

The "judge can only apply the law as he finds it," Morgen says, enunciating a conception of himself as applying the given law, which incorporated orders from Hitler. So conceived, his position afforded him no means of going after the mass extermination. But this view of adjudication is the positivist view from which Morgen himself departed in judging defendants according to their characters. So it was not respect for the limits of judicial power that inhibited Morgen from going after the leaders; it was fear of their unlimited political power.

In any case, Morgen is right that going after Hitler and Himmler would have accomplished nothing. So he considered other lines of attack:[7]

In this situation, the obvious thing is to consider extra-legal possibilities, namely, an assassination. But that was impracticable because—as one of the few—I had once visited the Führer's headquarters during the war. I was ordered to give a presentation to Himmler. You could go there only upon a written order from the Führer's headquarters itself. You had to go to a particular office in Berlin to pick up tickets for the special train that went there. There was very stringent security at the station and in the train. And then, after a night's journey, about noon on the following day, the train halted suddenly somewhere in East Prussia, in a green meadow amongst cows. A car came along a path and picked you up. You drove through a thick forest, through many wave traps. And there, scattered about, and protected by camouflage nets, heavily guarded, were the barracks. Who lived in each of these barracks, where Himmler or Hitler stayed, you couldn't figure out. By the way, I never got to the presentation, but after waiting for several hours I was sent off. The message was that Himmler was suddenly called away and had to fly to the front. And so I traveled back. I could judge from that first-hand view, and that's why the thought of such a possibility [as an assassination] never occurred to me.

One might think of bearing public witness to this development. But if one had done that, nobody would have believed it. One would have been declared mad and arrested.

Having ruled out these "extra-legal possibilities," Morgen says, he next considered possibilities abroad:[8]

At the end of that sleepless night, I had to acknowledge that this system could be combatted and toppled only from without. And I thought that I had to try. [Pause] It occurred to me that I had some time earlier spoken with a criminal commissar who oversaw an office for years in the border division at Switzerland, Constance, and in conversation he told me about the many possibilities of crossing the border, said—described the streets with houses where the front door was in German territory and the back door in Swiss territory. I thought I could find these crossing points. So I made up my mind to go to Switzerland.

The option was simple for me, since for my many official trips I always carried blank travel orders and a blank military pass. I needed only to fill them out as required by sudden investigations. So I presented a pass, a travel order saying "military judicial investigation in Vienna," and from Vienna on to Constance, and traveled straight through.

But then, Morgen says, he began to doubt the feasibility of this plan:[9]

About thirty-six hours later I neared my destination. In the meantime I had calmed myself enough to try and face what was about to happen. I thought that I would succeed in crossing the border, and I asked myself how things on the other side would play out in detail. Certainly an immediate interrogation: I'd be passed from one office to the next higher one. And while I tried to imagine it vividly—the questions, my answers—it suddenly became clear that my report and my story would have to sound so unbelievable and incomprehensible to an outsider, especially in a neutral country, that I wouldn't be believed. The question would definitely arise: Have you seen a gassing yourself, have you seen a corpse, a battered prisoner? And I would have to say in all honesty, No.

So the plan seemed unworkable. And even if it somehow worked, Morgen explains, the consequences would have been catastrophic:[10]

But I tore myself from that rumination and pictured it the other way around. I thought, If all goes well, and you are believed, then what? Surely, the Swiss regime would do nothing. But I would probably be presented to the press, and I'd make remarks to them. The result would be that war propaganda against Germany would go into high gear. And after what I had seen, I had to say to myself: In a total collapse, a complete defeat of Germany, the victorious powers would exterminate us, the whole German people, because of these events, draw and quarter each of us. [Pause] And to set such a thing in motion and answer for it—that was beyond my strength.

"The German people"—that is a big idea, but it is made up of many individuals. And then I thought of my near and dear. First of all, of course, my parents, who had sacrificed to put me through school and who I knew to be fine, decent people who didn't deserve such a fate. Then I thought of my comrades, whom I had left at the Russian front hardly three months ago.[11] At that time I was in the regiment SS-Germania, which was mostly composed of Danes, Belgians, Dutchmen, Norwegians—volunteers, young idealists, who frankly explained to me that they weren't National Socialists at all, but that it just came down to defending European culture against the tide of Bolshevism; and who, inadequately armed, fighting against a superior force, obeying senseless halt-orders and then—soldiers are familiar with this from the Russian front—sent to the slaughter in whole divisions but even so going to their deaths for their ideals. They too didn't deserve it. And so I then saw, no matter how I looked at the situation, that such a course of action could lead only to a fresh calamity, and I thereupon went back to Berlin.

Having abandoned his plan of escaping to Switzerland, Morgen says, he turned his thoughts back to the perpetrators:[12]

Along the way I became even calmer. And having thought about those hangmen in Auschwitz, but also thought, with hate and contempt and abhorrence, about the prisoners who helped them, I tried to put myself in their shoes. It is a salient trait of men, of life itself, to accommodate itself to given facts and to grasp at every straw and every chance to survive. And to that extent, as one couldn't resent the prisoners, so one couldn't be aggrieved with all humanity nor the whole German people on account of those SS members.

The thought of the SS "hangmen" and what set them apart from the rest of humanity led Morgen to frame a new, more realistic plan:[13]

And from this realization I suddenly saw a possible way of proceeding. Where the highest legal right, life itself, counts for nothing and is dragged in the mud, destroyed *en masse*, there too must all other legal rights [*Rechtsgüter*], whether of property or fidelity or whatever, must also collapse and lose their value. And therefore—and I had already convinced myself of this—these people, to whom these tasks had been delegated, could not help but become criminals. And so my job and the criminal code gave me the chance to pursue these crimes—that is, the ones that hadn't been ordered. And that's what I did.

The concluding step in Morgen's reasoning, as recounted here, followed directly from his conception of criminal corruption. Morgen reasoned that the perpetrators of mass extermination must have been corrupted by it, and being thus corrupted, must have committed other crimes—crimes that Morgen could prosecute, unlike the mass extermination itself. The existing criminal code therefore gave him the means of prosecuting the wrongdoers, even if not for their greatest wrong.

Morgen often speaks of the secondary crimes that flowed from the corrupting influence of mass murder. In one report written for the Americans immediately after the war, he says,[14]

> The SS Judiciary could not combat the root of the evil in the concentration camps. That was the "secret sphere" of the concentration camps, the prisoners' lack of rights, and the mass extermination of human life that was ultimately ordered by Hitler personally. This awful atmosphere necessarily undermined all morality and like a thousand-headed hydra brought forth ever more crime.

In a subsequent report for the Americans, Morgen writes, "The SS Judiciary made clear that the system of lawlessness and the factory-like slaughterhouse operation in the known extermination camps must morally corrupt [*demoralisieren*] the troops completely, and this became evident in all the shocking criminal cases."[15] Morgen writes these passages in December 1945 and January 1946, but he had said as much to Chief SS Physician Grawitz in the spring of 1944, warning him of "the consequences that these mass killings have: the epidemic of corruption, the brutalization of the men."[16] He claims to have written a report to his superiors about the gassings, in which

> My most emphatic and most crucial advice was [...] that the SS members who participated in the gassing were thereby so corrupted [*demoralisiert*] that they would in future prove no longer serviceable as normal soldiers or even as citizens, and furthermore that the leadership of the state was destroying its own moral foundations with these monstrous [*ungeheuerlich*] crimes.[17]

He told them that "through these methods the State was being led straight into an abyss."[18]

Unlike Morgen's first crisis, in Cracow, where he felt overwhelmed by individual cases of criminal corruption and merely asked for a transfer to a "healthier atmosphere," the mass extermination confronted him with inhumanity on a scale that challenged not just his identity as an SS judge upholding SS virtue, but his identity as a judge committed to justice as such. His first reaction was to abandon that identity and flee. On second thought, however, he chose a second-best course.

Morgen saw the inhumanity of the gassing as a form of systematic corruption, continuous with the individual corruption that he had been fighting all along. He therefore reasoned that, though powerless to fight the "Final Solution" directly, as he had the individual crimes, he could fight the former indirectly, by targeting the latter. He therefore decided to remain in Nazi Germany and continue his work.

Why does the Frankfurt court allow Morgen to ramble on about matters at best tangential to the crimes at issue in the trial? Well, the question that Morgen imagines being asked—If you saw what you claim, why didn't you do anything about it?—can be turned around like this: If you didn't do anything about it, then why should we believe that you saw what you claim? Morgen's explanation of his inaction is therefore essential to the credibility of the rest.

But surely Morgen needn't go on at such length. That he could not have prosecuted the executioners is obvious, or could easily be made obvious in fewer words. Morgen believed that the orders for Auschwitz had come from Himmler and Hitler, whose word was literally law in the Third Reich.[19] Anyone receiving such orders would be morally obligated to disobey them, but the legal system afforded Morgen no means of enforcing that obligation. So Morgen's long recitation of the ranks of Court Masters, and his fantasy of an über-Hitler—all of that is unnecessary, and worse than unnecessary, since it obscures the central point, namely, that Morgen had good reason to think that legal action was a non-starter.

Equally puzzling is Morgen's long digression about his trip to Hitler's compound. The ostensible point of this digression is to illustrate the difficulties he would have faced in trying to assassinate Himmler or Hitler. But no one would imagine today, or would imagine Morgen's having imagined then, that he could make an attempt on those two heavily guarded lives. The specifics of the security measures—the special train, the meadow full of cows—all are irrelevant.

Whereas Morgen belabors the obvious with respect to his powers as a jurist or his potential as an assassin, the reasons he gives against defecting to Switzerland seem grossly inadequate. What first strikes us is the disproportion between the deaths of millions, on the one hand, and the sacrifices made by two parents for their son's education, on the other.

Then there is Morgen's suggestion that revealing the "Final Solution" to the world would have produced war propaganda against Germany. War propaganda was indeed of concern to Morgen: he wrote a book about it as a cause of war. But since the "Final Solution" was real and impossible to exaggerate, sounding the alarm about it could not be dismissed as mere propaganda.

The key passage in Morgen's Frankfurt testimony is the paragraph about "a possible way of proceeding." Morgen uses this expression on several occasions, always with the same import.[20] He claims that, having recognized that he couldn't prosecute the gassing of millions, he sought to impede that process by prosecuting lesser crimes, "the ones that hadn't been ordered," or as he sometimes puts it, the "illegal killings."

Morgen had already explained this tactic at Nuremberg:[21]

> I saw a way open to me by way of justice; that is, by removing from this system of destruction the leaders and important elements through the means offered by the system itself. I could not do this with regard to the killings ordered by the head of the State, but I could do it for killings outside of this order, or against this order, or for other serious crimes. For that reason, I deliberately started proceedings against these men, and this would have led to a shake-up of this system and its final collapse.

The "killings outside of this order" included the murders committed at Buchenwald by Waldemar Hoven and Martin Sommer, whom Morgen was already investigating in November 1943 when he saw the mass-killing operation at Auschwitz.

Morgen therefore sought greater authority and more powerful tools for his prosecutions. He had earlier petitioned Himmler to establish a Special Purpose Court (*Gericht zur besonderen Verwendung*) dedicated to cases of corruption in the concentration camps. Now, on December 9, 1943, he asked for a Special Purpose Court whose jurisdiction would not be limited to financial corruption, since he wanted to prosecute murders as well.[22]

Morgen next zeroed in on Odilo Globocnik.[23] Globocnik had been SS and Police Leader in the district of Lublin. It was Globocnik who received the order for the "Final Solution" from Himmler and passed it on to Christian Wirth, who then oversaw the *Aktion Reinhard* extermination centers. Those centers ceased operation in late summer and early fall of 1943—having murdered 1.7 million Jews—and Globocnik was reassigned, along with his staff, to Trieste, where he was SS and Police Leader for the Adriatic Littoral.

It is unclear how much of Globocnik's role was already known to Morgen. He had seen the remainder of the victim's valuables in Lublin and the inventories that were being drawn up for Globocnik to submit to Himmler. As he said after the war, anyone seeing those riches would know that they were not "normal things."[24] He may have had other grounds for suspicion, perhaps based on his conversation with Wirth in Lublin, that Wirth and Globocnik were involved in a mass-murder operation.

So, at the beginning of 1944, Morgen flew down to Trieste to visit Globocnik. They talked through the night:[25]

> He laid out the story of his life and told me, among other things, what he had accomplished for the Reichsführer with *Aktion Reinhard*. [. . .] And from that I saw that because these killings had been ordered, the thing was legal in the sense of National Socialist law, and so as for doing anything directly against this sector, my hands were tied. And so my efforts turned to finding another way out.

Here Morgen learned that what he already believed about Auschwitz—that it was a mass-murder operation ordered by Himmler and Hitler—applied to a far larger complex, encompassing at least three other extermination centers. And he received confirmation that all of these operations were off-limits to prosecution.

The only operation that Morgen could still impede was Auschwitz, and so he went after Maximilian Grabner, Head of the Auschwitz Gestapo. On Grabner's orders, over 2000 prisoners had been shot solely for the purpose of making room in the Auschwitz arrest bunker when it became overcrowded.[26] As usual, the killings were covered up with fake medical certificates.

Grabner was tried in the fall of 1944, with SS Judge Werner Hansen presiding. In 1964, Hansen testified at the Frankfurt *Auschwitz-Prozess*, seconding Morgen's testimony about the background of the Grabner prosecution:[27]

> Before the trial against Grabner opened and took place, Dr. Morgen, who had led the investigation and brought the charges, had informed me that the background for this murder indictment was mass killings in Auschwitz. He had informed me that transports of prisoners came to Auschwitz [. . .] for the sole purpose being killed there. At the same time Dr. Morgen told me that this obviously took place on an order from the highest state leadership. It remained unclear whether it had been ordered by Hitler himself or someone else. It was certain that these, if I may say, actions were taking place beyond the authority of the judiciary. It would have been absolutely impossible for a court—whether a Court of Military Justice, or an SS and Police Court, or a court of the general judiciary—to institute an inquiry with the aim of bringing charges against the highest state leadership. [. . .] The possibilities for the judiciary were of course limited. The prosecution of Grabner was in my opinion the utmost that the SS Judiciary was in a position to do.

When one of the Frankfurt judges asks Hansen to confirm that Morgen had told him of the mass killings, and to describe Morgen's state of mind, Hansen replies,[28]

> I can see it before me as if it were yesterday. And I can still remember where I sat, and where Herr Doktor Morgen stood. [. . .] And Doktor Morgen told me about these mass killings and was appalled and disgusted about these measures that were being carried out by the highest offices. And he said that it must be our task, insofar as was possible for us, to contain this and to prosecute what we still could.

At the same trial, Morgen's assistant Gerhard Wiebeck testifies that when Morgen showed him indictments of several SS members for corruption, he was amazed to see references to the gassing as well.[29]

The question is how prosecuting individual crimes could contain the mass extermination, much less cause the entire system to collapse. Morgen elaborates:[30]

> It was to be expected that the perpetrators would refer to higher orders also for these individual crimes. This occurred; thereupon the SS Judiciary, on the basis of the material which I supplied, approached the highest government chiefs and officially asked, "Did you order these killings? Is the legal fact of murder no longer valid for you? What general orders are there concerning these killings?"

Here Morgen suggests that prosecutions for small-scale killings raised questions as to whether they had been ordered from above. His plan was that such questions would broaden out into the matter of "general orders" for killings: "Then the supreme state leadership would either have to abandon the perpetrators and finally surrender them into our hands for the mass extermination as well, or things must come to an open rupture through an external suspension of the entire judicial system."[31] In other words, inquiries into "illegal killings" would force the highest leaders to answer for the mass extermination, whereupon they would either toss the likes of Höss to the SS Judiciary or, by admitting to mass murder, cause the legal order to collapse.

Morgen says that the impact of his tactics was more modest at first:[32]

> [. . .] the immediate effects of the judicial investigation were that in all concentration camps the killing of prisoners by so-called "euthanasia" stopped immediately, because no doctor could feel sure that he would not be arrested from one moment to the next. Everybody bore in mind the example that was set by the case of the doctor

of Buchenwald. I am convinced that through this intervention and action the lives of thousands of prisoners were saved.

So far, so good. But now Morgen suggests that the envisioned challenge to the "Final Solution" was indeed undertaken, until being cut short by the collapse of Germany in 1945:

> If I may anticipate, on account of the trial in Weimar against Koch and Grabner [in fall 1944], this problem became acute as I had foreseen; the proceedings were suspended and the SS Judiciary put these questions, which I mentioned before, publicly and officially to the Reich Security Main Office. For this very purpose a judge was sent there, who had the task of investigating all sections of the Reich Security Main Office, to see whether such orders were in existence. As I heard, the result was negative. Thereupon an attempt was made to take direct steps against Hoess, but in the meantime the front had advanced, Auschwitz was occupied and the judge who had been sent there had to stop at the beginning of his fruitless investigations, and in January 1945 complete disorganization set in which made further legal prosecution impossible.

Now, Morgen is right that Grabner defended himself at trial by citing higher orders for his killings. A recess was then called to allow for a search of the files.[33] No orders materialized, but the trial was never resumed. So much is confirmed at the *Auschwitz-Prozess* by Judge Hansen, who presided at the Grabner trial. But Morgen intimates, further, that as he had foreseen, the lack of higher orders brought the perpetrators of mass extermination under the court's jurisdiction, so that "direct steps" could be taken against Rudolf Höss. Steps were indeed taken against Höss, but they were not directly aimed at his role in mass extermination, as Morgen here suggests. Morgen was never able to prosecute the perpetrators of the "Final Solution" for that, the ultimate crime.

Morgen's explanation of his tactics ends with a claim to have disrupted *Aktion Reinhard*:

> The killing system was severely shaken; for it is noteworthy that on my second visit to Lublin, shortly after I first approached Kriminalkommissar Wirth, I did not find him there. I learned that in the meantime Wirth had suddenly received orders to completely destroy all his extermination camps. He had gone to Istria with his entire command, and was guarding streets there, and while doing so he was killed in May 1944. When I heard that Wirth and his command had left Lublin I immediately flew there in order to find out whether he was merely transferring his field of activity and would continue elsewhere, but that was not so.

This part of Morgen's exposition at Nuremberg is nonsense. Wirth left Lublin for Trieste in September 1943, having finished dismantling his camps. Morgen didn't indict Koch and Grabner until the spring and summer of 1944, by which time Wirth was dead. So Morgen knows that his prosecutions had nothing to do with the closure of the *Aktion Reinhard* camps.[34] But he has already compressed the chronology by backdating his full knowledge of the "Final Solution" to his first conversation with Wirth. He then feels compelled to characterize his prosecutions as having been responsive to, and effective against, those operations, when in fact the only gassing operation that they could have affected was the one at Auschwitz-Birkenau, which continued into the summer of 1944—and on which they had no known effect.

Another path by which Morgen tried to stop the extermination, given that he was powerless to prosecute it, was to bring it to the attention of superiors who could prevail on Hitler to change course:[35]

> Hitler had to be induced to withdraw his orders. Under the circumstances, this could be done only by Himmler as Minister of the Interior and Minister of the Police. I thought at that time that I must endeavor to approach Himmler through the heads of the departments and make it clear to him, by explaining the effects of this system, that through these methods the State was being led straight into an abyss. Therefore I approached my immediate superior, the chief of the Criminal Police, SS Obergruppenführer Nebe; then I turned to the chief of the Main Office SS Courts, SS Obergruppenführer Breithaupt. I also approached Kaltenbrunner and the chief of the Gestapo, Gruppenführer Müller, and Obergruppenführer Pohl of the Economic and Administrative Main Office, and the Reichsarzt, Gruppenführer Dr. Grawitz.

Here Morgen recites a roster of officers with access to Himmler. Heinrich Müller, as Chief of the Secret Police (Gestapo), and Arthur Nebe, as Chief of the Criminal Police (Kripo), reported to Ernst Kaltenbrunner, who was Chief of the Reich Security Head Office. Oswald Pohl's organization, the Economic Administrative Head Office (WVHA), oversaw the concentration camps. Kaltenbrunner and Pohl reported to Heinrich Himmler; and Ernst-Robert Grawitz, Chief Physician of the Nazi regime, advised Himmler on the use of gas in the camps. Hence each of these men could indeed have been a conduit to Himmler, who was of course the conduit to Hitler. Finally, Franz Beithaupt was the Chief of the SS Judiciary Head Office in Munich, hence Morgen's boss.

Morgen speaks on several occasions of having met with these figures. Unfortunately, the context often fails to make clear how many meetings took place and whether they concerned the "legal" or the "illegal" killings, or perhaps both at once.

It is clear that on one occasion, at least, Morgen did not approach Müller but was summoned by him because of pursuing Grabner, who was Müller's man at Auschwitz.[36]

> So I had Grabner arrested immediately, whereupon I was ordered to report to the Chief of the Gestapo, SS-Gruppenführer Müller, at the Reich Security Head Office.
>
> As soon as I walked in, Müller roared at me: what sort of mischief was I up to, I had no understanding of state police matters, and so on in this tone. I tried to remain very calm and said to him something along these lines: Gruppenführer, I'm not a Gestapo officer but an SS judge, sworn to the law. Ultimately, we live in a nation of laws, and there are limits that even the Gestapo must respect. Müller, he turned white as chalk. He sprang up, he roared at me: how could I permit myself to speak to him that way, he a general in the Waffen-SS, and I—what was I?—a simple Obersturmführer, a little wurst. He would show me, I should get out! And he literally threw me out the door.
>
> There I stood in the great, empty, endless hallways of the building—the former Kaiser-Friedrich Museum, I think—and I was convinced that the man, in his hatred, in his rage, had called straightaway down to the guards. For anyone who wanted to enter had to fill out a visitor's pass, have his name recorded, and surrender it upon departure. I was convinced that when I went out, I would be arrested and would disappear in a cellar. I [Pause] considered my situation and said: You must, at all costs, change Gruppenführer Müller's mind. However bitter it is, however difficult it is for you, you must go back into the lion's den. In any case, you must try. And after I had considered this—five or ten minutes had passed meanwhile—I went back again into the antechamber and said that I had one more important message to give the Gruppenführer. "May I go in?"
>
> To my surprise, the door opened and [there was] Müller, who had also calmed down in the meantime. I excused myself for my un-military demeanor and said to him, "Gruppenführer, in fact I've come to ask your advice and instructions for the ongoing investigations." And it was as if Müller was suddenly transformed. He said at once, "Please, I am at your service." "Comrade Morgen," he said to me, "have a seat." I said to him "Gruppenführer, is it not true that in the personnel file of every concentration camp commandant, or a leader of the political [i.e., Gestapo] department in a concentration camp, there is copy of a declaration, signed by him, saying that the Führer decides about the life of an enemy of the state?"[37] "Yes," he said, "That's correct." I said, "It's also correct to assume, isn't it, that this power has been delegated to you, as Chief of the Secret State Police [Gestapo], and to no one else." He said, "Indeed, that's correct." Then I said, "What would you think, then, if someone far below you killed prisoners without reporting it to you, on his own initiative, at his own discretion?" "Well, that's impossible, it doesn't happen." So I said to him, "You see, Gruppenführer, that's how people are disregarding

your authority in the concentration camps. That's what Untersturmführer Grabner has done, and that's why I've arrested him." He said, "But that's a different matter. I hadn't seen it that way."

Morgen cleverly fends off interference from Müller by portraying Grabner's crimes as challenges to his, Müller's, authority.[38] These crimes were "illegal" killings, however, whereas Morgen says at Nuremberg that he approached Müller, among others, about the mass extermination by gassing.

These conflicting accounts can perhaps be reconciled to some extent, as indicated by Morgen's testimony at a lesser war-crimes trial, against Oswald Pohl:[39]

> Q. Witness, we do know that Mueller was the second in command, generally below Himmler, concerning the extermination of Jews. Did you speak with Mueller?
>
> A. Yes, I did. [. . .]
>
> Q. Was he surprised when you told him about your knowledge of the extermination of the Jews?
>
> A. Obergruppenfuehrer Mueller was surprised to hear about the illegal executions in the concentration camps, namely about the acts committed in the concentration camps against the law and he was also surprised at the large extent of crime, but he was not at all surprised that there was an extermination of the Jews, that there were [sic] inhuman treatment which had been ordered, and, he said to me, ironically, "Why don't you arrest me."

So it appears that both the "illegal" and the "legal" killings came up in one and the same conversation.

At this point in his testimony at the Pohl trial, Morgen is asked whether he reported to yet another figure, Horst Bender, an SS judge who was Himmler's personal liaison to the SS Judiciary Head Office:[40]

> Q. Witness, did you ever speak to Judge Bender, who was chief judge of the Reichsfuehrer-SS about this matter, and what impression did you have then? Did he know anything about those things?
>
> A. I have the impression, at least I thought at the time, the man was absolutely surprised about it. Of course, I did tell him, I did tell Oberfuehrer Bender because he was a judge who reported to the Reichsfuehrer-SS directly, and he also consulted him. I also told the Chief of Main Office SS Court, Obergruppenfuehrer Breithaupt. I can state under oath that both personalities were horrified to hear about those things. I am a man who studied in all sorts of fields, and I was quite familiar with International Law, and about principles for all the laws which existed for all the legal countries,

and that is the reason why I left no doubt that if a State committed such crimes, that those things can have a dire and horrible result against the State as such. And I am positive as a result of my investigations that I was able to [show] with concrete cases that the agents which were used for the bloody practices became absolutely criminals. Absolute[ly] putrid.

In this passage it is clear that Morgen is speaking of the state crime of extermination.

Thus, whether or not Morgen was trying to get Hitler's order reversed, he did report the extermination to superiors, especially superior jurists, with the expectation that they would recognize it as a war crime under international law.

The international law on which Morgen could have relied in these conversations was the Hague Convention of 1907. The convention did not yet contain the concept of "crimes against humanity," which would later serve as the basis for prosecuting Nazi atrocities, but it did contain a precursor formula. The Preamble of the Hague Convention speaks of "the laws of humanity" as providing "principles of the law of nations" to protect belligerents and civilians in times of war. It states that these principles should hold "until a more complete code of the laws of war has been issued."[41]

Before the Nuremberg trials, however, many jurists doubted whether the laws of humanity amounted to anything more than "positive morality," hence whether they could underwrite prosecutions and punishments. Only when Nazi perpetrators were tried and sentenced for "crimes against humanity" were the laws of humanity accorded the force of law.[42]

Morgen must have recognized that the mass extermination violated the laws of humanity, thus violating the Hague Convention. But what could he have expected to accomplish by citing international law to his superiors in 1944, when Nazi Germany had been openly violating international law for years? The answer is that Morgen's aim was not to alert Bender and Breithaupt to illegality as such. The "dire and horrible result" of which he warned them was that perpetrators of the Holocaust were corrupted to the point of being "absolutely putrid." This is the point that he had tried to impress on Grawitz by speaking of "the epidemic of corruption, the brutalization of the men."[43]

In these protests, Morgen was speaking a language that his superiors understood. Himmler himself recognized the risk of brutalization. In a speech to SS officers on October 6, 1943, Himmler declared,[44]

One had to make the difficult decision to make this people disappear from the earth. For the organization that had to carry out the task, it was the most difficult one we ever had. It was carried out, I believe I can say, without our men and our leaders having suffered damage to mind and spirit. [. . .] The path between the possibilities obtaining here—either to become vicious, heartless and to no longer respect human life, or to become soft and spin out of control to the point of nervous collapse—the course between this Scylla and Charybdis is terribly narrow.

In a speech two days earlier, Himmler had insisted that the SS successfully navigated this strait:[45]

Most of you will know what it means when 100 bodies lie together, when there are 500, or when there are 1000. And to have persevered through it, and—with some exceptions of human weakness—to have remained decent [*anständig*], has made us hard and is a page of glory never mentioned and never to be mentioned.

These speeches were delivered shortly before Morgen's discovery of the Erntefest massacre and his momentous visit to Auschwitz. His subsequent warnings to Bender, Breithaupt, and Grawitz thus spoke to concerns that were already on the minds of SS leaders. Unlike Himmler, however, Morgen denied the possibility of committing mass murder without "damage to mind and spirit." Indeed, he saw mass murder as corrupting the entire state, undermining its moral foundations and leading it into the abyss. But when speaking to his superiors, he emphasized the threat to SS virtue.

As we will see, Morgen's strategy for undermining the "Final Solution" did not succeed. No one listened, and by the time the key defendants came to trial, the gas chambers had finished their work.

FIFTEEN
ADOLF EICHMANN

In targeting the men responsible for the "Final Solution," Morgen eventually set his sights on Adolf Eichmann, who played the crucial role of organizing the deportation of victims to the extermination centers. Morgen recounts the episode in his testimony at Nuremberg:[1]

> I petitioned the SS Court at Berlin to carry out the investigations into Eichmann on the basis of my leads.[2] The SS Court in Berlin thereupon submitted to the chief of the Reich Security Main Office, SS Obergruppenführer Kaltenbrunner, in his capacity as highest judge, a warrant to arrest Eichmann.
>
> Dr. Bachmann reported to me that this submission resulted in dramatic scenes.[3]
>
> Kaltenbrunner immediately called in Müller, and now the judge was told that an arrest was in no event to be considered, for Eichmann was carrying out a special secret task of utmost importance entrusted to him by the Führer.

Morgen says that these events took place in the middle of 1944.

In 1961, this episode comes up at Eichmann's trial in Jerusalem. The Israeli Attorney General volunteers, "We even have the actual warrant for arrest."[4] Unfortunately, no warrant survives. All we have is Eichmann's testimony, as follows:[5]

> A. The whole thing occurred not in 1944, but in 1943. In 1943 two men of the Criminal Police came to see me at my Section. They asked about a pouch with diamonds or other precious stones, and I told them, yes, I did know something about this, but I said I do not know how and what, I cannot remember. And then the policemen left. Months later I was informed that I had to report to the SS and Police Court in Berlin. I went there late one afternoon and reported, because I assumed that they wanted some information or something, but instead I was examined by a judge called Baumann or Baumgarten. This was about what had happened to the pouch with the precious stones. And after I made a statement there to the effect that I did know something, but I could not remember any of this business, I was questioned, and a record was made by a sergeant of the Order Police who was present.
>
> Q. And the result was that this charge turned out to be baseless?
>
> A. The result was that when I came back, I put my head of registry to work, and he and his staff spent the whole night going through the files, and then they found

a communication between Müller and Glücks where [. . .] I forget today [. . .] Müller informed Glücks that there was a pouch with precious stones in the safe of the Berlin Secret Police Headquarters. And this letter, which dates back to my predecessor's time—Lischka—must somehow have got to me when I took over the Section; so I remembered such a matter of precious stones and a pouch with diamonds, I had said I did, and that was it.

I took this letter to my superior—Gruppenführer Müller—informed him of the proceedings on the previous day, and then later I heard that Judge Baumann had made an application for my arrest to my judicial superior, Kaltenbrunner, and had been turned down there. I myself was dealt with very harshly by the police court authorities. For my staff, as long as [. . .] for my staff in the Section, as long as this letter had not been found, there remained a bad taste, because it was after all a criminal matter, and therefore I asked for this Judge Baumann or Baumgarten to apologize to me in the presence of the members of my Section. And the man came and apologized to me for the treatment I had received.

Eichmann's version of events agrees with Morgen's in many particulars. Although Eichmann is unsure of the judge's name, his guesses are very close to "Bachmann," the name given by Morgen. Morgen says that the attempt to arrest Eichmann occurred in the middle of 1944, and Eichmann says that the first inquiries came in 1943 and the warrant for arrest "months later"—another close match. Like Morgen, Eichmann recalls that the arrest was vetoed by Kaltenbrunner. And the apology that Eichmann recalls extracting from the judge sounds like one of the "dramatic scenes" of which Morgen was later informed.

Eichmann's description of the charges is virtually unintelligible: all we can tell is that they involved a pouch of diamonds. But then, a pouch of diamonds would have been right up Morgen's alley—precisely the sort of minor offence that he was qualified to investigate, and by investigating which he tried to impede the "Final Solution," according to his postwar testimony. To judge from Eichmann's account, the diamonds were a cold case dating from the time of his predecessor. Dredging it up and pinning it on Eichmann would have been a stretch but, again, a stretch is what Morgen claims to have made in order to disrupt the extermination process.

Morgen had to ask the SS court in Berlin to investigate Eichmann because he himself lacked the authority to do so. His authority from Himmler was to investigate crimes within the concentration camps, whereas Eichmann's responsibilities ended at the railheads where deportees were deposited by his trains. Why did Morgen go so far outside his province?

The connection went through Budapest. In the middle of 1944, when Morgen approached the SS court, Eichmann was working out of Budapest on the deportation of Hungarian Jews to Auschwitz. Eichmann had entered Hungary with his commando on March 19, 1944, just behind the invading German forces, and he remained active in Budapest until Christmas.[6] The bulk of the deportees, numbering more than 400,000, were shipped to Auschwitz over the course of ten weeks, beginning in late April. Two-thirds were gassed upon arrival.[7]

Eichmann's work in Hungary required him to visit Auschwitz to coordinate the flow of deportees with the receptive capacity of the camp—or, more precisely, the capacity of its gas chambers.[8] Since the deportations took place from late April to early July, Eichmann's visits would have coincided with Morgen's investigations in the camp, which included, for example, the interrogation of a commandant's adjutant in May.[9] So Morgen and Eichmann could well have crossed paths.

Moreover, Morgen received a new assignment that sent him into Eichmann's sphere of operations. In a letter of June 16, 1944, requesting additional manpower, Morgen complains about his burden of open cases and adds, "I'm supposed to be getting from the Reichsführer-SS a further complex that is playing out between Hungary and Auschwitz."[10] He asks for an assistant to carry out the initial investigations in forthcoming cases.

Morgen did visit Hungary, although his visit didn't amount to much.[11] In a postwar deposition, he says that he vaguely remembers being in Budapest for two days in the early summer of 1944. He explains that he wanted to interrogate Eichmann, who was accused of having misappropriated "a number of precious watches, other valuables and stocks from a safe in Berlin," a description that matches Eichmann's 1961 testimony in Jerusalem.[12] Morgen's attempt to question Eichmann failed.[13] When he arrived in Budapest, he found the office of the Higher SS and Police Leader, Otto Winkelmann, "in a nearly chaotic state," either because of the approaching front or because Winkelmann had been the target of an assassination attempt—Morgen doesn't recall. Since Winkelmann's adjutant wouldn't reveal his whereabouts, Morgen considered it pointless to stay on in Budapest, and he flew back to Germany.

Morgen's desire to interrogate Eichmann was incidental to the official purpose of his visit, which was to investigate corruption by SS men and Hungarian police, at the personal behest of Himmler. Suspicion had arisen that the SS men accompanying the Jewish deportees were robbing them of their valuables and were then involved in illegal currency trading. Morgen adds that those investigations came to nothing, because the deportations stalled and the SS men were reassigned.[14]

Morgen's work in Hungary would cause him considerable headaches after the war. In December 1945, a former superior of Morgen's, SS Judge Kurt Mittelstädt, swore an affidavit accusing Morgen of having drafted a leaflet encouraging Hungarian Jews to bring their valuables with them to Germany. Mittelstädt paraphrases the text of the leaflet as follows:[15]

> Jewish men and women! Be without fear, nothing will happen to you in Germany. You will be put to work there as Germany needs the labor of every man and every woman. Don't throw away your valuables, don't give them to the Hungarian policemen, but take them with you to Germany. You may need them there.

Mittelstädt claims that this leaflet was shown to him by Günther Reinecke, Chief of Legal Affairs at the Head Office of the SS Judiciary, in the summer of 1944.

In the early 1950s Morgen was investigated on suspicion of complicity in the murder of Hungarian Jews. One of Morgen's former assistants, Gerhard Wiebeck, submitted an affidavit claiming to have been shown the telltale leaflet in 1944 by Oswald Pohl.[16] Wiebeck assumed that Jewish deportees had been showing up in Auschwitz empty-handed, depriving the Reich of its usual haul. The leaflet was supposedly Morgen's attempt to restore the flow of valuables.

In a 1954 deposition in connection with the investigations against Morgen, Mittelstädt backpedals from his 1945 testimony, stating that he does not know whether such a leaflet was ever published.[17] Reinecke's deposition in the case states that he prevented the publication of any summons to deportees that would give the "unfavorable impression abroad" that Germany needed Jewish labor.[18]

In his testimony about these allegations, Morgen flatly denies having written any leaflet.[19] He says that he was probably confronted with the question how to protect the deportees from extortion by their guards and would have agreed that they should be informed of their rights. He claims to have pointed to "the main cause of such offences, namely the prisoners' lack of rights and their feeling of being helplessly exposed to every arbitrariness."[20] He may have reported such discussions to the Chief of the Head Office of the SS Judiciary, he says, but he would have done so only by way of a "reporting activity," since the SS Judiciary had nothing to do with the deportations of Jews.[21] He adds, "As for the absurd contention that I ever planned to summon Jews in the outlying ghettos with leaflets to report voluntarily for their evacuation and to bring with them as many treasures and valuables as possible, I have only a complacent smile."[22]

The case against Morgen was dismissed in May 1955 by the Ministry of Justice of Baden-Württemberg. The Ministry ruled that there was no proof of the leaflet's having been published and "no indication [. . .] that the accused Dr. Morgen intended to promote the killing of Hungarian Jews with the will of a perpetrator."[23] Hardly a ringing acquittal.

The investigation of Morgen was resumed in 1970 but finally laid to rest in 1972 with the judgment that the charges were unsubstantiated.[24] In fact, they were implausible on their face. Morgen was a judge and criminal investigator, not a collection agent. If he had become involved in securing Jewish property for the Reich, his involvement would have consisted in prosecuting SS officers who embezzled it. Propaganda was not his métier. In the summer of 1944, Morgen had just completed a report denouncing the commandant of Buchenwald for failing to restore personal property to Jewish inmates upon their release, and he was trying to have Eichmann arrested. It would have been utterly out of character for him to urge Jewish deportees to furnish themselves with valuables to be expropriated at Auschwitz.

As it turns out, both Mittelstädt and Wiebeck were on bad terms with Morgen.[25] Wiebeck's affidavit conjures up a scene of ex-SS officers jockeying for credibility with their American captors—by discrediting one another, if necessary. The accusations against Morgen must be viewed in this light.

We know of no prosecutions that resulted from Morgen's visit to Hungary. What we do know is that at the time of the Hungarian deportations, when Morgen and Eichmann were both active at Auschwitz, Morgen tried to get an SS court to arrest Eichmann, not for corruption in Hungary, but for mishandling a pouch of diamonds in or before 1943.

The most plausible interpretation of these events is the one that Morgen himself offered after the war—namely, that finding himself powerless to prosecute the crime of mass murder, he tried to impede it by prosecuting the perpetrators for lesser crimes. Morgen could only nip at Eichmann's heels, but no heels would have been more tempting to an investigator intent on interfering with the "Final Solution."

THE WEIMAR TRIALS

Morgen installed an investigative commission in Auschwitz in the fall of 1943. He then opened an investigation into Maximilian Grabner, Chief of the Auschwitz Gestapo, on suspicion of murdering roughly 2000 inmates of the camp's arrest bunker. Grabner was tried by a Special Purpose Court (*Gericht zur besonderen Verwendung*) that Himmler had established within the SS Judiciary, at Morgen's request. Significantly, the idea for establishing the court originated with Konrad Morgen.

Morgen had earlier persuaded Himmler to establish a *ZbV*-court dedicated to cases of corruption in the concentration camps.[1] After his visit to Auschwitz, Morgen recommended another *ZbV*-court, with a broader scope.[2] The purview of the new court would not be limited to financial corruption in the camps. Morgen wanted to prosecute murders, and so he needed a court with wider jurisdiction than the *ZbV*-court dedicated to financial corruption. The new court was to be located with the SS Judiciary Head Office in Munich, above the heads of unreliable local SS judges.

Why Himmler agreed to establish this court remains unclear, but we can assume that ideological considerations played a role. The cover letter conveying Morgen's recommendation to Himmler's office mentions that the Army and Air Force already had general *ZbV*-courts, whose secret charters might serve as models for the SS. Since the SS styled itself as hewing to a higher standard of uprightness than these other organizations, Himmler could hardly refuse to bring its system of internal discipline into line with theirs.

Himmler finally established the general *ZbV*-court in May 1944, but he was by no means giving Morgen a free hand. Already at the beginning of 1944, he had ruled that no new investigations should be opened: Morgen must confine himself to pending cases.[3] Morgen managed to bypass this order by claiming that new initiatives were necessary for winding up the case against Koch, but Himmler then declared that the Koch case itself must be decided. All Himmler really wanted, Morgen says, was "to stand before Koch's dangling feet and give a harrowing speech" to the assembled concentration camp commandants, "at night, by firelight," so that they would confess their crimes: "Himmler, that romantic—that's what he had in mind."[4]

Morgen succeeded in getting the investigation continued, but not without further opposition. His main enemy was Oswald Pohl, who as Chief of the SS Head Office for Economy and Administration oversaw the concentration camps. Morgen had first tangled with Pohl back in 1941, during his assignment in Cracow. There Morgen had developed evidence against Pohl's adjutant and had referred the case to the Head Office of the SS Judiciary. Pohl then sent his legal advisor, Kurt Schmidt-Klevenow, to keep an eye on Morgen, while trumpeting it about that he was "rolling around in the *Dreck* and splattering others with it." Recounting the case to the CIC, Morgen ironically comments, "That was the beginning of my cordial relations with Pohl."[5]

Back then, Pohl had peppered Himmler with complaint after complaint against Morgen. And now again, in 1944, "He abused me, vilified me, threatened me, kept filing serious grievances against me with my superior officers, watered down and twisted the elements of offenses, stirred up the local Court Masters and commandants," as well as pressuring the Security Service and Criminal Police to thwart him.[6] Finally, in the summer of 1944, Pohl instructed all concentration camp commandants that no SS judge should be granted entry to a camp without an identification card issued by him.[7]

Pohl's attitude was shared by Gestapo Chief Müller. With his boss, Kaltenbrunner, Müller went to speak with Himmler about Morgen:[8]

> "The man has done outstanding work, cleared up a lot, made a howling success. But now justice has been done. Any further detective work in the concentration camps will cause disarray. The discipline of the inmates will be endangered." "I cannot guarantee security," said the one. "The work in the concentration camps is being hampered. I can make no more guarantees to the armament industry," said the other. Pohl said he would resign all his positions if I didn't disappear.

Caught in the middle between Morgen and Pohl was Kurt Mittelstädt, who led the new investigative office attached to the *ZbV*-court. Frustrated to the point of despair by the number of files flooding into the office, Mittelstädt had appealed to Morgen for help.[9] At first he stayed in the background and let Morgen take the lead, but then he decided to do it all himself and took the documents away. As Pohl's attacks intensified, Mittelstädt advised Morgen to back off. "We have enough manpower whom we could train," he said. "Stay in the background and supervise." Morgen remarks, "I got the impression that Mittelstädt was playing a double game. How it came about, I don't know. He was always sort of nasty to me."[10]

Morgen described Mittelstädt's erratic behavior toward him in a letter to his fiancée, Maria Wachter:[11]

M. is definitely a difficult boss. At times he was not interested in me at all. Today he is fretting about everything. Often he lapses into a rude military tone which hurts even in a uniformed drill but paralyzes sober factual work on questions that can be decided only by trained intelligence. He's easily offended. An incurable mistrust induces him to smell grave insubordination in harmless events, to which he reacts with inappropriate sharpness.

At the end of October, Morgen wrote a letter to Günther Reinecke complaining of Mittelstädt's behavior and asking to be transferred out of the Munich office.[12]

During this period, Himmler was gradually divesting himself of Morgen. When Morgen began working for the central ZbV-court in Munich, he was still formally affiliated with the Reich Criminal Police Office, under the Reich Security Head Office. He was therefore in the untenable position of reporting up two distinct chains of command. In August 1944, the Chief of the SS Judiciary, Franz Breithaupt, sent Himmler a request that Morgen's posting to the Criminal Police be suspended: Morgen should henceforth be responsible solely to Breithaupt and, through him, to Himmler.[13]

Himmler granted this request, via his legal advisor Horst Bender. Morgen was now attached solely to the ZbV-court, as head investigator. Expressing his thanks for Morgen's good work in the concentration camps, Himmler asked to receive a recommendation for Morgen's promotion, and he granted Morgen three weeks' vacation, stipulating that he was "not allowed to involve himself in juridical questions" during that period.[14] He also instructed Bender to discuss with Morgen "fundamental questions about the conduct of investigations." With these directives Himmler was subtly neutralizing Morgen, arranging for him to be schooled by Bender and rewarded, conveniently, with three weeks out of action.

The case of the Buchenwald defendants—the Kochs, Waldemar Hoven, and Martin Sommer—went to trial in September 1944 before the ZbV-court, sitting for the occasion in Schloss Kranichfeld, a Renaissance castle about 30 km from the scene of their crimes.[15] Morgen was present as the investigating judge. The trial turned out to be a daunting experience for him. As he remarks bitterly in a postwar memo, "the real trial was not against the accused but against me as investigator and attorney."[16] What turned the tables against him was the presence of several SS officers whose attention had been caught by word of the trial. Oswald Pohl sent Kurt Schmidt-Klevenow, whom he had once dispatched to hound

Morgen back in Cracow.[17] Schmidt-Klevenow held forth to the Weimar court after hours, when its members joined the SS auditors for meals. He said that Morgen had exaggerated the case to draw attention to himself and had falsified reports to Himmler, the whole trial was nonsense, it was damaging the reputation of the SS and disrupting the concentration camps.[18]

By this point, Morgen was generally regarded as a "dead man."[19] His colleague Gerhard Wiebeck heard that a warrant for Morgen's arrest had already been issued by the Reich Security Head Office. When Wiebeck objected that Morgen, as the prosecuting counsel, could not be arrested during the trial, he was told that Morgen would be locked up after the proceedings.

Schmidt-Klevenow objected especially to the connection Morgen drew between corruption and killing. He argued that Morgen should have accused Koch only of embezzlement, and perhaps instituted a separate trial against Hoven for murder, though only after obtaining Himmler's consent.[20] He went so far as to challenge the legal basis of all the murder charges, which was an order issued by Himmler that the Führer alone could decide the life or death of an enemy of the state. Schmidt-Klevenow questioned whether Himmler had meant this order literally or had rather held a *reservatio mentalis*—as it were, crossed his fingers behind his back.[21] Of course, if fundamental rules could be disregarded on the basis of such metaphysical speculation, then political and ideological considerations, such as the reputation of the SS, could take precedence, and any attempt to prosecute crimes against concentration camp prisoners would be doomed to failure. Morgen expressed his frustration in a letter to Maria Wachter:[22] "Defenseless, I stood alone in the storm as the object of the tribunal. [. . .] Yes, the 'sovereign judge'! It is a sad and thankless business to be the state's prosecutor of state institutions."

After evidence had been presented, Koch suddenly put forward a new explanation of his actions. He said that the doctors at Buchenwald had received an order to carry out whatever killings were requested by their commandant, from which he had inferred that he, as commandant, had the right to make such requests.[23] The trial was therefore adjourned for further fact-finding, over written objections from Morgen.

After this adjournment, the *ZbV*-court took up the case of Maximilian Grabner. As Morgen had foreseen, even hoped, Grabner claimed to have received "higher orders" for the killings in the Auschwitz arrest bunker. He claimed that the Reich Security Head Office had sent orders of execution, together with the order to destroy them.[24] A search for the alleged orders came up empty,[25] but the trial was then in recess, never to be resumed. In March 1945, Morgen heard that Grabner had been released. He told the chief judge of the *ZbV*-court, "If we lose the war, you're the first one they'll hang"—an outburst of frustration more vivid for being patently false.[26] At the end of the war, Grabner was arrested in Vienna and sent for trial to Poland, where he was convicted and hanged.[27]

At Nuremberg, Morgen implies that when no higher orders were found for Grabner's killings, the existence of higher orders for mass extermination also came into question, leaving the commandant of Auschwitz-Birkenau, Rudolf Höss, vulnerable to prosecution for his role in the "Final Solution"—at last, a prosecution of the ultimate crime.[28] In fact, however, prosecution of that crime would have to await the Nuremberg Tribunal. As in other cases, Morgen had to proceed against Höss on lesser charges.

The Buchenwald trial reconvened in mid-December.[29] The outcome was a disappointment. Koch was sentenced to death, but only for embezzlement and fraud.[30] He was shot shortly before the end of the war. Ilse Koch was acquitted for lack of evidence. Hoven was tried twice, but a judgment was continually deferred.[31] He remained under arrest in Buchenwald and was ultimately released in March of 1945.[32]

After the war, Hoven was convicted of war crimes and crimes against humanity in the "medical trial" at Nuremberg. He was hanged in 1948. Ilse was tried by the Americans and sentenced to life in prison. A key issue in the trial was whether she had made lampshades out of prisoners' skin—a question on which Morgen testified in the negative, on the basis of his thorough search of the Koch residence in 1943.[33] Frau Koch created a sensation during the trial by announcing that she was eight months pregnant, a revelation made especially titillating by the fact that many of the men with whom she had come into contact in pre-trial detention were Jews. Her baby son was taken from her and he didn't discover their connection until the age of 19. Ilse's sentence was reduced and she was released after four years in prison, but she was later re-tried and re-incarcerated in Germany. She committed suicide in prison in 1967.

Ilse Koch's postwar reputation has far exceeded her role in the crimes committed at Buchenwald during her husband's tenure as commandant. Few today have heard of Waldemar Hoven, who killed hundreds with phenol injections, but many have heard of *Die Hexe von Buchenwald*—the Witch of Buchenwald—who supposedly made lampshades out of human skin.

SEVENTEEN

RUDOLF HÖSS AND
ELEONORE HODYS

Eleonore Hodys was a political prisoner from Austria who came to Auschwitz in 1942. No sooner had she arrived than the commandant, Rudolf Höss, began to show an interest in her. He arranged for her to work in his household repairing carpets and making tapestries for his wife. In 1942, while his wife was away, Höss began making overtures to her. Höss's wife dismissed her and had her locked up, but Höss kept up the relationship, visiting her cell at night.

Morgen takes up the story in his testimony at the *Auschwitz-Prozess*:[1]

> Standartenführer Höss, who was married, had started a love affair with a Czech prisoner named Hodys, and this female prisoner became pregnant. To keep the fact from getting out, Höss had his lover brought to block 11, the bunker. And down in that cellar there were standing cells. I later had them removed. They were chambers about one to one-and-a-half meters square. And down low there was a small hole into which one could only crawl. The prisoner had to stand there as long as the camp administration liked. And in the case of Hodys, [Höss] had ordered that this woman, who was pregnant, should be given nothing to eat. She should starve to death down there. But even those de-humanized guards, some of them, could not carry out this order. From time to time there was one who gave her something to eat. In this way she could eke out her meager life.

Hodys was finally released from the bunker. She managed to get an abortion and worked as a janitress in the camp. She even escaped a selection for the gas chamber. Hodys came to Morgen's attention via his assistant Gerhard Wiebeck, who joined the investigative team in Auschwitz in March 1944.[2] Morgen managed to have her transferred to a clinic in Munich, where he gradually gained her trust and got her to give a deposition against Höss. Her deposition was later included in a pamphlet published by the American Seventh Army in May 1945, immediately after they had liberated Dachau.[3]

Hodys's testimony shows that Morgen's investigation was a genuine threat to Commandant Höss. She describes a meeting with Höss that took place under the eye of Morgen's colleague Gerhard Wiebeck:[4]

> [Höss] got rather excited and put his hand on the bed to steady himself. He affirmed that my behavior had been orderly, and that I had been placed in the bunker for my own protection. He did not know why I was locked up in the standing cell.

Höss's evident discomfort—and blatant dishonesty—indicates that despite his powerful position, he viewed Morgen's investigation with alarm.

Morgen's work with Hodys is documented in letters that he wrote to his fiancée, Maria Wachter. The letters were written in mid-October 1944, after the Koch trial had been adjourned and just as the Grabner trial was getting underway. Morgen hoped that Hodys's testimony would bolster his position:[5] "Yesterday evening I came back from Munich, having been there for 2 days. I now have new evidence that will bring the stagnating trials in Weimar to a just end, and to that extent will prove me right." Several days later, Morgen writes,[6]

> This afternoon I will go again to Munich to see my prisoner. I already wrote to you about her. I am hoping to get great results for my work—and the heads of a great number of serious criminals. Aside from that she is in every respect a remarkable person. Charming and feminine in the Vienna style, academically educated, well travelled in Abyssinia, Africa, Palestine, Italy, a pharmacist and bacteriologist, cagey, intelligent, and artful as almost no other daughter of Eve, but no bluestocking, a needleworker whose hands must have produced marvellous pieces of tapestry. On the other side: a convicted political criminal, divorced, and bed-ridden and sick for a year. The woman is a phenomenon of will. It is incredible what she has gone through without her character or looks having suffered.

When Morgen calls Hodys "my prisoner," he doesn't mean that he was her jailer; he is rather expressing paternalistic solicitude, mixed perhaps with possessiveness. He seems taken with her, and he therefore finds himself entering into her ordeal with genuine empathy:[7]

> Last night I came back from Munich. After a 10-hour, highly informative interrogation of my prisoner. You cannot imagine the bleak desolation of [her former] cell [at Auschwitz], the bad air, the confinement behind bars, heavy iron doors, bolts and chains. I was so exhausted that I could not make use of all the time before my train. For almost an hour I paced up and down at the station Munich-East.

Soon the entire scene at the clinic begins to work on his sensibilities:[8]

> This afternoon I came back from Munich. I spent two days in the orthopedic clinic where my prisoner is now. It is a big house with many cupolas. Small children, blossoming girls with dragging, amputated legs, war wounded soldiers. All are cared for by Catholic sisters wearing shapeless white bonnets, like scarecrows. Still, I could tell that they are women enough to enjoy nice friendly words and gestures.
>
> There is a good atmosphere in this house, and I thought how it is still part of our sinking standard of behavior to stand up for the helpless, disfigured, and crippled with respect and active love.
>
> At noon there was a long alert, I sat in the cellar with all the sick. Suddenly the sisters started to pray with a choir of children to pray the rosary. ". . . blessed among women, blessed is the fruit of your womb . . . in the hour of our death . . ." in an endless litany. Must it be that way?
>
> My prisoner was very difficult and felt unwell. So did I. So we got nowhere on the first day. At 5 in the afternoon I went to bed exhausted in my quarters and woke up the next morning at 9:30.
>
> The next day we caught up. I am happy to have closed this most dismal chapter. Still, I'm depressed at being powerless to fully stand up for this unfortunate woman. No matter how clear the case, if there's no bigwig to stand behind it, everything bogs down in paperwork. Who will ask after her when I am no longer in charge of the case! Only her enemies. And maybe she will have to suffer one day for having given me her trust. A hint of that came to her as we finished. She was in despair. And I could offer her nothing but my good will. What is that for a woman who has been disappointed so often?

These letters reveal a side of Morgen that he never betrays in his official dealings, not even in his informal conversations with American interrogators, whom he got to know over the course of nearly three years in custody.

Höss was never tried by the SS Judiciary for any of his crimes. He found justice only in 1946 in Poland, where he was sentenced to death.

EIGHTEEN

OUT OF THE FRAY

In the fall of 1944, the SS Judiciary Head Office was bombed and forced to move to Prien am Chiemsee, a lakeside resort in Bavaria, about 80 km from Munich. While working in Prien, Morgen was often melancholic. Even in rural Bavaria the war could now be felt. In a letter to his fiancée, Maria Wachter, he writes,[1]

> It is not only the oncoming fall which turns one's thoughts to mortality. Every day it suddenly comes into view in a different form. Today and yesterday noon there were alerts. Some 350 bombers, shining like silver, passed at 4000 meters towards their site of destruction. Further away a small payload fell on peaceful farmhouses. One could feel the ground shake.

Mindful of the fate awaiting the Third Reich, Morgen turned to literature. He re-read Ernst Jünger's book *On the Marble Cliffs* (1939), in which an idyllic culture is destroyed by a dictatorial power.[2] The book was often interpreted as a critique of National Socialism.[3] Morgen now read it as a potential epitaph for Germany: "This book, which already struck me as bearing a deeper meaning when it was published, is very relevant today, in stating the problem of an old order defeated by the onslaught of chaos."[4] The "old order" that Morgen has in mind could not have been the National Socialist order, which wasn't old and, by this time, wasn't much of an order. He must mean the previous order, for which he is feeling nostalgic. The same nostalgia comes through when he speaks of reading "a book from before the 1st World War," Romain Rolland's *Meister von Heute* (*Musiciens d'aujourd'hui*, 1908). "It's nice that one has something left over for the coming years to enjoy as a distraction."[5]

Morgen's letters to Maria chart the evolving military outlook:[6]

> Comrades from the front report a high level of morale among the troops and the indisputable superiority of the soldiery. What's lacking—quantitative and qualitative superiority in weaponry—is being made up. There too I've heard a lot of good news. It's hard to believe, from the look of our ruined cities. [. . .] Still, we want to believe. Thus far, we have come through, and we can keep going.

For encouragement, Morgen looks to the speeches of national leaders:

> This morning I read Dr. Goebbels's speech. It's true, as he says, that the losses of industrial manufacturing are offset by new construction of unprecedented proportions. Unfortunately it was started too late. I have renewed hope that we will gain enough time, now that the Americans have attacked the Philippines. My great fear was that the Americans would throw their entire strength against us first.[7]

Morgen had been granted a vacation by Himmler in late August. He now took the vacation in November. He then received a transfer, which fulfilled both his own desire to escape from Mittelstädt and Himmler's desire to sideline him.[8] His new assignment was in Cracow, the scene of his first investigations as an SS judge. In a letter to Maria, he depicts his arrival:[9]

> What does the city have in store for me this time? As the train approached Cracow, out of a patch of rainy weather, the towers of the city came into view below. A fog and layer of clouds lay gently upon them. The clouds parted and bright light fell on the valley, which shimmered like the silvery mirror of a lake. It was magically unreal and beautiful. So let us take it as a sign that much will be illuminated here.

But the glorious sight of Cracow from the train soon gives way to the gritty reality of an eastern city at war:[10]

> By 4:30 it's already dark. Lying in gloom, the city is unsafe. The pubs close around 9:00. [. . .] As far as I can see, life is dull, like the conditions in the Reich. More black-marketeering, of course. For example, one would have to put down a whole month's pay for a kilo of tobacco. A black-marketer got 1000 marks for a pair of shoes, etc.

Morgen wanted Maria to join him in Cracow, but by January 1945 he frankly warns her that the situation has become dangerous:[11]

> Though the western front has undoubtedly been relieved, a new unhealthy development is currently making its way up from the Southeast. The Soviets are clearly planning to capture the approach to Czechoslovakia in order to bring the final collapse of the East through internal disorder. It isn't yet clear whether the advance forces will try the path through Vienna or through Pressburg. A panzer captain from that theater tells me that the Russians are attacking not only with their famous material superiority but also surprisingly with extraordinarily well-equipped, well-disciplined, and well-led elite troops.

And yet Morgen remained optimistic—or at least made a show of optimism for Maria's sake: "I have no doubt that a massive deployment of the territorial army [*Volkssturm*] will close the gap and deflect the threat." His own spirits were again raised by the words of a leader—this time a speech of Himmler's from the summer, which was read out to bolster the morale of the staff at the court:[12]

> [The speech] is still having a tremendous effect on us today, and has influenced me and everyone deeply. He spoke of the virtues of an officer. From that, one realized how un-German we have become. The speech was delivered with an openness not previously seen. The RFSS [Reichsführer SS] showed himself to be a great man with a sensitive heart, unexpectedly practical in matters concerning the troops.

Finally, the situation in Cracow becomes untenable. On January 14 Morgen writes,[13]

> The Russians are at the gates of Cracow. The main defenses have been overrun, because they were manned inadequately, or not at all. Again one has mis-calculated. Again everything has turned out so differently. It's late at night—or early in the morning, whichever. I've had our documents and typewriters packed up and will send them to the Reich today. My suitcase, too. Destination: the local court in Tarnowitz, Upper Silesia, where the Court has a few chambers. We will stay here and await the Russian tanks, to destroy them or be mowed down. I'm very quiet and calm. I don't think about the worst.

The Germans abandon Cracow. Morgen, accustomed to being chauffeured, gets behind the wheel of an unreliable Opel and drives through darkened streets clogged with traffic. He manages to make progress by driving on the sidewalks. After 11 unnerving hours, he eventually makes it to Bielitz, a city south of Auschwitz.[14] Though he hopes to set up a small court in Bielitz, the approaching Russian front forces him to flee again. From Bielitz he makes his way to Teschen (Český Těšín) on the border between Poland and Czechoslovakia. The prospect changes again, and he writes to Maria, "We're having a great time. Good food, a nice warm room. Nothing to do."[15] But the war continues to approach.

From Teschen, Morgen moved to Olmütz, from there to Brünn, and finally to Breslau, where he worked at an SS court until war's end. He then got caught up in a Russian tank offensive and was imprisoned by the Czechs.[16] How he escaped, he never says.

Morgen showed up back in Prien am Chiemsee in September. There he learned that the Americans were looking for him: an American officer, accompanied by Morgen's former colleague Gerhard Wiebeck, had visited Maria Wachter to learn his whereabouts.[17] A few days after his arrival in

Prien, Morgen reported to the Americans in Mannheim and was taken into custody.

The Americans moved Morgen to Dachau, where they were collecting suspected war criminals. He was then transferred to Nuremberg to testify as a witness for the defense of the SS, which was charged with having been a criminal organization.[18] Morgen was then interrogated by the Army Counter-Intelligence Corps from August 1946 until March 1948—by which time his cooperative spirit had worn thin. In April 1947, he complains,[19]

> At this point I have to mention that I've already been in prison for ten months, and that with no explanation I'm being kept in strict solitary confinement, the reason for which is not clear to me; and I feel that under these circumstances I can give no further testimony. I would like first to know what my position is, and whether I am here merely as a witness or someone has charges to make against me.

Morgen was eventually released to the Germans for denazification—a process that extended up to May 1951.[20]

Morgen and his Maria had long wanted to marry. As an SS officer, though, Morgen had needed the permission of the Head Office of Race and Settlement (*Rasse- und Siedlungshauptamt*), which demanded proof that there were no racial, ideological, or health-related obstacles to the match. Here problems arose. Himmler wanted SS officers to marry hardy young women who would bear lots of racially pure Aryan children. But Maria Wachter was a widow, four-and-a-half years older than Morgen.[21] Their marriage was blocked in 1942 on the grounds of their disparity in age.[22]

Desperate to prove Maria's fertility, they had conceived a child—fertility being more important than legitimacy—but she lost the pregnancy after being wounded in an air raid. In an account of his personal circumstances submitted to the SS Judiciary Head Office, Morgen concedes that the prospects for a new pregnancy are not favorable.[23] Even so, the Head Office raised no objections.[24] The Public Health Department in Frankfurt certified Maria's health and ancestry,[25] but permission to marry was still not forthcoming. Morgen recounts this ordeal to one of his CIC interrogators:[26]

> Q. Did you know the RuSHA [Rasse- und Siedlungshauptamt]?
> A. I once had contact with it when I handed in a marriage application and it was rejected. [...]

Q. Why was it rejected? Wasn't it racially valid?
A. It was rejected. I can't tell you why.
Q. I mean, your bride-to-be was German?
A. Yes.
Q. And it was rejected—impossible. [. . .]
A. Yes, it was absolutely crazy. [. . .] A cousin of mine went through the same thing. He was an "old fighter" [for National Socialism], his wife too, and they had to wait over a year—during which they lost National Socialism.

Morgen and Maria had to wait until after the war, and his imprisonment by the Americans, before they could marry. They never had children.

NINETEEN

POSTSCRIPT

What can we make of the case of Konrad Morgen? In what sense was Konrad Morgen a "fanatic for justice"?

Morgen was anything but fanatical about National Socialism. Any contempt he felt for concentration camp prisoners was reserved for the common criminals, not for Jews or Gypsies or homosexuals. When thinking of a possible German defeat, his sympathies went first to his parents and then to his former comrades in the SS Regiment Germania, most of whom were foreigners. There is barely a mention of Hitler in his papers both during and after the war. Thus, Morgen was not much susceptible to racist or nationalist or totalitarian sentiments.

Morgen's sentiments—other than love of his mother and his fiancée—were invested in his professional role as an SS judge, a role in which he immersed himself with a passion. But that role was itself conflicted. On the one hand, an SS judge applied the same body of law as civil and military judges: there was no distinct SS legal code. On the other hand, the SS judge was supposed to apply the civil and military codes in a distinctive manner appropriate to members of the SS. Morgen therefore had a second allegiance not incumbent on other judges applying the same body of law. His second allegiance was to the value system of the SS.

At first, Morgen found a means of reconciling these commitments. By conceiving of crime mainly as a manifestation of bad character he could uphold both the law and SS standards at once. Morgen's fascination with the varieties of bad character therefore suited him to the role of SS judge.

Morgen had a distinctive interpretation of the SS virtues. Sensitivity to criticism of his SS membership, together with enthusiasm for the traditional conception of honor, moved him, at the age of 28, to challenge Karl Julius Speck to a duel over a trivial insult. But he soon arrived at his own, more nuanced conception of honor. The official SS motto was *Meine Ehre heißt Treue*—"For me, honor means loyalty"—but loyalty to what? Except for a few boilerplate sentences, Morgen paid scant loyalty to Party and Führer. Toward Heinrich Himmler, Reichsführer of the SS, he was obedient in the performance of his duties but not personally, and he even stretched the limits of obedience. Yet puzzles remain. How could he still be moved in January 1945 by Himmler's talk of "the virtues of an officer," and how could he characterize the Reichsführer as "a great man with a sensitive heart," given his knowledge of the Erntefest massacre and the "Final Solution"?

Morgen's loyalty was rather to an ideal SS of his own envisioning, an elite corps marked by secular virtues such as honesty and integrity. Morgen remained loyal to that ideal SS even after the war, as he defended the organization while condemning those whom he viewed as traitors to its ideals.

Though not fanatical about the political ideology of the Party or the SS, Morgen belonged to both and was at home in their culture, with all its appalling features. As German forces were ghettoizing, deporting, and shooting Jews in Cracow, he was busy prosecuting embezzlers. When speaking of the war, he spoke as a German soldier in solidarity with the German cause. He enjoyed a daily steam bath and massage in Buchenwald, while underfed prisoners were sleeping on wooden shelves four-high. After viewing the gas chambers of Auschwitz, he could still be shocked by SS men fraternizing with Jewish girls. He condoned hard treatment of subject peoples in the East. He referred to mass execution by shooting as "the old, tried method"—whatever that may have meant. When he returned to Cracow at the end of 1944, he was gratified to hear that his reputation as a hanging judge (*Blutrichter*) had preceded him, striking fear into the hearts of prisoners.[1]

Morgen was certainly a fanatic about his work. He was constantly on the go. The Sauberzweig investigation required trips to Warsaw, Auschwitz, Berlin, Hamburg, the Hague, and Amsterdam.[2] At the end of 1941, he had to rush back and forth between Cracow and Warsaw while juggling multiple cases, several of them for capital crimes.[3] His later investigations in the concentration camps involved travels from Buchenwald to Lublin, Auschwitz, Berlin, the Netherlands, and the Adriatic Littoral.

Nothing dampened Morgen's appetite for work. In December 1944, the war was obviously lost, the prosecution of Grabner had failed, the Buchenwald trial was in adjournment—and Morgen's mind turned to business as usual. After returning from his November vacation, he wrote to his fiancée, "Of course I straightaway applied new energy to investigating. I can't leave it alone."[4] Over the Christmas holidays, he wrote, "I am eager to get back to work."[5] Of course, Morgen would have said that he was a fanatic for his work because it was the work of dispensing justice, for which he was a self-confessed fanatic. The question, then, is what Morgen meant by "justice" when he described himself as a fanatic for it.

The most uncharitable interpretation would be that "justice" for Morgen meant merely rigid adherence to rules and regulations, as if his hostility to corruption was no more than what Himmler articulated in his speech to SS officers at Posen, when he said, "We had the moral right [. . .] to destroy this people [. . . b]ut we have not the right to enrich ourselves with so much as a fur, a watch, a mark, or a cigarette or anything else."[6] The evidence militates strongly against this interpretation. Even in his wartime communications, Morgen manifested a genuinely humane sensibility. His descriptions of the *Appellplatz* and *Steinbruch* at Buchenwald would be fitting texts for the memorials at those sites today, so vividly did they portray the willful cruelty of the SS officers in charge. He invoked the transcendent value of an individual human life in reporting the case of a murdered Jew. We must remind ourselves that these passages were written by a member of the SS for the eyes of his superiors. Morgen's moral indignation was so strong that he was not afraid to voice it in quarters where it was not likely to receive a favorable hearing.

But Morgen's antenna for injustice was tuned only to the criminal variety; social and political injustice were not on his radar. What mattered most to him was ensuring that criminal individuals got what they deserved— criminal individuals being, not just individuals who committed illegal acts, but people who did bad things because they were bad people. He was capable of overlooking the larger political context of the misery before his eyes. Whereas he was much exercised by the way Jews were treated when entering Buchenwald, he had nothing to say about the nationwide pogrom that brought them there. He deplored the concentration camp system not in principle but for its corrupting effects on individuals who went on to commit individual crimes. Even in the case of crime, he was more sensitive to the viciousness of criminals than to the suffering of their victims. His moral sentiments were strong, but their range was narrow. Perhaps he would have been equal to the moral challenges of other times, but for his own times, his moral range was certainly inadequate.

This inadequacy was abetted by Morgen's self-conception as a jurist, which allowed him to indulge in a self-deceptive complacency. When he moved from the Civil to the SS Judiciary, he brought with him the self-satisfaction of being a dispenser of justice, overlooking the nature of the institutions that he served. It never occurred to him that it was impossible to dispense real justice in a radically unjust system. Nor did he consider that as an officer of that system, he was perforce an agent of its injustices, not just of his own principles.

The same can be said of Morgen's relationship to the SS. He was politically naïve and therefore blind to the vicious political role of the SS. He was trying to enforce secular moral purity in an institution dedicated to ideological and racial purity—which was like straightening the pictures in a madhouse. Again, he was content with his own moral equilibrium, though the world around him was morally askew.

Morgen's failures of judgment about that world are clearest in his return to business as usual in 1945. Trying to clean up the SS in July 1943 was one thing; continuing that project in 1945 was quite another, now that he had seen the gas chambers of Auschwitz and the deportations from Budapest.

We credit Morgen's claim that he pursued Eichmann, Höss, and Grabner in order to "do something" about the mass extermination. Given the cases that were on his docket in the summer of 1944, a pouch of gems would not have drawn his attention had it not offered a pretext for arresting the man organizing the transports from Hungary to Auschwitz. As for the prosecution of Grabner, the presiding judge confirmed after the war that its connection to the mass extermination had been confided to him by an outraged Morgen at the time.

Yet even if Morgen's aim in these cases was to do something about the "Final Solution," the question remains: What exactly did he think was wrong with it? The question itself sounds absurd. What was wrong with the "Final Solution"? That's obvious, one thinks, and Morgen, having witnessed it first-hand, could not have helped but know. From the perspective of moral theory, however, the answer is not at all obvious. For from that perspective, the question asks how the immorality of the "Final Solution" can be adequately grasped and expressed.

The philosopher Gilbert Harman has written, "it sounds odd to say that Hitler should not have ordered the extermination of the Jews, that it was wrong of him to have done so. That sounds somehow 'too weak' a thing to say."[7] Harman isn't denying that genocide is immoral; he is asserting that some ways of talking about its immorality are inadequate.[8] Suppose someone were to say, "The gassing of six million Jews was a violation of their rights." Of course it *was* a violation of their rights. Surely, though, a violation of rights is not the half of it: the language of rights and wrongs is too legalistic. Something much more profound, more profoundly immoral, was underway at Auschwitz-Birkenau.

Greater insight into that immorality can be found, we think, in Hannah Arendt's remarks on the death sentence handed down to Adolf Eichmann.

She writes, "Because he had been implicated and had played a central role in an enterprise whose open purpose was to eliminate forever certain 'races' from the surface of the earth, he had to be eliminated."[9] She then addresses Eichmann himself:[10]

> [...] just as you supported and carried out a policy of not wanting to share the earth with the Jewish people and the people of a number of other nations—as though you and your superiors had any right to determine who should and who should not inhabit the world—we find that no one, that is, no member of the human race, can be expected to want to share the earth with you.

This notion of being unwilling to share the earth with other people—of placing oneself above the human condition of sociality, above the condition of being a person among other persons—comes a bit closer to expressing the immorality of the "Final Solution" than mere talk of violated rights. The "Final Solution" was not just the most colossal wrong in modern history; it was the most colossal instance of inhumanity. In the term coined for the Nuremberg Tribunal, it was a crime against humanity, because it was a crime against the fellowship of human beings as sharers of one world.

Morgen sometimes came close to an appropriate response, as when he says, in looking back on the Erntefest massacre, "I considered myself obligated as a human being to look into this monstrosity." But with his head down and his nose to the grindstone, he was usually too deeply embedded in his professional identity to take the larger view. He was finally forced out of that perspective by seeing the machinery of industrialized mass murder, and he then considered fleeing from the whole business. Instead he chose to resume his role as an SS judge and, with the defective tools it afforded him, to subvert the system from within—a choice that led to a dead-end at the Weimar trials, whereupon Morgen returned to his regular job.

Still, we cannot conclude that flight would have been a better course for Morgen than remaining in his position, equivocal though it was. Whether he should have stayed on the train to Switzerland rather than return to prosecute individual killings in the midst of mass murder—whether he should instead have taken arms against that sea of criminality—these are questions on which we hesitate to second-guess him. He was cognizant, however imperfectly, of facing a moral catastrophe, and he tried to do something about it—which is far more than can be said for other fanatics at the time.

What can students of moral and legal theory learn from the case of Konrad Morgen? To begin with, we can learn that the moral psychology of people living through mass atrocities such as the Holocaust cannot be dissected with the blunt concepts of "good" and "evil." Konrad Morgen was neither black nor white, but grey. He endorsed, and never rebelled against, the ethos of the Nazi SS, and his conscience slept through the news of pogroms and executions, to be fully awakened only by murder on an industrial scale. Yet he showed genuine compassion for the Jewish inmates of Buchenwald and recognized their right to life. Despite his allegiance to the SS, he was a thorn in the side of its hierarchy, and in the end, he used his powers against some of the foremost perpetrators, at considerable risk to himself. Morgen was no saint, not by a long shot, but neither was he evil. He was, as we have said, a study in moral complexity.

Many of Morgen's failings were due to uncritically accepting distorted characterizations of what lay before his eyes—the characterization of oppression as pacification, liquidation as euthanasia or reprisal, maltreatment and murder as medical research. His case illustrates the inadequacy of upholding values or applying principles without exercising skepticism about received terms for stating the facts. As the philosopher Barbara Herman has argued, even Kant's Categorical Imperative cannot properly guide our choices unless we first describe them in morally relevant terms.[11]

Morgen's case also stands as a warning against shallow "virtue ethics." Morgen was even more fanatical about virtue than about justice. He judged actions primarily by what they said about the agent's character and attitudes. Insofar as he misjudged some actions, however, the reason was not that he attributed them to the wrong traits of character; it was rather that his catalogue of character traits was impoverished. Aristotle's virtue ethics was grounded in eudaimonism, his theory of living well, which was grounded in his teleology, the view that there is a way that we humans are meant to live. The Aristotelian virtues are traits whose exercise makes for the full realization of human nature in a flourishing human life. The SS conception of virtue bore no relation to human flourishing: it was designed to make SS men serviceable instruments of the state. Morgen therefore ended up judging by defective standards. An ethic of virtue can be a dangerous thing if not grounded in an understanding of the role that virtue must play in the realization of human potential considered universally, not as the exclusive property of a particular group. The National Socialist state interpreted morality as a parochial ideological enterprise.

This parochial morality had a distorting effect on the law, since National Socialist legal theorists favored a marriage of the two. Moralizing rhetoric concealed the extent to which the regime turned law into a means of authoritarian political control and, eventually, terror and murder.

Morgen's professional conduct bore the imprint of these developments. The conversion of criminal law into an instrument of unbridled deterrence, the replacement of the principle *nulla poena sine lege* by the principle *nullum crimen sine poena*—such transformations Morgen willingly accepted and incorporated into his practice. The zealous indignation that imbues his reflections on the "corruption criminal" is in line with the moralization of law in National Socialist legal theory.

Yet Morgen's conscience was not completely silenced by ideology. His reports about Buchenwald express his awareness that justice and morality are tied to respect for humanity as such. He tried to use the rule of law, insofar as it was still available in the National Socialist system, to live up to what he once called the "natural sense of justice." But when the Weimar trials failed, and the prospect of a special court to prosecute the greatest crimes evaporated, he should have realized that the National Socialist state was not one in which universal norms could be enforced.

In his book *Law's Empire* the legal scholar Ronald Dworkin imagines an ideal judge, whom he dubs Hercules, and his Nazi-era counterpart, "Judge Siegfried," both equipped to interpret the law as Dworkin recommends, by "assum[ing], so far as this is possible, that the law is structured by a coherent set of principles about justice and fairness and procedural due process," principles that can guide the application of statutes and precedent to novel cases. Although Siegfried aims to follow this prescription, Dworkin concedes that it is impossible to follow under National Socialist law, which is "too wicked" to accommodate interpretation in light of moral principles.[12] Thus Dworkin recommends that "Siegfried should simply ignore legislation and precedent altogether, if he can get away with it, or otherwise do the best he can to limit injustice through whatever means available to him."[13] Judge Siegfried, Dworkin argues, should remedy the overall injustice of the Nazi system by doing "all in his power—even lie about the law if this could help."[14]

Morgen did not follow this prescription. He fell much further from the moral ideal than Dworkin's Siegfried. But Morgen's case provides us with a more realistic picture of adjudication under distorted legal conditions. We cannot altogether dismiss Morgen's statement that as a judge, he had to work with the law as he found it. To "lie about the law," disregarding rules and precedents altogether so as to follow morality alone, would have tested Dworkin's caveat to Siegfried—"if he can get away with it"—more seriously than Morgen's activities already did.

Tightening the connection between law and morality has been a common prescription for the ills of the National Socialist legal system. If morality and justice form an integral part of law, so the argument goes, such deterioration in the law will not be possible. The concept of legal validity has often be tied so closely to moral criteria that certain norms of National Socialist law are no longer accorded the title of valid law.

Morgen's case warns us to be cautious here. The National Socialist strategy of claiming that law, morality, and politics form a unity was directed at undermining morality's critical function of providing grounds for reforming the law and, if necessary, resisting it. The claim that legal imperatives are also ethical imperatives can only strengthen the power of an unjust regime, since it is an attempt to gain control of the individual's deepest personal convictions.

Morality should of course be the ultimate standard for legal systems. But maintaining separation between the normative spheres of law and morality preserves the corrective function of moral insight. Instead of promoting a moralization of law, we should rather require the law to meet formal conditions such as publicity, transparency, and non-arbitrariness. The mere requirement to publicize legal orders might already have prevented the worst excesses of the National Socialist regime.

We would be pleased if this book discouraged at least some of our colleagues from using the Holocaust as a convenient source of toy examples of immorality. Far better to look closely at the moral failings of real people—the capricious cruelty of a Commandant Koch, the uncritical conscientiousness of a Norbert Pohl or a Kurt Mittelstädt, the depravity of an Oskar Dirlewanger—or the flawed conscience of a Konrad Morgen.

Figure 1 Konrad Morgen. Estate of Konrad Morgen, courtesy of Fritz Bauer Institut

APPENDIX 1: SAMPLE DOCUMENTS

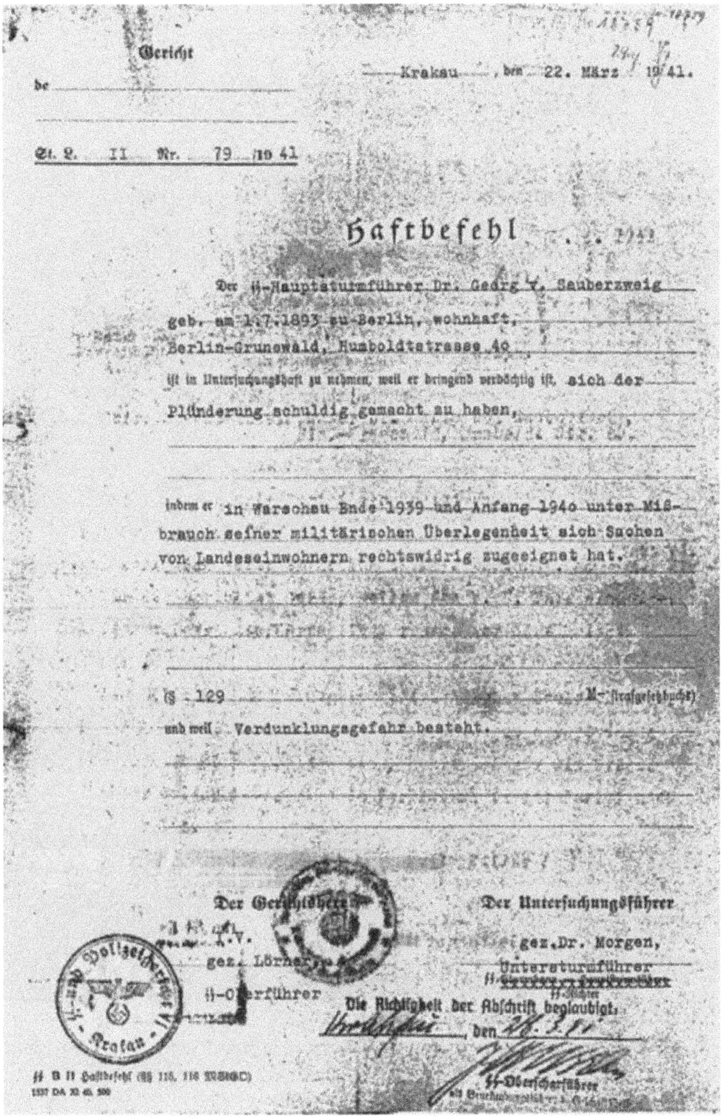

Gericht

Krakau, den 22. März 1941.

St. L. II Nr. 79 /1941

Haftbefehl

Der SS-Hauptsturmführer Dr. Georg v. Sauberzweig

geb. am 1.7.1893 zu Berlin, wohnhaft,

Berlin-Grunewald, Humboldtstrasse 40

ist in Untersuchungshaft zu nehmen, weil er dringend verdächtig ist, sich der Plünderung schuldig gemacht zu haben,

indem er in Warschau Ende 1939 und Anfang 1940 unter Mißbrauch seiner militärischen Überlegenheit sich Sachen von Landeseinwohnern rechtswidrig zugeeignet hat.

(§ 129 M-Strafgesetzbuchs)

und weil Verdunklungsgefahr besteht.

Der Gerichtsherr

i.V.

gez. Lörner

SS-Oberführer

Der Untersuchungsführer

gez. Dr. Morgen,

Untersturmführer

Die Richtigkeit der Abschrift beglaubigt.

den 28.3.41

SS-Oberscharführer

SS B II Haftbefehl (§§ 115, 116 MStGO)

Figure 1.1. *Arrest warrant (Haftbefehl) for Georg von Sauberzweig, signed by Morgen. Courtesy of Bundesarchiv Berlin-Lichterfelde*

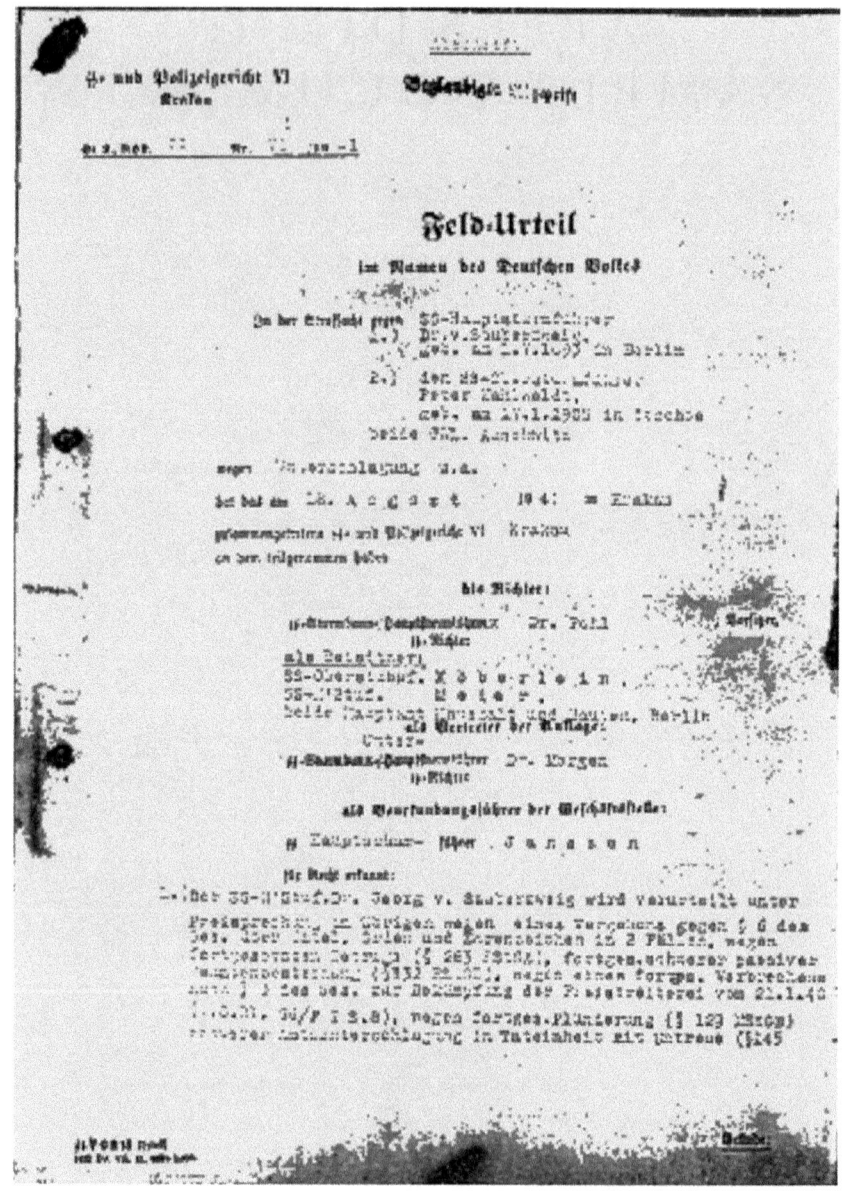

Figure 1.2. Judgment against Sauberzweig. Courtesy of Bundesarchiv Berlin-Lichterfelde

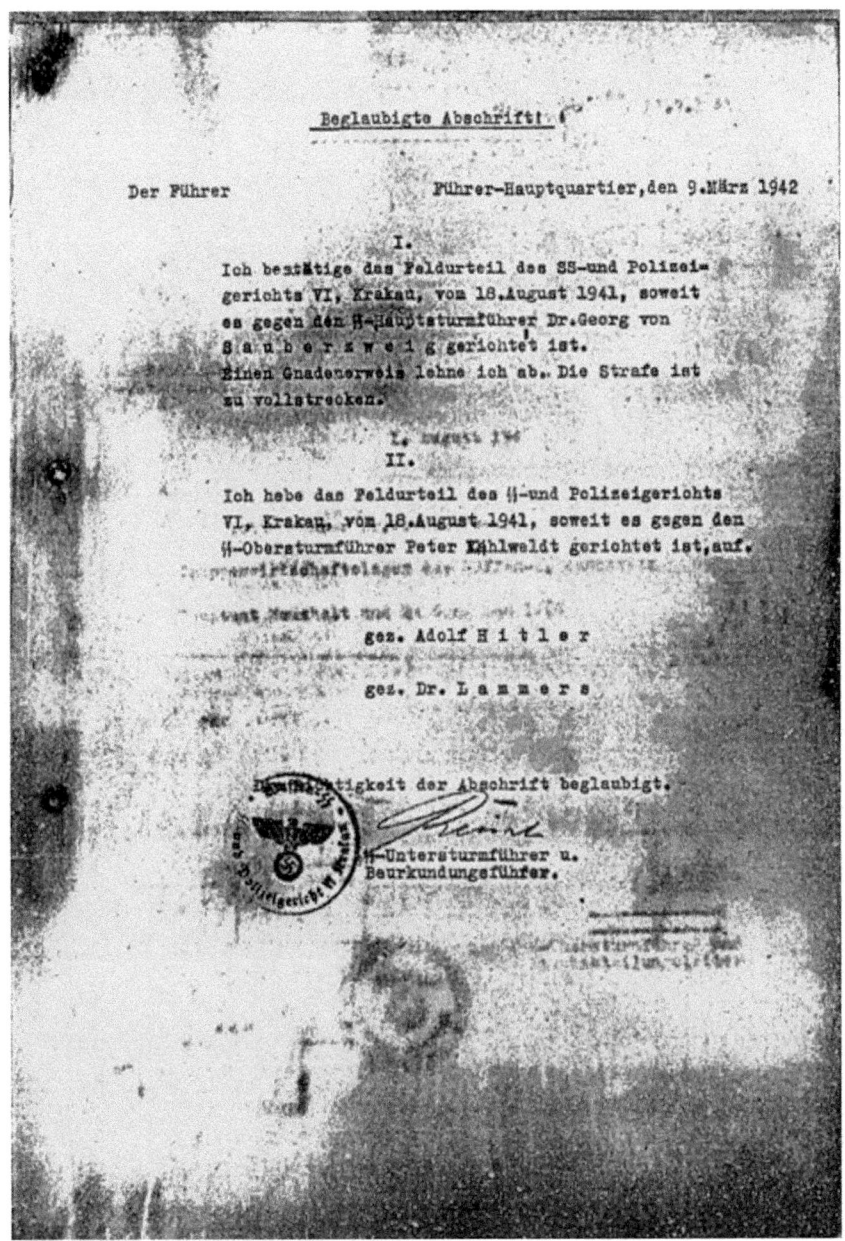

Figure 1.3. Hitler's rejection of Sauberzweig's appeal. Courtesy of Bundesarchiv Berlin-Lichterfelde

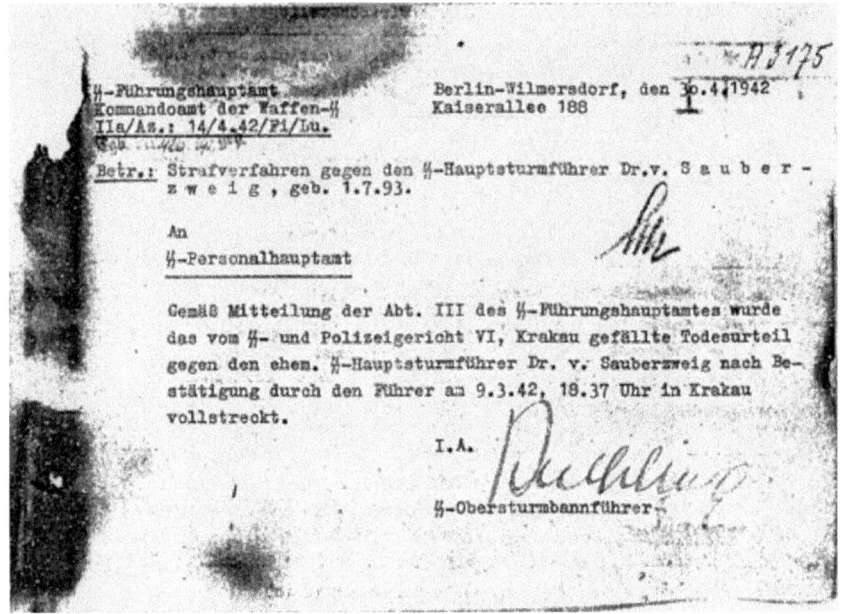

Figure 1.4. Confirmation of Sauberzweig's execution. Courtesy of Bundesarchiv Berlin-Lichterfelde

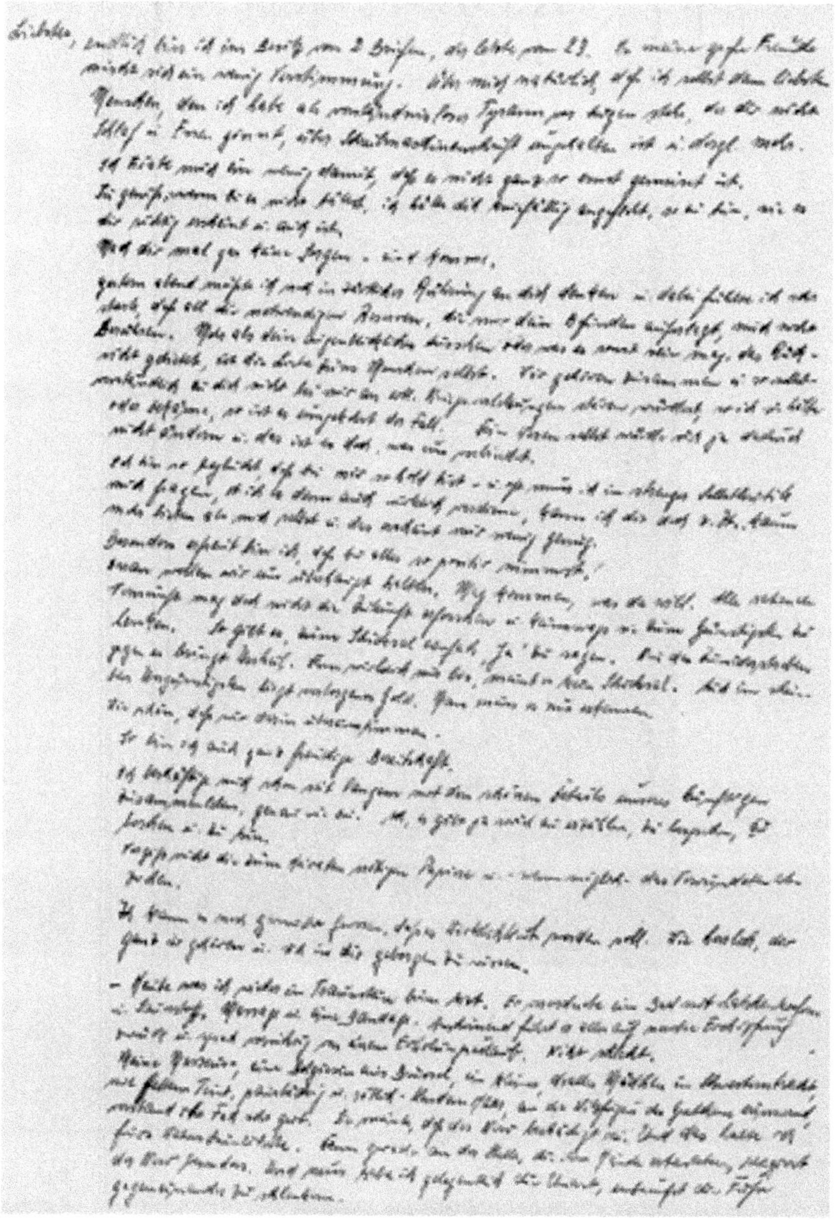

Figure 1.5.   Letter from Morgen to Maria Wachter. Estate of Konrad Morgen, courtesy of the Fritz Bauer Institut

APPENDIX 2: PHOTOS

Figure 2.1. Konrad Morgen 1938. Estate of Konrad Morgen, courtesy of the Fritz Bauer Institut

Figure 2.2.   Konrad Morgen in his SS uniform. Estate of Konrad Morgen, courtesy of the Fritz Bauer Institut

Figure 2.3. Karl Otto Koch. Courtesy of the US National Archives

Figure 2.4.   Karl and Ilse Koch with their son, at Buchwald. Corbis Images

Figure 2.5.   Odilo Globocnik

Figure 2.6. Hermann Fegelein. Courtesy of Yad Vashem

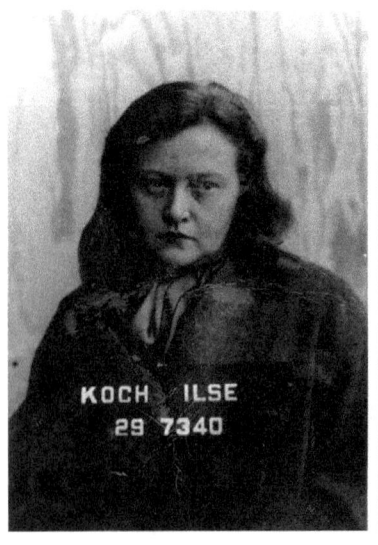
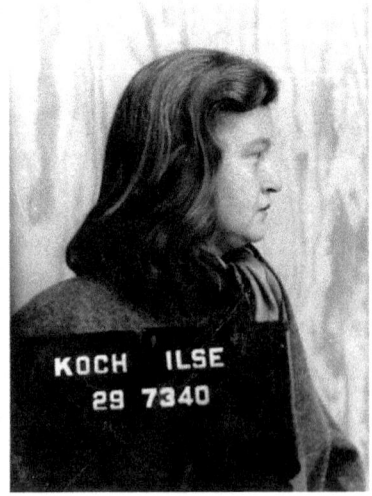

Figure 2.7. Ilse Koch. Courtesy of Yad Vashem

Figure 2.8.   Waldemar Hoven. Courtesy of Yad Vashem

Figure 2.9.   Christian Wirth. Courtesy of Yad Vashem

Figure 2.10. Jaroslawa Mirowska. Private collection

NOTES

Preface

1. The execution of Karl Otto Koch, former commandant of Buchenwald, is well documented. The execution of Hermann Florstedt, former commandant of Majdanek, is disputed by a member of his family (Lindner (1997)).
2. The most notable exception is the account Morgen gave at Nuremberg about how he discovered the "Final Solution." We discuss this case in Chapter 12.

1 Introduction

1. **KMF**, pp. 5557–70.
2. A kapo was a prisoner functionary assigned by the SS to supervise other prisoners or to carry out other tasks. The etymology of the term is disputed.
3. See Bein (1990).
4. Herzl (2004).
5. For a detailed study of the impact of this law see Mommsen (1966).
6. See Koellreutter (1938), p. 19; Huber (1939), pp. 55–6.
7. Best (1936), p. 126. Our translation. Quoted also by Herbert (2001), p. 164.
8. Cesarani (2004), p. 71.
9. Browning (2004), pp. 28–35.
10. Ibid., p. 26.
11. Ibid., p. 111.
12. Ibid., p. 45.
13. Ibid., p. 27.
14. Ibid., pp. 54–68. As Browning (2004) puts it, "While the Nazis never wanted openly to admit it and struggled against such a conclusion for months, it turned out that, at least temporarily, consolidating Lebensraum in the incorporated territories and solving the Jewish question were not complementary but competing goals" (p. 43).
15. Ibid., pp. 175–8.
16. Ibid., pp. 111–68.
17. Ibid., p. 81.
18. Ibid., p. 69.
19. Ibid.
20. Ibid., pp. 69–70. Translation slightly modified for clarity. See also the remark of a subordinate of Hans Frank, Governor General of unincorporated

Poland, to which the Jews were to be deported: "In the end one cannot simply starve them to death" (ibid., p. 71).

21. Ibid., p. 102.
22. Ibid., p. 89.
23. Ibid., p. 104.
24. Ibid., p. 253.
25. Ibid., p. 110.
26. Dieckmann (2000), p. 247. Dieckmann writes, "The murder of the Jewish men was seen as a way of executing the order to 'liquidate' the Soviet leadership stratum" (p. 249). See Browning (2004), p. 259: "As in preinvasion memoranda and plans, German officials in the field hid ideological bias behind practical rationalizations, mostly by presenting anti-Jewish measures as part of a wider policy of 'pacifying' the occupied area." See also p. 110: both Soviet commissars and Soviet Jews "would have to be eliminated" because "ultimately they were perceived as one."
27. Browning (2004), p. 261.
28. Ibid., p. 353: "Bach-Zelewski claimed to have told a shaken Himmler after the latter had witnessed a relatively small execution in Minsk: 'Look at the eyes of the men in this commando, how deeply shaken they are! These men are finished for the rest of their lives. What kind of followers are we training here? Either neurotics or savages!'" Bach-Zelewski's postwar testimony claimed that Himmler, having seen the execution in Minsk, asked *Einsatzgruppe* B commander Arthur Nebe to consider other methods of killing (ibid., p. 354).
29. Ibid., p. 321.
30. Friedlander (1995), p. 87. The term "euthanasia" is in quotation marks because showing mercy to the victims was not in practice the regulating goal of the program.
31. Ibid., p. 62.
32. Ibid., chapter 13, "Killing Handicapped Jews."
33. Ibid., table 5.3, p. 109.
34. Ibid., pp. 142ff.
35. Ibid., p. 144.
36. Ibid., p. 297.
37. These centers were preceded in operation only by Chelmno, which used gas vans of a kind that had been developed for the *Einsatzgruppen* and were operated by an officer who had used such vans to kill the handicapped in Poland. See Friedlander (1995), p. 286; see also p. 139.
38. Ibid., pp. 297ff., 237–45.
39. Ibid., p. 300: "First, subterfuge was used to fool the victims upon arrival with the appearance of normality. In the euthanasia centers, physicians and nurses checking medical files made the killing center look like a regular hospital, while in the camps of Operation Reinhard, the trappings of the reception area

and the welcoming speech by a staff member made the killing center look like a labor camp. The victims were told in both places that they had to take showers for hygienic reasons, and the gas chambers were disguised as shower rooms, while the belongings of the victims were carefully collected and registered to maintain the illusion of normality. [. . .] Second, in both the Reich and the East, the victims were crowded into the gas chamber, and their corpses were burned immediately after they had been killed."

40. The other exception, beside Auschwitz-Birkenau, was Majdanek.

2 The SS Man

1. Morgen narrates this episode in **KMP**, p. 6674. See also Morgen's handwritten letter about his surrender in **F65**. Morgen's detention is confirmed by CIC Seventh Army Detention Report, **SKV** EWL 903/3.
2. This material is preserved in Nuremberg document **NO-2366**.
3. **KMI** 30.8.46, pp. 1–2.
4. **KMB**, p. 110.
5. **KMI** 4.9.46, pp. 2–3.
6. **PKM**, p. 1.
7. Koehl (1983), p. 79.
8. Kershaw (1998), p. 479.
9. Affidavit of Wilhem Felgenauer dated January 2, 1948, **SKV** EWL 903/3. Note, however, that Felgenauer himself avoided joining the SS.
10. Longerich (2008), pp. 265–395; see also Hambrock (2009).
11. The Teutonic Order (*Deutscher Ritterorden*) played a crucial role in the colonization of Eastern Prussia, parts of Poland, Latvia, and Lithuania. For Himmler's appeal to the *Deutscher Ritterorden* and other historical ideals, see Reinicke (2003), pp. 73–8, 93–105.
12. Buchheim (1965), p. 190.
13. See Schulte (2009); see also Smelser and Syring (2003).
14. See Kogon (2006), esp. ch. 22.
15. See Wildt (2009).
16. Schmitt (1934), p. 327.
17. See Huber (1939), pp. 30–7, 216–17.
18. See Huber (1939), pp. 30–7, 216–17.
19. **KMI** 30.8.46, p. 5. See also **KMP**, p. 6671.
20. **KMI** 4.9.46, pp. 2–3. Morgen says that this incident prevented him from getting employment in Frankfurt, so that he had to go to Stettin. That Morgen's refusal to vote caused trouble with the Nazi Party is confirmed by a letter to Morgen from the local Party leader demanding that Morgen inform the Party where he had voted, because his vote could not be found in the records of the local office (letter of Fleischer to Morgen dated August 28, 1934 **SKV** EWL 903/3).

21. **SKV**, affidavit of Wilhelm Müller, Frankfurt am Main, 28 February, 1948.
22. **KMB**, p. 105.
23. **KMP**, p. 6671 (English original).
24. Protocol of the public session of the civilian court handling denazification, June 24, 1948 (**SKV**, EWL 903/3, J/75/5326).
25. Morgen's only known reaction to the Röhm putsch can be found in a short statement at his 1948 denazification trial. In response to a question about the Röhm affair, Morgen says that members of the SS were told about the "voluptuous life" of the SA leadership, as well as the fact that Röhm was a homosexual. (Homosexuality was a crime at the time.) Morgen adds, mistakenly, that Röhm was sentenced and shot by a court martial (*Standgericht*). In defense of this statement, he says "that he had no reason for doubt because he heard it from people he trusted" (protocol of the public session of the civilian court handling denazification, June 24, 1948, J/75/5326, in **SKV**, EWL 903/3).
26. Gruchmann (1988), p. 303. See also Schmerbach (2008).
27. Roland Freisler, State Secretary in the Ministry of Justice and later president of the Volksgerichtshof, was actively engaged in shaping the educational program in Jüterbog.
28. **HAW**(3), p. 9.
29. Schmerbach quotes the recollection of one participant: "We listened calmly and patiently to the lectures and exercises. In the discussion we were cautious: no open dissent; in especially critical cases, frosty silence." Schmerbach (2008), 140.
30. **HAW-3**, p. 136. Morgen's comment on his evaluation in the camp Jüterbog; letter of Morgen to the Reich Minister of Justice, April 8, 1938.
31. **PKM**, letter dated 8.3.1938 and accompanying documents.
32. **KMI** 30.8.46, pp. 3–5. Morgen retells this story in his affidavit of 28.1.47, pp. 1–2. Morgen's story is confirmed by documents in his personnel file at the superior provincial court in Frankfurt am Main. See **HAW**(3), pp. 233–41, letter of the President of the Superior Provincial Court Stettin from April 25, 1939, informing Morgen that the court in Stettin will recommend his dismissal from the judiciary to the Reich Ministry of Justice. Morgen protested in a letter to the Minister of Justice on May 9, 1939, **HAW**(3), pp. 243–51. Morgen was dismissed from the court in Stettin and lost his status as an official of the Reich, but he was not completely dismissed from the judiciary. In order to return to service, he would have had to start over with temporary positions replacing judges who were on leave for combat training. Morgen was offered such a position in Königsberg in August 1939, but he declined it because he had meanwhile contracted to work for the German Labor Front for at least one year. See **HAW**(3), pp. 264–6.
33. See Morgen's curriculum vitae and the protocol of the public session of the civilian court handling denazification, June 24, 1948, J/75/5326 (**SKV** EWL 903/3).

34. **KMN**, letter of 30.10.1939.
35. **SKV** EWL 903/3; also contained in KMN.

3   The SS Judiciary

1. The creation of the SS Judiciary on October 17, 1939 was announced in the *Reichsgesetzblatt* October 30, 1939 (RGBl 1939, I, Nr 214, p. 2107). See Vieregge (2002), appendix, p. 247.
2. Early in the invasion of Poland, members of the *Wehrmacht* lodged complaints about the atrocities committed by SS units. These complaints were based, not on moral grounds, but rather on grounds that these activities would adversely affect the discipline of the troops. See "Notes of Eastern Territories Commander, Johannes Blaskowitz," Klee, Dressen, and Riess (eds.) (1991), pp. 4–5. See also Wette (2006), pp. 101ff. The question whether the SS Judiciary was established to prevent military prosecutions of the Waffen-SS was raised at the IMT trial in Nuremberg, in connection with the prosecution's indictment of the SS as a criminal organization. See **IMT** vol. XX, testimony of Günther Reinecke, p. 429.
3. Though there were plans for a specific codification of SS law, they were never put into practice. See Vieregge (2002), pp. 81–5.
4. An article on the education of young SS men, published in the regular memoranda of the Head Office of the SS Judiciary, emphasizes that education within the SS has to be "tackled from the ethical side." The text states, "The SS man must not be educated in such a way that he follows orders merely out of fear of punishment, but in a way that he gradually comes to the point of fulfilling his duties out of a voluntary commitment resting on a deep conviction." See "Zur Erziehung und Belehrung von SS-Rekruten," **MHG**, Band II, Heft 3, 1942, p. 85.
5. See Vieregge (2002), pp. 92–4.
6. §92 of the military penal code (§92 MStGB) states, "(1) Whoever does not follow an order in official matters [Dienstsachen] and who thereby intentionally or by negligence causes either a considerable disadvantage, or a danger to human life, or a significant danger to the property of others, or a danger to the security of the Reich or the vigor or training of the military troops, will be punished by severe detention (not less than a week) or imprisonment or fortress detention [Festungshaft] of up to ten years. (2) If the deed is committed in military combat or constitutes an especially grave case, it can be punished by either the death penalty or lifelong or temporary arrest." For the German original see Vieregge (2002), p. 96, n. 162.
7. The law for ordinary citizens was §2 of the "Gesetz zum Schutz des deutschen Blutes und der deutschen Ehre"; the punishment was specified in §5.
8. Himmler reiterated this order in a memo to Friedrich-Wilhelm Krüger dated June 30, 1942, in Heiber (ed.) (1970), document 120. Here Himmler explicitly

says that violations are punishable as military disobedience. Morgen says the same at **KMI** 15.10.47, pp. 5–6. On Himmler's order see also Vieregge (2002), pp. 107–9.

9. Franz Breithaupt, "An die Führer der SS und Polizei," **MHG**, Band II, Heft 3, 1942, p. 73. Franz Breithaupt was Chief of the SS Judiciary Head Office from 1942 until 1945. According to a directive of Himmler from August 1, 1942, the chief of the SS Judiciary, who was also proxy to Himmler, had to be a military person, not a jurist. See Vieregge (2002), pp. 41ff.; Wegner (2010), p. 319.

10. NS7/13 "Bericht über die Dienstbesprechung der Chefs der SS- und Polizeigerichte am 7. Mai 1943 in München," Bl. 13–21, Bl. 14.

11. Weingartner (1983), p. 280.

12. This is confirmed by Günther Reinecke in his witness testimony at the International Military Tribunal trial in Nuremberg. Reinecke states, "Neither I nor the other SS judges had special training at special schools. The SS judges came from positions in the legal profession and were before the war high-ranking legal personalities, public prosecutors or lawyers, or some of them were transferred during the war from the courts of the Wehrmacht to courts of the SS." **IMT** XX, p. 416.

13. **KMI** 15.10.47, pp. 5–6.

4 Criminals and Spies

1. See Schenk (2010).

2. Ibid., pp. 144, 53, 77, 136.

3. **KMI** 30.08.46, pp. 6–7.

4. **KMI** 30.08.46, p. 7. See also **KMI** first affidavit of 28.1.47, pp. 3–4.

5. **PGS**. These documents are reproduced in Appendix 1.

6. See **KMI** 30.8.46, p. 8. According to Oswald Pohl's defense attorney, Pohl refused to petition for a pardon of Sauberzweig; he then issued an order to "administrative leaders [. . .] to tell them to be absolutely clean"; and the Hauptamt SS-Gericht used this order "as exemplary proof for the support of the SS justice in the Main Office SS court" (**KMP** 6703–4, English original).

7. **NO-2366**, letter from Morgen to Hinderfeld dated March 27, 1942, p. 3; and NS7/318, Pohl's letter to Scharfe dated January 22, 1942, p. 12.

8. **NO-2366**, memo from Norbert Pohl to Martin Tondock dated Krakau, April 21, 1941, p. 1 (also in **NS19/3878**). In Morgen's later summary of the case, he says in the course of investigating Sauberzweig that he noticed that Sauberzweig and Fegelein addressed each other as "du" (**NO-2366**, Morgen memo to Tondock dated September 6, 1941, p. 3).

9. Morgen's postwar testimony about this case in **KMI** 30.8.46, pp. 13ff. is confirmed by memos and letters in **NO-2366**.

10. Riess (2003), pp. 160–72. For the history of the *Hauptreitschule München* see Bahro (2007).
11. O'Donnell (1978), p. 186.
12. Kershaw (2000), p. 816. O'Donnell (1978), pp. 180ff., attempts to reconstruct the circumstances of Fegelein's death.
13. These events are documented in **NS19**/3878 by memos from the Gestapo, including an inventory of goods found in the *Hauptreitschule*; a letter from Fegelein to Himmler dated 14.3.1940; a letter from Himmler to Heydrich dated March 1940 (day illegible); and a *Schlussbericht* from the Security Service dated April 9, 1940.
14. **NS19**/3878, Morgen report to the SS Judiciary Head Office dated [day illegible] March 1941, pp. 3ff.
15. Morgen's colleague SS Judge Martin Tondock reported to Himmler that Fegelein and other SS officers were suspected of having sexual relations with Polish women. He cited the claim of Fegelein's Polish mistress, Genoveva Raczkowska, that when she became pregnant, Fegelein forced her to have an abortion. **PHF**, letter from Tondock to Himmler dated May 21, 1941, p. 15; also in **NS19**/3878, p. 15, letter from Tondock to Himmler dated 21 May 1941; also **KMI** 30.8.46, pp. 14–15.
16. **NO-2366**, memo from Morgen to Tondock dated September 6, 1941, pp. 3–4.
17. **KMI** 30.8.46, p. 15.
18. **NO-2366**, memo dated Krakau, April 21, 1941, p. 2.
19. **KMI** 30.08.46, p. 14. See also **NO-2366**, Pohl's letter to Scharfe, dated September 8, 1941.
20. **NS19**/3878, letter from Himmler to Tondock, dated May 19, 1941, p. 1.
21. See **NS19**/3878, letter from Himmler to Tondock, dated May 19, 1941, p. 2. See also Tondock's telegram to Himmler, dated 5.8.1941, asking for clarification of this order.
22. **KMI** 30.8.46, p. 14.
23. **NO-2366**, memo from Morgen to Tondock dated September 6, 1941; and record, dated Krakau, September 8, 1941, of conversation between Morgen and Tondock on September 7, 1941. According to Morgen's postwar account (**KMI** 30.8.46, p. 16), he had been ordered by Himmler to drop the case, but the SS Judiciary Head Office demurred. They said to Morgen, "Of course, this won't go as Herr Himmler thinks"; and to Himmler, "It goes without saying that the matter has to be investigated."
24. **NO-2366**, record, dated Krakau, September 8, 1941, of conversation between Morgen and Tondock on September 7, 1941, pp. 1–2.
25. **NO-2366**, record, dated Krakau, September 8, 1941, of conversation between Morgen and Tondock on September 7, 1941, p. 3.
26. **NO-2366**, record, dated Krakau, September 8, 1941, of conversation between Morgen and Tondock on September 7, 1941, p. 4.

27. **NO-2366**, record, dated Krakau, September 8, 1941, of conversation between Morgen and Tondock on September 7, 1941, p. 5.
28. **NS19/3878**, memo from Tondock to Himmler dated 16.9.1941.
29. **KMI** 30.8.46, p. 17.
30. **KMI** 30.8.46, p. 17.
31. **NO-2366**, letter of Pohl to Scharfe, dated September 8, 1941, p. 1.
32. This threat is also mentioned by Morgen in **KMI** 30.8.46, p. 15.
33. **NO-2366**, letter of Pohl to Scharfc, dated September 8, 1941, p. 4. See also a letter to Scharfe from Morgen's colleague Martin Tondock complaining that Horst Bender, Himmler's liaison to the SS Judiciary Head Office, was trying to separate the Fegelein case from the others, presumably so as to accord him special treatment (**NS19/3878**, letter of Tondock to Scharfe dated October 17, 1941).
34. **KS**, p. 4. The theme of this letter is the need to preserve the perceived independence of the SS Judiciary. Among the threats to that independence, according to the writer, are suspicions of favoritism that might arise from the dilatory enforcement of an order by Himmler to demote Morgen for the mishandling of a case.
35. Kogon (2006), p. 288.
36. **KMN**, letter to Maria Wachter, December 13, 1944.

5 The Criminal Character

1. Questions of legal theory discussed in this chapter are raised again in the Postscript.
2. The commission was founded in 1933 by an order of Hitler with the assignment to draft a new criminal law "according to the ideas and needs of the new state." See Hartl (2000).
3. *Das kommende deutsche Strafrecht* (1935) and (1936).
4. Gruchmann (1988), pp. 821, 822. See also Hartl (2000), p. 277.
5. The original formulation of §2 in the German Penal Code (*Strafgesetzbuch für das Deutsche Reich*) of 1871 is: "Eine Handlung kann nur dann mit einer Strafe belegt werden, wenn diese Strafe gesetzlich bestimmt war, bevor die Handlung begangen war," <http://de.wikisource.org/wiki/Strafgesetzbuch_für_das_Deutsche_Reich_(1871)#.C2.A7_1>. In the current version of the German Penal Code (based on the *Strafgesetzbuch* of 1871) the principle *nulla poena sine lege* is formulated in §1 in the following way: "Eine Tat kann nur bestraft werden, wenn die Strafbarkeit gesetzlich bestimmt war, bevor die Tat begangen wurde," <http://www.gesetze-im-internet.de/bundesrecht/stgb/gesamt.pdf>.
6. See Freisler (1935), p. 22. See also Gleispach (1936), p. 1070, Dahm (1934a), p. 92. The denomination of the principle *nulla poena sine lege* as the "Magna Carta of the criminal" is due to the fact that the historical source of this

principle is article 39 of the English Magna Carta of 1215. See Mezger (1938), p. 29.

7. Schäfer (1935), p. 202.
8. Ibid., p. 204.
9. Ibid., pp. 213–14. The amendment was published in the *Reichsgesetzblatt* RGBL. I (1935), p. 839.
10. Siegert (1934), p. 380.
11. As the theorist Edmund Mezger (1938) explained, "The sole justification of penalty is that it is an indispensable means to sustain the *volks*-community," p. 135.
12. *National Socialist Guidelines for a new German Criminal Law*, edited by the Reich Legal Office of the Nazi Party, declared that "National Socialist criminal law must be based on the duty of loyalty to the *volks*-community," p. 12.
13. The notion of a *Volksschädling* also had a more specific definition referring, for example, to looters who exploited the conditions of war and weakened the resistance of the *Volk*.
14. Dahm (1934a), p. 89.
15. On the moralization of law, see Sauer (1934).
16. Freisler (1938), p. 56.
17. "[T]here can be no doubt that the National Socialist idea of a *volks*-community is inseparably bound up with the idea of authoritarian leadership. In the political leadership, especially in the Führer, the *Volk* finds its true representative, which constitutes the basis of the authority of the Führer and the state." Dahm (1934a), p. 90.
18. See Dahm (1934a), pp. 89–92.
19. See Dahm (1934b), pp. 827–31; see also Hartl (2000), pp. 116–26.
20. Freisler (1935), p. 22.
21. Freisler (1935), p. 22.
22. Krug (1935), p. 99; Freisler (1935), pp. 34, 35.
23. Sauer (1934), p. 188. A related development was the embrace of honor-punishment. See Dahm (1934b), p. 826. Friedrich Schaffstein (1934) argued that whereas in the liberal state, with its value-relativism, honor-punishment made no sense because the concept of honor had no clear meaning, "the National Socialist unity of legal and ethical evaluation" gave the concept of honor a clear meaning that could be attached to honor-punishment (p. 279).
24. Mezger (1936), p. 29.
25. Mezger (1938), p. 135. Nazi legal theorists later changed their minds about character-based adjudication. An example is Georg Dahm, a professor of criminal law at the University of Kiel. In an essay in 1935, Dahm had claimed, "The concept and word of corpus delicti [*Tatbestand*] should be removed from criminal law altogether. The doctrine of the corpus delicti is not only fruitless but harmful. It obscures the essence and inner nature of a crime"

(Dahm 1935, p. 89.) But in 1944, Dahm frankly deplores recent developments in criminal law. He claims that the corpus delicti is a crucial factor in adjudication. He argues that it is impossible to develop a typology of perpetrators that would enable the judge to reach a fair verdict. He warns that a perpetrator-based criminal law, lacking the objective criteria of an offense-based law, might deteriorate to an assessment of the defendant based on the judge's "mere subjective impressions and vague assumptions" (Dahm, 1944, p. 18). A purely perpetrator-based criminal law, he says, "is just merely a dream, indeed an ugly dream" (ibid.).

26. **NS7/318**, letter of Norbert Pohl to Scharfe, January 22, 1942, p. 4.
27. **NS7/318**, letter of Norbert Pohl to Scharfe, January 22, 1942, p. 4.
28. **NS7/318**, letter of Norbert Pohl to Scharfe, January 22, 1942, p. 6.
29. **NS7/318**, letter of Norbert Pohl to Scharfe, January 22, 1942, p. 5.
30. **NS7/318**, letter of Norbert Pohl to Scharfe, January 22, 1942, p. 6.
31. **KMK**.
32. **KMK**, p. 119.
33. **KMK**, p. 117.
34. **KML**, translated in its entirety.
35. Dworkin (1998), ch. 1, ch. 7.
36. Freisler (1938), p. 56.

6   The Issue of Race

1. Riess (2003), pp. 160–72, 163, 165–6.
2. Fest (2007), p. 110.
3. Arad (1987), pp. 384ff.
4. See Aly (2000); see also Aly and Heim (2002).
5. **NO-1744**, in *Reichsführer! Briefe an und von Himmler*, document 165, dated 26.10.42.
6. §92 dealt with the crime of military disobedience; §149 with misuse of a firearm.
7. Herf (2006), p. 52.
8. Herf (2006), pp. 166–7.
9. **NO-2366**, text of telegram to Norbert Pohl, dated 2 November 1941.
10. **KMI** 30.8.46, pp. 20ff.; 6.12.46, pp. 18ff.; 10.12.47, pp. 2ff. See also **KMI**, second affidavit of January 28, 1947; and **KMM**, pp. 4071–8 (English) and 4198–4205 (German).
11. A copious file of the case survives, containing mainly documents for the defense, including the recommendation for dismissal. That recommendation confirms that Morgen reported accusations against Dirlewanger, though in the course of a different prosecution (**ODD**, memo signed Fritz Schmidt, dated October 17, 1942, p. 4). Remarkably, Dirlewanger admitted to the gravest acts,

offering justifications rather than denials. He claimed, for example, that he killed Jews by injection because he had been ordered to kill them and reasoned that shooting would ruin their clothes, which would then be useless to his men.

12. **KMI** 30.8.46, p. 22. A different account of this incident appears in **ODD**, memo of Fritz Schmidt dated October 17, 1942, pp. 3–4.
13. **KMI** 12.10.46, p. 10.
14. Günther (1933), p. 14. For example, the introductory remarks in Wilhelm Stuckart's and Hans Globke's commentary on the Nuremberg laws rely on Günther's definition of "race" (Stuckart and Globke (1936), p. 1).
15. Huber (1939), p. 153.
16. Forsthoff (1933), pp. 38–9 (the passage remains unchanged in the 1934 second edition of Forsthoff's book).
17. Stuckart and Globke (1936), p. 25.
18. **KMB.**
19. **KMB**, p. 15.
20. See, for example, Morgen's references to Hitler's Reichstag speech of May 21, 1935, **KMB**, pp. 106–7.
21. **KMB**, p. 4. Morgen describes this misjudgment in **KMI** 30.8.1943, pp. 2–3.
22. **KMB**, p. 74.

7   From Cracow to Buchenwald

1. **NO-2366**, letter to Hinderfeld dated March 27, 1942, p. 3.
2. **KMI** 30.8.46, pp. 18–19. See also **KMP**, p. 6673.
3. **KMN**, "Besitzzeugnis," indicating that as of April 1943 Morgen was a Sturmmann in the Panzer regiment "Germania," which was part of Division Wiking. As Morgen explains in his testimony at the *Auschwitz-Prozess* in Frankfurt, the regiment was composed mainly of volunteers from other countries in northern Europe.
4. **KMI** 15.10.47, p. 6. The case that got Morgen into trouble involved an SS man named Breitling (**KS**, p. 1). It moved Himmler to admonish the SS and Police Leader in the General Gouvernement, Friedrich-Wilhelm Krüger (letter of 30.7.1942, in *Reichsführer! Briefe an und von Himmler* (1970), document 120, pp. 156–7).
5. See Rhodes (2002), p. 63, quoting the testimony of Günther Otto at Nuremberg, **NO-434**.
6. At **KMI** 30.8.46, pp. 19–20, Morgen says that during his time in the field, his company lost 570 men and was left with only 17. On Soviet atrocities, see **KMW**, pp. 2793–2795.
7. **HPS**, p. 4. **PS-1919**, p. 4, official English translation.
8. **KMI** 4.9.46, pp. 3–5. Morgen had begun the story in **KMI** 30.8.46, p. 20. See also Paulmann's affidavit, **WPA**, p. 544. In **KMO**, Morgen says that his

investigation in Buchenwald started at the end of June; in **KM5**, p. 556, and **KMI** 4.9.46, p. 11, he says it was July.

9. Morgen says that the court wanted someone who was also an SS judge, because the investigation would extend into Buchenwald, and the regular police couldn't make inquiries inside the camp (**KMI** 4.9.46, p. 4).

10. **KMI** 4.9.46, p. 5. More specifically, Bornschein was innocent of crimes in Buchenwald; he was tried and sentenced for crimes committed in the civilian sector. See also **KMP**, p. 6677, and **KMW**, p. 2871.

11. **KMI** 4.9.46, pp. 5–6. See also Morgen's report, **IZ** 7.1.46, p. 4; his affidavit **KM5** at Nuremberg, pp. 552ff.; his testimony at Nuremberg, **IMT XX**, pp. 489–90; and his testimony in the trial of Oswald Pohl, **KMP**, pp. 6681.

12. *Buchenwald Concentration Camp 1937–1945* (2004), pp. 60–1, p. 34.

13. The Soviets had already liberated Auschwitz, in January.

14. These were published in *Life* magazine. See <http ://life.time.com/history/behind-the-picture-bourke-white-and-the-liberation-of-buchenwald/>.

15. This film is accessible at <http://www.youtube.com/watch?v=52swR3dRkjs&list=PLFEEC6992905580AA>.

16. **KMW**, pp. 2797–9, 2870, 2880ff. Morgen's assistant Nett testified to the same effect, **KMW**, p. 2926.

17. See excerpts from Pister's testimony in Greene (2003), pp. 281ff.

18. **IZ**, 7.1.46, p. 5; **KMF**, pp. 5609–10.

19. *Buchenwald Concentration Camp 1937–1945* (2004), p. 149. In another example of Morgen's unreliability on camp conditions, he says that he never saw a Jew treated worse than any other prisoner (**KMI** 12.10.46, p. 12).

20. See <http://life.time.com/history/behind-the-picture-bourke-white-and-the-liberation-of-buchenwald/#5>.

21. *Buchenwald Concentration Camp 1937–1945* (2004), pp. 150–1.

22. *Buchenwald Concentration Camp 1937–1945* (2004), p. 145.

23. **KMI** 4.9.46, pp. 14–15. Morgen does not say that he lived at the camp. He may instead have lived at the "Elephant" Hotel in Weimar.

24. *The Buchenwald Report* (1995), p. 125.

25. **IMT XX**, p. 489.

26. **IZ** 7.1.46, pp. 5ff. See also Morgen's affidavit at Nuremberg **KM5**, pp. 555–6.

27. For example, **IZ**, 7.1.46, p. 4: "At the time of my investigations in the concentration camps—middle of '43 to the spring of '44—the German camps presented a very appealing outward appearance."

28. See Kogon (2006), pp. 66–7: "After about 1941 the 'standard atrocities' described in this book were to a large extent slowed down in the base camps. The admission of newcomers took place under tolerable conditions. The bathhouse, the delousing dip, and the various processing rooms functioned fairly well. Apart from the 'official' imposition of corporal punishment, there was in general far less beating and kicking. The camps were still way stations of human degradation, but they lost those shameless and exquisite torments that

had long characterized them. [. . .] These changes must be emphasized, in the interest of truth. They do not by any means imply that the concentration camps were transformed into rest homes! Far from it. The stories of what happened to various special groups of prisoners prove that to the hilt. What it does mean is that the daily onslaught of terror that exceeded all human capacity in the early years tended to dwindle more and more in some of the camps. What remained was the 'standard' hardship affecting the daily lives of from twelve to thirty-five thousand men herded together in an area of less than half a square mile. These conditions remained inhuman enough, even when they were not intensified by all manner of deviltry."

29. **KMP**, pp. 6685–95.

30. See also **KMO** (official English translation): "I have tried to make it clear time and again that the basic evil of the concentration camp system itself is responsible for the wave of crimes and criminals"; **KMW**, p. 2881: "My opinion is that concentration camps to that extent and as an institution generally, were evil"; **IMT** XX, p. 497: "The concentration camps were establishments which, to put it mildly, were bound to give rise to crimes as a result of the application of a false principle."

8   Karl Otto Koch

1. The following narrative is drawn from **KMI** 4.9.46, pp. 6ff. Details of the case are also described in **KMW**, pp. 2809ff. See also **KMO** and Paulmann's affidavit, **IMT** XLII, pp. 544–5. Paulmann and Morgen differ over minor details.

2. Koch was removed from the command of Majdanek in August 1942 because of a mass escape. At the time of Morgen's visit to Buchenwald, Koch was commanding a postal protective unit in Eger (**KMO**).

3. Josias Erbprinz zu (Hereditary Prince of) Waldeck und Pyrmont joined the Nazi Party in 1929 and the SS in 1930. Like other members of the nobility, he was valued by the Nazis as lending social respectability to their cause. In 1939 Waldeck became Higher SS and Police Leader in Weimar, thereby taking on supervision of Buchenwald. The Americans sentenced him to life imprisonment in 1947, but he was released under an amnesty in 1950. For further details of his biography, see Petropoulos (2006), pp. 261–6.

4. Orth (2000), pp. 189–90. Morgen describes this order in **KMI** 4.9.46, p. 8.

5. **KMO**.

6. **KMI** 4.9.46, p. 8. The word "fanatic" shows up in Victor Klemperer's study *The Language of the Third Reich* (2006), pp. 52–6. Klemperer was a Jewish academic who survived the war in Dresden and his wartime diary is among the most valuable records of the period. In non-ideological German, Klemperer explains, "the word is invariably very negatively loaded, it denotes a threatening and repulsive quality. Even when one occasionally comes

across the expression in an obituary for a research scientist or an artist—he was fanatical about his discipline or his art—the tribute always conjures up associations of petulant introvertedness and embarrassing remoteness" (p. 54). In the Third Reich, however, the word became "an inflation of the terms 'courageous,' 'devoted' and 'persistent': to be more precise, it is a gloriously eloquent fusion of all of these virtues, and even the most innocuous pejorative connotation of the word was dropped" (p. 55).

7. **KMI** 18.1.47, p. 2.
8. **KMI** 21.10.46, p. 8.
9. **KMI** 4.9.46, pp. 12–13.
10. **KMO**.
11. *The Buchenwald Report* (1995), p. 341. See also p. 126: "Morgen was very unpopular with the SS officers, who were afraid of him."
12. **KE** pp. 20–1.
13. **KE**, p. 21.
14. **KE**, pp. 21–2.
15. **KE**, p. 33.
16. **KE**, p. 28.
17. Some of these accusations against Ilse Koch are discussed in the Buchenwald trial, **KMW**, pp. 2902ff. For example: "There were also reports that Mrs. Koch had kicked her own mother out of this [*sic*] house and the old woman was sitting on a rock outside the house without a bite to eat and she cried."
18. A prisoner who worked in the Koch household recalls, "By day the 'handsome Waldemar' [Dr. Hoven] frequently came to her; by night, however, Deputy Commandant Florstedt." *The Buchenwald Report* (1995), p. 336.
19. **KMI** 11.10.46, pp. 12–13.

9 From Corruption to Murder

1. **KE**, pp. 46–7. The following description is drawn from this passage.
2. **KE**, p. 47. See also Morgen's affidavit in Nuremberg, **KM5**, p. 554.
3. This version is in **IMT XX**, pp. 490–1. See also **KE**, p. 51, where Morgen mentions the comparison of records.
4. **IMT XX**, p. 491.
5. **KE**, pp. 47–8, 52–7.
6. The former clerk of camp doctor Waldemar Hoven confirms that Hoven killed prisoners on orders from Koch (affidavit of Ferdinand Roemhild, **NO-434**, p. 5).
7. **KMP**, p. 6740: "as far as the shootings while attempting to escape are concerned, investigating I found out that numerous cases had occurred which were nothing but pure raw-blooded murders, and which were also charged against the defendants as murders."
8. **KMI** 30.8.46, p. 15; **KMI** 4.9.46, p. 8; **KMI** 11.6.47, p. 2.

9. **KMI** 4.9.46, p. 8.
10. **KMI** 4.9.46, p. 9.
11. **KE**, p. 48.
12. **KE**, p. 48.
13. **KE**, pp. 50–1.
14. **KML**, p. 2.
15. **KE**, p. 53.
16. **KMW**, p. 2848. See also the testimony of Chief SS Judge Günther Reinecke at Nuremberg, **IMT** XX, p. 442; and testimony of Werner Paulmann, **WPA**, p. 550.
17. **KE**, p. 55. At **KMF**, p. 5651, Morgen identifies him as a member of the Socialist Party (SPD). This case is also discussed by Werner Paulmann in **WPA**, p. 547.
18. Morgen says only that the Prince knew Krämer (**KE**, p. 56). That Krämer had treated him is reported by a survivor of the camp (*The Buchenwald Report* [1995], p. 341).
19. **KMF**, p. 5651.
20. **KE**, p. 55.
21. *The Buchenwald Report* (1995), p. 184. Rudolf Gottschalk, former member of the communist underground in the camp, also names Blank as the murderer (**HA** Hoven Document 2, p. 4 of original).
22. **KE**, p. 56.
23. *The Buchenwald Report* (1995), pp. 123–4.
24. **KE**, pp. 53–4. After the war, Johannes Jaenisch was tried for participation in these executions (**JJ**, unsigned document dated September 8, 1952). Morgen submitted an affidavit to this trial (affidavit dated September 22, 1952), in which he claims to have investigated these killings fully. (Morgen misstates the date as November 11, 1938—an understandable mistake, given that November 9–10, 1938, was the date of *Kristallnacht*.)
25. **KE**, p. 60.
26. **KE**, pp. 61–2.

10 Partners in Crime

1. *The Buchenwald Report* (1995), pp. 203–4.
2. *The Buchenwald Report* (1995), pp. 154, 200.
3. *The Buchenwald Report* (1995), p. 35.
4. **KE**, p. 59.
5. **KE**, p. 58.
6. In postwar testimony, Morgen appears to believe that Sommer was indeed taken in by Koch's claim of higher authority. See also **KMW**, p. 2811, where Morgen says that Koch "read to Sommer a letter of the Reichsfuehrer SS in which the Reichsfuehrer gave the SS Colonel Koch the authority to have

executions and special treatments carried out in the arrest bunker for state political reasons. This letter, in fact, did not exist at all, and Koch had only played a comedy before this quite primitive man Sommer."

7. **KE**, pp. 59–60.
8. *The Buchenwald Report* (1995), p. 229. See also **NO-434**, affidavit of Hoven's former clerk, Ferdinand Roemhild.
9. According to surviving prisoners, lethal injections were no longer administered in late 1944, "a consequence of the trial of [Dr.] Hoven, who stood under accusation of murder for the lethal injection of prisoners. Since the proceedings reached a favorable outcome for Hoven and no conviction resulted, the SS resumed lethal injections for the prisoners in Block 61 at the end of January 1945." *The Buchenwald Report* (1995), p. 317.
10. **KE**, p. 66.
11. **KE**, p. 67.
12. This item appears in Morgen's report, but see also *The Buchenwald Report* (1995), p. 211, where the ghostwriters are named as prisoners Wegerer and Sitte.
13. **KMI** 11.10.46, pp. 8–9.
14. **KMI** 11.10.46, p. 10.
15. **KE**, pp. 70–2.
16. **KE**, p. 70.
17. **KE**, p. 67.
18. **NO-429**, pp. 5–6; **WHI**, interrogation of October 22, 1946, pp. 20–2, 26–30.
19. Morgen also describes the case of Freudemann and May in **KMW**, pp. 2758ff.
20. See *The Buchenwald Report* (1995), pp. 229–30.
21. **KE**, pp. 74–5.
22. **KMR**, affidavit dated May 23, 1947, Joachim Mrugowski document No. 114, p. 50.
23. **KMI** 11.10.46, p. 17. Morgen also describes the procedures for selecting experimental subjects at **KMW**, pp. 2761ff.
24. **KMR**, affidavit dated February 26, 1947, document Joachim Mrugowski No. 23, p. 161.
25. **KMI** 11.10.46, pp. 10ff. This episode is also described in **KMR**, affidavits dated February 26, 1947, documents Joachim Mrugowski Nos. 23 and 29.
26. **KMI** 11.10.46, p. 12. The suspicion that Koehler was killed is reported by Morgen's co-investigator Bernhard Wehner, **JJ** excerpts of testimony dated 12.6.1950.
27. Kogon (2006), pp. 291–2.
28. **KMR**, affidavit dated February 26, 1947, Joachim Mrugowski document No. 29, p. 189; affidavit dated May 23, 1947, document Joachim Mrugowsky No. 114, p. 55.
29. **KMR**, affidavit dated May 23, 1947, document Joachim Mrugowsky No. 114, p. 55 (emphasis in the original).

30. The court in Morgen's second denazification trial, in Ludwigsburg, asked the local court in Bad Homburg to take up the matter. Because Kogon had not responded to several letters asking him to clarify his accusations (**SKV EWL** 905/4), the court considered those accusations an obstacle to Morgen's denazification. In his deposition at the Bad Homburg court, Kogon states that he only heard about Morgen's presence at the experiment from Dr. Ding-Schuler. He adds that, given the structure of the camp, members of the SS Judiciary had no authority to order such an experiment, let alone the execution of prisoners of war. But he adds that the proposal for the experiment may have come from the SS court. Kogon also states that he is not sure whether the prisoners taking part in the experiment were identical with those who were strangled in the crematorium. Kogon declares himself certain that a serious antagonism arose between Ding-Schuler and Morgen. The reason was that Morgen had begun to interrogate Ding-Schuler, presumably in the course of investigating Hoven. According to Kogon, Ding-Schuler remarked, "Now, Morgen is getting sassy [*wird frech*]; he even dares to come after me."
31. **KE**, pp. 80–1.
32. **KMB**, pp. 107–8; **KMK**, p. 117.
33. **KMF**, p. 5585.
34. **KE**, p. 82. **WHI**, interrogation of October 23, 1946, p. 7.
35. **KA**, p. 1.

11   "Legal" Killing

1. **KMI** 11.10.46, pp. 15–16. After "order of Hitler," the transcript reads "(Himmler?)," indicating that Morgen's speech was unclear.
2. Morgen dates the conversation with Grawitz to the spring of 1944.
3. **PS-630.**
4. **KMT**, tracks 5–6. Material from this interview appears in Toland (1992), pp. 761, 774, 820.
5. **KMI** 19.9.46, pp. 5ff.
6. **KMI** 19.9.46, pp. 7–8.
7. See Friedlander (1995), s.v. "14f13."
8. **NO-434**, pp. 3–4. See also *The Buchenwald Report* (1995), pp. 165, 212, 242–3. In a letter dated February 2, 1942, Hoven sent Bernburg a list of Jews for "further treatment"—a euphemism for gassing. (The original is reproduced in *Buchenwald Concentration Camp 1937–1945*, p. 127. A translation appears in *The Buchenwald Report* (1995), p. 243.)
9. **NO-429**, pp. 4–5; **WHI**, 22 October 1946, pp. 16–17, 31–2. Hoven claims that his only role was to sign false death certificates for the victims after the fact.
10. **WHI**, October 22, 1946, p. 17; October 23, 1946, p. 8.

11. **KMI** 6.12.46, p. 17.
12. *Buchenwald Concentration Camp 1937–1945* (2004), pp. 121–4.
13. **KMW**, pp. 2793–5.
14. **KMW**, pp. 2777ff.
15. The text of this decree is accessible at <http://archive.jta.org/article/1942/03/12/2856861/full-text-of-cruel-nazi-decree-against-jews-and-poles-beheaded-in-washington>.
16. **NG-558** (official English translation). Original German also at **PHB**, pp. 237–9; see also pp. 80–1.
17. Morgen makes the same error in an interrogation (**KMI** 12.10.46, pp. 7, 10). It thus appears to be a genuine misunderstanding on his part.
18. **KMW**, pp. 2782–3.
19. **KMW**, pp. 2874–5.
20. **KMI** 11.10.46, p. 3.

12   The "Final Solution": Conflicting Stories

1. Gerhard Wiebeck testified at the *Auschwitz-Prozess* in Frankfurt that Morgen showed him this gold, which was stored in a safe in Buchenwald (**GWT**, pp. 19590–1).
2. **KMI** 4.9.46, p. 29.
3. In fact, Morgen had already visited Auschwitz once before, while investigating Georg Sauberzweig (**NO-2366**, letter to Hinderfeld dated March 27, 1944, p. 2). But that visit must have occurred before August 1941, when Sauberzweig was convicted—and probably before March, when he was arrested—hence before the first, "experimental" gassings had occurred, and long before the gas chambers were built (**PGS**).
4. **IMT** XX, pp. 492–3.
5. On Wirth, see Riess (2011), pp. 239–51. On the "euthanasia" program, see Friedlander (1995).
6. Arad (1987), pp. 182–4.
7. Sereny (1983), p. 54.
8. <http://www.ushmm.org/wlc/en/media_nm.php?ModuleId=10005190&MediaId=413>.
9. See "Die Zwangsarbeitslager am 'Alten Flughafen' Lublin," pp. 48–9, in **GM**, pp. 19498–9. According to this report, based on testimony of former prisoners, the wedding was held on the same day that the singer Jimmy (Samuel Jacob) Kleerekoper was hanged. The Jewish Historical Museum in Amsterdam dates his death June 27, 1943 (http://www.joodsmonument.nl/person/529432?lang=en). See also Kuwalek (2004), 112–34, p. 129, n. 47.
10. **IMT** XX, p. 492.
11. Sereny (1983), pp. 260–1.
12. **POG**, pp. 1–3.

13. **KMI** 11.10.46, p. 1.
14. **KMP**, p. 6683.
15. **KMI** 10.11.46, p. 5. See also **KMI** 21.10.46, p. 10, where he says that it took him until the turn of the year 1943–44 to discover the "killings" (Tötungen); the context suggests that he is referring to the mass extermination.
16. In one affidavit Morgen says that his initial visit took place in the first half of November (**KMN**, affidavit dated November 1945). Elsewhere he says that this work at Auschwitz began just as Arthur Liebehenschel was replacing Rudolf Hoess as commandant; Liebehenschel's assignment in Auschwitz began on November 11 (**KMI** 4.9.46, p. 29; **PAL**).
17. **IMT** XX, p. 495.
18. The English version has the word "frightful" here, but the word used by Morgen is "ungeheuerlich," which is much stronger.
19. **KMP**, p. 6752.
20. See Reports from Globocnik to Himmler, Nuremberg Documents PS-4024, **IMT** XXXIV, pp. 81ff.
21. See also **IMT** XX, p. 496, where Morgen insists that figures shown in a photograph of atrocities are not wearing SS uniforms; and **KMP**, pp. 6686–95, where Morgen lists all of the deaths that cannot be charged to the SS administration of the camps, including deaths in the gas chambers. He insists that these deaths were attributable to the men who had devised the concentration camp system. Morgen also lists causes of deaths that are not attributable to the SS at **IMT** XX, pp. 499–502.
22. **KM7**, pp. 563–64. See also **IMT** XX, p. 494. Wirth's status with respect to the SS was at least complicated: **PCW**.
23. Examination of Günther Reinecke, **IMT** XX, pp. 436, 444–5.
24. **IMT** XX, p. 502.

13 Aktion Erntefest

1. **PFL**, memo dated 25.10.1943.
2. **KMD**(1), pp. 4, 10. See also **KMD**(2), p. 8.
3. This dubious distinction is also claimed for the September, 1941 massacre at Babi Yar.
4. **KMD**(1), p. 5, p. 7.
5. **KMD**(1), p. 8. In fact, the massacre was investigated not by Morgen alone but by a full commission, which may well have been Dennerlein's. See the report of Walter Toebbens (**WTR**, p. 30); the report of Hans Lauffs (**LA**, pp. 2–3); and an affidavit of Erich Muhsfeldt (**EM**, August 16, 1947, pp. 5–6).
6. **EKI**, interrogation of October 12, 1945, pp. 9–13. Portions of this passage appear in *Nazi Conspiracy and Aggression* (1948), pp. 1309–11.
7. These German police were probably members of Reserve Police Battalion 101, whose participation in the massacre is described by Browning (1998), ch. 15.

8. **CHK**. See *Erntefest, 3–4 listopada 1943: Zapomniany epizod Zagłady* (2009).
9. **KMD(1)**, p. 5. For the effects of the massacre on the labor force, see the report of Max Horn, director of Ostindustrie G.m.b.H., **NO-1270**.
10. **KMD(1)**, p. 9.
11. **KMD(1)**, p. 8.
12. In Morgen's 1973 testimony, he describes having seen "mountains of clothing" in the location where the victims had been forced to undress (**KMD(1)**, p. 6). Independent testimony makes clear that, as one would expect, the victims had also left behind gold, jewelry, and money (**WTR**, p. 28).
13. **EM**, affidavit of August 16, 1947, p. 6.
14. **SR**, p. 266.
15. **LA**, p. 25.
16. Hannah Arendt (2006) later wrote that "the lie most effective with the whole of the German people" was that they "must annihilate their enemies or be annihilated," p. 52.
17. When one of his questioners in 1980 points out that fear of an uprising could only have been a pretext for the massacre, given that its victims included women and children, Morgen says he didn't know that there were many women and children among the victims (**KMD(2)**, p. 8). Perhaps relevant in this connection is that Morgen's wife was present (p. 1).
18. **KMD(1)**, p. 8.
19. **KMF**, pp. 5576–7: "The question would definitely arise: Have you seen a gassing yourself, have you seen a corpse, a battered prisoner? And I would have to say in all honesty, No."
20. **KMT**, track 6.
21. Toland's attitude toward Morgen comes out clearly in his 1992 book, where he speaks of "the inexorable Konrad Morgen" (p. 820) as "the man who did most to hinder the atrocities in the East" (p. 761) through "his lonesome attempt to end the Final Solution" (p. 774).

14 Auschwitz

1. Riess (2003), pp. 160–72, 163, 165–6.
2. The Division Wiking, in which Morgen served, had carried out such executions earlier in the war. See Rhodes (2002), p. 63, quoting the testimony of Günther Otto at Nuremberg, **NO-434**. In all probability, Morgen served in the division not as a combatant but rather in one of the field tribunals that accompanied combat units.
3. In April 1942, an officer was arrested and tried for executing Jews by this method with more than the usual cruelty—and for taking photographs, which he then circulated among family and friends (Büchler (2003)). Note that Morgen was dismissed from the SS Judiciary in May or June 1942, and the officer was not tried until May 1943.

4. His rank as of April was *Sturmmann*: private first class (**KMN**, "Besitzzeugnis," April 1943).

5. **KMF**, pp. 5570–4.

6. "In besonderem Einsatz," the term for execution squads behind the front lines in Poland and the Soviet Union.

7. **KMF**, pp. 5574–5.

8. **KMF**, pp. 5575–6.

9. **KMF**, pp. 5576–7.

10. **KMF**, pp. 5577–8.

11. Morgen elsewhere describes his service at the front as follows: "I went through with all the withdrawal fights through the steppe, and I also participated in the counter-attack at the Donez. After that the division was completely disrupted, and a company contained only seventeen men" (**KMP**, p. 6673).

12. **KMF**, pp. 5578–9.

13. **KMF**, p. 5579.

14. **F65**, "The fight of SS judges against injustice in the concentration camps," report dated December 21, 1945, p. 11.

15. **F65**, "SS–KZ–Gerichtsbarkeit," 7.1.46, p. 8.

16. **KMI** 11.10.46, p. 16.

17. **KMV(2)**, p. 11719. At **KMF** , p. 5641, Morgen says that participation in the killings would make SS members "not just brutal and sadistic and corrupt but utterly useless as soldiers for later life."

18. **IMT**, XX, pp. 506–7.

19. See **KMI** 19.9.46, pp. 7–8.

20. See **KMI** 10.11.46, p. 3 ("Mein Bestreben ging dahin, einen anderen Ausweg zu finden"); **KMI** 13.12.46, p. 29 ("Ich musste nur einen anderen Weg finden"). Morgen makes the same general point at **KMP**, p. 6696.

21. **IMT** XX, p. 507.

22. **KMI** 4.9.46, p. 17.

23. **KMI** 11.10.46, pp. 2–4.

24. **KMP**, p. 6752.

25. **KMI** 11.10.46, p. 3.

26. **WHM**, pp. 26053–4.

27. **WHT**, pp. 25991–2.

28. **WHT**, pp. 26013–14.

29. **GWT**, pp. 19591–2.

30. **IMT** XX, p. 507.

31. Our translation. See *Der Prozeß gegen die Hauptkriegsverbrecher*, <http://www. zeno.org/Geschichte/M/Der+Nürnberger+Prozeß/Hauptverhandlungen/Ein hundertachtundneunzigster+Tag+Donnerstag,+8.+August+1946/Vormittags sitzung>.

32. **IMT** XX, pp. 507–8.

33. **WHT**, p. 25994. See also **KMI** 4.9.46, p. 33.

34. Morgen tends to overestimate the impact of his investigations. At **KMW**, p. 2900, he says "immediately after I had intervened in a mass extermination camp such as Lublin, these mass extermination camps were destroyed to the ground. I could prove that the Commander of Auschwitz Hoess had committed overt acts such as murders [. . .] . Hoess was taken out of office immediately, and as a result of that the activities of Birkenau slowed down."

35. IMT, XX, pp. 506–7.

36. **KMF**, pp. 5582–5.

37. In one of his CIC interrogations, Morgen cites this principle as the basis on which he prosecuted murders in the concentration camps: "Ueber das Leben eines sogenannten Staatsfeindes entscheidet der Fuehrer selbst" (**KMI** 18.1.47, p. 4).

38. Elsewhere Morgen says that he was first called to speak with Kaltenbrunner, then Nebe, then Müller (**KMI** 04.9.46, p. 31).

39. **KMP**, pp. 6695–6.

40. **KMP**, pp. 6696–7.

41. The Preamble reads, "Until a more complete code of the laws of war has been issued, the High Contracting Parties deem it expedient to declare that, in cases not included in the Regulations adopted by them, the inhabitants and the belligerents remain under the protection and the rule of the principles of the law of nations, as they result from the usages established among civilized peoples, from the laws of humanity, and the dictates of the public conscience. They declare that it is in this sense especially that Articles 1 and 2 of the Regulations adopted must be understood." See Convention (IV) respecting the Laws and Customs of War on Land and its annex: Regulations concerning the Laws and Customs of War on Land (The Hague, October 18, 1907), accessible at <http://www.icrc.org/ihl.nsf/FULL/195>.

42. Morgen is obviously aware of this change in his postwar testimonies. In the typescript of one affidavit, for example, he inserted handwritten corrections listing "crimes against humanity" as one of the charges against Karl Koch (**KMI** affidavit of 29.1.47, p. 2).

43. **KMI** 11.10.46, p. 16.

44. Himmler (1974), Posen speech of October 6, 1943, pp. 169–70.

45. **PS-1919**, p. 66.

15 Adolf Eichmann

1. IMT XX, p. 514. See also **KMP**, p. 6696; **KM5**, p. 556; and **KMW**, p. 2900: "I should like to add something. I went as far as to place an arrest order before Kaltenbrunner for the man in charge of all European Jewish extermination, Eichmann. So far as I am concerned, I did not only confine myself to cases of corruption or similar cases; however, I did everything to keep these conditions from spreading." Morgen's explanation at **KM5**, pp. 559–60, makes clear that

he knew a fair amount about Eichmann's activities. See also the testimony of Günther Reinecke, **IMT** XX, p. 443: "Names like Hoess and Eichmann did come up during our investigations and proceedings were, in fact, instituted against both, but at the end of the war they were still in their initial stages."

2. The official English translation reads, "I asked the SS Court at Berlin to investigate Eichmann on the basis of my report." The original German reads, "Ich habe das SS-Gericht Berlin ersucht, die Untersuchungen gegen Eichmann auf Grund meiner Hinweise durchzuführen" (http://www.zeno.org/ Geschichte/M/Der+Nürnberger+Prozeß/Hauptverhandlungen/Einhundert achtundneunzigster+Tag+Donnerstag,+8.+August+1946/Vormittagssitzung).

3. The official English translation reads, "on this submission rather dramatic incidents took place." The German reads, "dass es bei dieser Vorlage zu dramatischen Auftritten gekommen ist."

4. *The Trial of Adolf Eichmann* (1992), Session 39, May 15, 1961, vol. II, p. 712; also accessible at <http://www.nizkor.org/hweb/people/e/eichmann-adolf/ transcripts>. Eichmann's defense attorney reads from the relevant portion of Morgen's Nuremberg testimony in Session 87, July 6, 1961, vol. IV, pp. 1550–3.

5. *The Trial of Adolf Eichmann* (1992), Session 105, July 20, 1961, vol. IV, p. 1801.

6. *The Trial of Adolf Eichmann* (1992), vol. VII, *Statement by Adolf Eichmann to the Israel Police*, pp. 268–9, 304–5, 1070–1.

7. Cesarani (2004), p. 173.

8. *The Trial of Adolf Eichmann* (1992), Session 10, April 19, 1961, vol. I, pp. 137, 143. As Eichmann tells Willem Sassen, who interviewed him in Argentina, "I had, of course, to keep in constant touch with the receiving camps, especially Auschwitz, before the arrival of a large sector, let us say, Hungary" (quoted in Session 75, June 20, 1961, vol. III, p. 1367). At trial, Eichmann recalls having visited Auschwitz four to six times, though without specifying the times of these visits (Session 93, July 12, 1961, vol. IV, p. 1633; Session 99, July 17, 1961, p. 1712). At least one visit occurred much earlier, at the behest of Heinrich Müller.

9. **GWA**, p. 5.

10. **F65**, p. 112.

11. **KMI** 4.9.46, p. 19. That Morgen was in Hungary on a special mission, outside of ordinary SS court business, and stayed only briefly, is confirmed by a deposition of the SS judge at the SS and Police Court in Budapest, Anton Baumgartl, in the course of court proceedings against Otto Winkelmann, the former Higher SS and Police Leader in Budapest. Baumgartl states that he had never heard of Konrad Morgen or of his investigations in Hungary, adding that such investigations could not have occurred without coming to the attention of his court. **HAW(1)**, pp. 43–4, Interrogation of Anton Baumgartl on November 10, 1960, as witness in proceedings against Otto Winkelmann. .

12. **HAW(2)**, pp. 8–10, Testimony of Konrad Morgen to the State Prosecutor Provincial Court (*Landgericht*) Frankfurt am Main, April 1, 1954, pp. 1–6 (1).
13. **HAW(2)**, pp. 8–10, Testimony of Konrad Morgen to the State Prosecutor Provincial Court (*Landgericht*) Frankfurt am Main, April 1, 1954, p. 1.
14. **HAW(2)**, pp. 8–10, Testimony of Konrad Morgen to the State Prosecutor, Provincial Court (*Landgericht*) Frankfurt am Main, April 1, 1954, p. 1.
15. **F65**, p. 71, affidavit of Kurt Mittelstädt, 14.12. 1945, official English translation. A copy of the affidavit **NO-1875** is part of **HAW(1)**, p. 4. Hauptstaatsarchiv Hessen, Abteilung 461, Nr. 31 502 (413 AR-Z 28/ 1970.) Ermittlungsverfahren gegen Dr. Konrad Morgen 1970.
16. **F65**, pp. 72–4, affidavit of Gerhard Wiebeck, 22.3.1954, p. 2.
17. **HAW(2)**, pp. 9–10. Testimony of Kurt Mittelstädt in Bad Tölz, March 24, 1954.
18. **HAW(2)**, p. 19 (4a JS 1841/54), Testimony of Dr. Reinecke, Munich, March 29, 1954.
19. **HAW(2)**, pp. 8–10, Testimony of Konrad Morgen, p. 2.
20. **HAW(2)**, p. 9, Testimony of Konrad Morgen, p. 3.
21. **HAW(2)**, p. 10, Testimony of Konrad Morgen, p. 4.
22. **HAW(2)**, p. 10, Testimony of Konrad Morgen, p. 5.
23. **HAW(2)**, pp. 45–7. Ministry of Justice Baden-Württemberg, May 24, 1955. Blatt 45–7, Justizministerium Baden-Württemberg: Stuttgart 24.5.1955.
24. **KMU**, decision dated March 6, 1972, also in **HAW(1)**, p. 57. The State Prosecutor of the Provincial Court Frankfurt am Main states that no witnesses confirmed the accusations against Dr. Morgen and that none of the witnesses "could remember the object of the investigations, the leaflet, or could remember that Dr. Morgen was ever active in Budapest." Morgen refused to testify in the 1970 investigations; he just wrote a letter to the court stating that earlier investigations had already disproved the accusations.
25. Wiebeck's affidavit says that their relations were tense. On Mittelstädt, see **KMN**, Morgen letter to Reinecke dated October 23, 1944; and **KMI** 4.9.46, p. 22. See also **HAW(2)**, pp. 8–10, where Morgen testifies that Mittelstädt was afraid that Morgen would provide incriminating evidence against him and wanted to discredit him in advance. And indeed, in Mittelstädt's own 1954 deposition, he says that he was informed by an interrogator in 1945 that Morgen had accused him of sentencing 45 fire-fighters to death in Vienna. Mittelstädt actually faced charges stemming from that incident. **HAW(2)**, pp. 9–10, testimony of Kurt Mittelstädt, Bad Tölz, March 24, 1954.

16   The Weimar Trials

1. **KMI**, 4.9.46, p. 17. The court was set up at the beginning of November 1943 (**NS7/128**, letter of December 23, 1943).

2. NS7/128, letters dated December 23, 1943 and January 7, 1944. According to these documents, Morgen's request was dated December 9, 1943.
3. **KMI** 4.9.46, p. 20.
4. **KMI** 4.9.46, p. 21.
5. **KMI** 30.8.46, p. 12.
6. **KM5**, p. 558.
7. **KM5**, p. 559; **KMI** 4.9.46, p. 22.
8. **KMI** 4.9.46, p. 21.
9. **KMI** 4.9.46, pp. 18–19.
10. **KMI**, 4.9.46, p. 22.
11. **KMN**, Letter to Maria Wachter, September 22, 1944.
12. **KMN**, report to Günther Reinecke, October 23, 1944.
13. **PKM**, letter dated 3.8.1944.
14. **PKM**, letter from Bender to Breithaupt, 26.8.1944. The promotion was granted in November (**PKM**, memo from Herff, November 9, 1944). The vacation was put off until at least October (**KMN**, letter to Maria Wachter dated October 9, 1944).
15. **WHT**, p. 26018. Here the prosecutor cites a report from defendant Wilhelm Boger, written in 1945.
16. **NO-2366**, "Short remarks to the Bill of Indictment against SS Standartenführer Koch, formerly commandant of the KZ Buchenwald," p. 3.
17. As Pohl's legal advisor, he had the authority to appoint the legal officers of the WVHA in the concentration camps, which it supervised. He therefore regarded the SS Judiciary, and Morgen in particular, as unwelcome intruders.
18. **KMI** 18.1.47, p. 3. See also **NO-2380**, p. 1.
19. **KMI** 18.1.47, p. 5.
20. **KMI** 18.1.47, p. 6.
21. **KMI** 18.1.47, p. 4. See also **NO-2380**, p. 1.
22. **KMN**, letter to Maria Wachter dated Weimar, September 11, 1944.
23. **NO-2380**, p. 1.
24. **WHT**, p. 25993.
25. **KMI** 4.9.46, p. 33. Grabner asserted, while under arrest in Vienna after the war, that his orders had come from Höss—that Höss had admitted as much when he appeared as a witness at Grabner's trial (**GR**, p. 35).
26. **KMI** 4.9.46, p. 33.
27. Testimony of Heinrich Dürmayer, *Der Auschwitz-Prozess* (2007), p. 11529.
28. **IMT** XX, pp. 507.
29. **KMN**, letter to Maria Wachter, December 22, 1944.
30. Elsewhere Morgen suggests that murder was indeed one of the counts on which Koch was convicted (**KMO**, p. 1; **KMT**, track 2, 20:20). Günther Reinecke, in his testimony at Nuremberg, says that Koch was condemned to death for his whole "system of murder," though the indictment focused

on a handful of cases for which the evidence was most accessible (**IMT** XX, p. 441).

31. **NO-2366**, "Short remarks to the Bill of Indictment against SS Standartenführer Koch, formerly commandant of the KZ Buchenwald," pp. 2–3; **KMI** affidavit of 28.1.47, pp. 7–8.

32. **KMI** affidavit of 28.1.47, p. 8.

33. **KMW**, pp. 2806–7; **KMO** and accompanying documents from the Dodd Archive. See also **KMT**, track 5, 15:00.

17   Rudolf Höss and Eleonore Hodys

1. **KMF**, p. 5587.
2. **GWA**, pp. 4–5.
3. Eleonore Hodys made this testimony under oath to Konrad Morgen. The German original of Eleonore Hodys's testimony is in the Institut für Zeitgeschichte Munich, accessible online at <http://www.ifz-muenchen.de/archiv/zs/zs-0599_1.pdf≥. An English version of Hodys's testimony is reprinted in *Dachau Liberated* (2000), ch. 5. That she testified under oath is confirmed by Morgen's assistant Gerhard Wiebeck (**GWT**, p. 19597). Günther Reinecke testified at Nuremberg that Hodys agreed to speak with Morgen in return for a guarantee of safety, which was made good by her transfer to Munich (**IMT** XX, pp. 475–6). Hodys says, "About the fears which I had in connection with my transfer to Munich, I spoke to my fiancée [*sic* . . .]. He advised me under all circumstances not to mention the commander's name" (*Dachau Liberated* (2000), p. 90). In other words, Hodys was transferred for the express purpose of being interviewed by Morgen and his staff.
4. This passage appears in *Dachau Liberated* (2000), p. 89; here retranslated from the original, p. 23.
5. **KMN**, letter to Maria Wachter, October 9, 1944.
6. **KMN**, letter to Maria Wachter, October 13, 1944.
7. **KMN**, letter to Maria Wachter, October 16, 1944.
8. **KMN**, letter to Maria Wachter, October 22, 1944.

18   Out of the Fray

1. **KMN**, letter dated September 22, 1944.
2. Jünger (1939).
3. It was almost banned by Philipp Bouhler, Head of the Official Party Examiners for Protection of National Socialist Literature—in other words, the Nazis' head censor. Goebbels wanted to send the author to a concentration camp. See Martus (2001), pp. 375–9, Schwilk (2007), Keller (1997).
4. **KMN**, letter to Maria Wachter, September 22, 1944.
5. **KMN**, letter to Maria Wachter, December 12, 1944.

6. **KMN**, letter to Maria Wachter, October 16, 1944.

7. **KMN**, letter to Maria Wachter, October 27/28, 1944.

8. For Morgen's request, see **KMN**, letter to Reinecke dated October 23, 1944. For Himmler's response see **PKM**, letter from Bender to Breithaupt, 26.8.1944.

9. **KMN**, letter to Maria Wachter, December 12, 1944.

10. **KMN**, letter to Maria Wachter, December 12, 1944.

11. **KMN**, letter to Maria Wachter, January 7, 1945.

12. **KMN**, letter to Maria Wachter, January 15, 1945

13. **KMN**, letter to Maria Wachter, January 14, 1945.

14. **KMN**, letter to Maria Wachter, January 19, 1945.

15. **KMN**, letter to Maria Wachter, January 22, 1945.

16. **KMI** 4.9.46, p. 22; 6.12.46, p. 21.

17. **F65**, Morgen's handwritten account dated 14.12.1955.

18. Morgen arrived in Nuremberg on July 1, 1946 (**IMT** XX, p. 483).

19. **KMI** 4.4.47, p. 1.

20. **SKV** EWL 903/3. In its sentence of June 24, 1948, the denazification court classified Morgen as an "exonerated person" (*Entlasteter*), meaning that he was not guilty of any complicity in war crimes. The court concluded that Morgen had not only shown courage in prosecuting high SS leaders but had thereby engaged in active resistance against the Nazi regime. This first sentence was revoked by the Ministry for Political Liberation (see Ch. 10, n. 30 for further details). The Ministry argued that Morgen had merely been fighting corruption in the SS, which did not amount to resistance against National Socialist tyranny. A second trial was held at the central German civilian court of North Württemberg handling denazification. In its decision of September 18, 1950, the court brought all proceedings against Morgen to a close under the "Law for Completion of Political Liberation" of April 3, 1950, which ended all pending denazification proceedings. This second court sentence became effective in May 1951. Note that the North Württemberg court was highly critical of Morgen, classifying his judicial activities as SS *Säuberungsmaßnahmen*—house cleaning. (See Beschluss der Zentral-Spruchkammer Nordwürttemberg, September 18, 1950, J 75/5326, **SKV** EWL 903/3.)

21. **KMH**, *Fragebogen*.

22. **KMN**, "Meldung des SS Hauptsturmführers Dr. Morgen über persönliche Verhältnisse" ("Notice of SS Hauptsturmführer Dr. Morgen re: personal circumstances"), September 30, 1944. In 1942 Morgen had asked the SS Race and Settlement Office to approve the marriage as quickly as possible, because he was about to be sent to the front (**KMH**, handwritten letter, June 27, 1942, to the SS Race and Settlement Main Office).

23. **KMN**, "Meldung des SS Hauptsturmführers Dr. Morgen über persönliche Verhältnisse" ("Notice of SS Hauptsturmführer Dr. Morgen re: personal circumstances"), September 30, 1944.

24. **KMH**, permission signed by Günther Reinecke, November 11, 1944.

25. **KMH**, "Erbgesundheitliche Beurteilung" (Hereditary Health Evaluation) of Maria Theresia Blank, December 20, 1944.
26. **KMI** 15.10.47, pp. 1–2.

19   Postscript

1. **KMN**, letter to Maria Wachter, December 12, 1944.
2. **NO-2366**, letter to Hinderfeld, March 27, 1942, p. 3.
3. **NS7/318**, letter from Norbert Pohl to Scharfe, January 22, 1942, p. 13.
4. **KMN**, letter to Maria Wachter, December 12, 1944.
5. **KMN**, letter to Maria Wachter, December 26, 1944.
6. Himmler (1974), Posen speech of October 6, 1943, pp. 169–70.
7. Harman (1975), p. 7.
8. Note that we are not endorsing Harman's diagnosis of the inadequacy. Harman argues that calling Hitler's decision wrong would presuppose that he could have been deterred by consideration of its wrongness, whereas Hitler was "beyond the motivational reach of the relevant moral considerations" (Harman (1975), p. 8). In our view, the very category of wrongness may be inadequate to the immorality of the case.
9. Arendt (2006), p. 277.
10. Arendt (2006), p. 279.
11. Herman (1993) and (2007). We discuss this issue further in our (2011).
12. Dworkin (1998), p. 106.
13. Dworkin (1998), p. 105.
14. Dworkin (1998), p. 106.

BIBLIOGRAPHY

Except where noted, the originals are in German and the translations are ours.

Archival Sources

BG   *Birmes-Gollak*. Anklage Birmes, Heinrich; Gollak, Ernst; Winkler, Benno; Bundesarchiv Ludwigsburg AKT B162/4693 II 208 AR-Z 74/60.

EH   *Eleanora Hodys*. Testimony published in *Dachau Liberated: The Official Report by U.S. Seventh Army, released within days of the camp's liberation by elements of the 42d and 45th division*, ed. Michael W. Perry (Seattle: Inkling Books, 2000). In English.

EKI   *Kaltenbrunner Interrogations*. US National Archives, Record Group 238 Microfilm Publications, M1270, Rolls 4 and 25. In English.

EM   *Erich Muhsfeldt Affidavits*. Dated Krakau 14.8.1947, 16.8.1947, 19.8.1947, 8.9.1947. Copy provided by Barbara Schwindt (2005, p. 81, n. 47) as "Übersetzung in 'Akten des Majdanek-Prozesses,' HA, Bd. 56, Bl. 11551 ff."

F65   *Institut für Zeitgeschichte*. File deposited by Gerhard Wiebeck, Akz. 2693/61, F-65.

GM   *Georg Michalsen*. Ermittlungen gegen Georg Michalsen u.a. Landgericht Hamburg. Bundesarchiv Ludwigsburg B162/1748 208 AR-Z 74/60.

GR   *Grabner Report*. Document written by Maximilian Grabner while in custody in Vienna. DÖW Vienna (Documentation Centre of Austrian Resistance), File Number 23680/15. Copy of File of the Hessisches Staatsarchiv, Proceedings against Georg Reno, concerning Euthanasia (StA Frankfurt/Main 4 Js 444/59).

GWA   *Wiebeck Affidavit*. Affidavit of Gerhard Wiebeck, dated 28 February 1947, Nuremberg document NO-2331. Harvard Law School Library. *Nuremberg Trials Project: A Digital Document Collection*, HLSL Item 2326.

GWT   *Gerhard Wiebeck Frankfurt Testimony*. Day 95 of the Frankfurt *Auschwitz-Prozess* (1.10.1964), Fritz Bauer Institut, HH StAW Abt. 461 Nr. 37638. Published as *Der Auschwitz-Prozess: Tonbandmitschnitte, Protokolle, Dokumente, 95. Verhandlungstag 1.10.1964* (Berlin: Direct Media Publishing, 2004), pp. 19570–19698.

HA   *Hoven affidavits*. Affidavits regarding Waldemar Hoven. NMT 01. Medical Case—*USA v. Karl Brandt et al*. Numbered as "Hoven Document *x*." Harvard Law School Library. *Nuremberg Trials Project: A Digital Document Collection*, HLSL Item 672.

HAW(1) Hessisches Hauptstaatsarchiv Wiesbaden 461/31502 (Abteilung 461, Nr. 31 502, 413 AR-Z 28/1970), Staatsanwaltschaft Frankfurt am Main. Ermittlungssache gegen RA Dr. Konrad Morgen 1970.

HAW(2) Hessisches Hauptstaatsarchiv Wiesbaden 461/32808 (Abteilung 461, Nr. 32 808, 4a JS1841/54), Staatsanwaltschaft Frankfurt am Main. Ermittlungssache gegen RA Dr. Konrad Morgen 1954.

HAW(3) Hessisches Hauptstaatsarchiv Wiesbaden 631/325 (Abteilung 631, Nr. Personalakten des Oberlandesgerichts Frankfurt am Main über Dr. Konrad Morgen).

HPS   *Himmler Posen Speech*. Extracts from speech of Heinrich Himmler in Posen, October 4, 1943, official translation. Harvard Law School Library. *Nuremberg Trials Project: A Digital Document Collection*, HLSL Item 2974.

HSG   *Hauptamt SS-Gericht*. Files of the SS Judiciary Main Office. Captured German Records Filmed at Berlin (American Historical Association), US Archives Record Group 242, microfilm T-580, rolls 212–15.

IMT   *Trial of the Major War Criminals before the International Military Tribunal 14 November 1945–1 October 1946* (Nuremberg: Secretariat of the Tribunal, 1947) ("Blue Series").

IZ   *Institut für Zeitgeschichte*. Two reports dated 21.12.45 and 7.1.46 concerning the SS-*Gerichtsbarkeit* (filed with F65).

JJ   *Johannes Jaenisch*. Trial of Johannes Jaenisch, Landesgericht Waldshut. Bundesarchiv Ludwigsburg B162/29657 AR 10 361/87.

KA   *Koch Anklageverfügung*. Dated 17 August 1944. Dodd Archive uconn_asc_1994–0065_box288_folder7343—7344.

KE   *Koch Ermittlungsergebnis*. Dated April 11, 1944. Document NO 2366. Harvard Law School Library. *Nuremberg Trials Project: A Digital Document Collection*, HLSL Item 2328; also US National Archives. Record Group 238, ARC Identifier 597043 / MLR Number NM70 174.

KM5, KM7 Morgen's IMT Nuremberg affidavits, Nuremberg Documents SS-65, SS-67, "Blue Series," vol. XLII, pp. 551–65.

KMB   Konrad Morgen, *Kriegspropaganda und Kriegsverhütung* (Leipzig: Universitätsverlag von Robert Noske, 1936).

KMC   *Army Counter-Intelligence Corps*. Dossier on Morgen (XE004520), US National Archives, Record Group 319, Box 365.

KMD   *Konrad Morgen Majdanek-Prozess Testimony*. **KMD(1)**. Morgen affidavit to the Majdanek-Prozess, dated Düsseldorf September 19,

1973. Landgericht Düsseldorf I 4/71. Bundesarchiv Ludwigsburg B162/2359. **KMD(2):** *Majdanek-Prozess Testimony* 2. Morgen's deposition for the Majdanek-Prozess, Frankfurt January 22, 1980.

KMF   *Konrad Morgen Frankfurt Testimony.* Day 25 of the Frankfurt *Auschwitz-Prozess*, Fritz Bauer Institut, HHStAW Abt. 461 Nr. 37638. Published as *Der Auschwitz-Prozess: Tonbandmitschnitte, Protokolle, Dokumente*, 25. *Verhandlungstag* 9.3.1964 (Berlin: Direct Media Publishing, 2004), pp. 5550–5693. Some of this testimony appears, heavily abridged, in Hermann Langbein, *Der Auschwitz-Prozess: Eine Dokumentation* (Frankfurt am Main: Europäische Verlagsanstalt, 1965).

KMH   *Konrad Morgen marriage papers.* Bundesarchiv Berlin-Lichterfelde, BArch (ehem BDC/RS) Morgen, Konrad (Akte des Rasse- und Siedlungshauptamtes der SS).

KMI   *Konrad Morgen Interrogations.* "Interrogation Records Prepared for War Crimes Proceedings at Nuernberg 1945–1947." US National Archives, Record Group 238, Microfilm 1019, Roll 47.

KMK   *"Der Korruptionsverbrecher."* Article by Morgen published in *Kriminalistik. Monatshefte für die gesamte kriminalistische Wissenschaft und Praxis*, Vol. 17, *Heft* 12, Berlin December 1943, pp. 117–19.

KML   *Konrad Morgen Paul Kleesattel Memo.* Memo from Morgen to Horst Bender dated 19.2.1942. Bundesarchiv Berlin-Lichterfelde (ehem. BDC), SM J5, Kleesattel, Paul.

KMM   *"Ministries Case" Testimony.* Morgen's testimony at the trial of Ernst von Weizsäcker et al. before the Nuremberg Military Tribunal. US National Archives, record group 238, microfilm M897. In German and English.

KMN   *Konrad Morgen Nachlass.* Fritz Bauer Institut, Frankfurt am Main.

KMO   *Konrad Morgen Oberursel Affidavit.* Morgen's affidavit executed 28 December 1945. German with English translation. Dodd Archive uconn_asc_1994–0065_box288_folder7346.

KMP   *Konrad Morgen Pohl Testimony.* Morgen's testimony in the trial *USA v. Pohl et al.*, NMT Case 4. Testimony of August 21–22, 1947, trial transcript pp. 6669–6753. University of Southampton Library MS200/4/13/1–2. In English.

KMR   *Konrad Morgen Mrugowsky Affidavits.* Translations of 3 affidavits by Morgen submitted in the trial of Joachim Mrugowsky NMT 01. Medical Case—*USA v. Karl Brandt et al.* English transcripts pp. 5118 (dated 26.02.47), 5150 (dated 26.02.47), 10675 (dated 23.05.47). Harvard Law School Library. *Nuremberg Trials Project: A Digital Document Collection*, HLSL Items 736, 741, 794.

KMT	*Toland Interview.* Interview of Morgen with John Toland, October 25, 1971, audio recording. FDR Library, Hyde Park, NY, John Toland Papers, box 53.
KMU	*Morgen Verfahren wegen Beihilfe zum Mord.* Documents concerning the investigation of Morgen's alleged complicity in the deportations from Hungary. Bundesarchiv Ludwigsburg B162/9000 VI 413 AR-Z 28/70.
KMV	*Frankfurt Vorvernehmungen.* Pre-trial interrogations for Auschwitz Prozess, in Morgen Nachlass, Fritz Bauer Institut.
KMV(1)	Dated 24/27.1.1961, LG Köln, 30 UR 9/58, 4 Ks 2/63, Bd. 46, Bl. 8514–24.
KMV(2)	Dated 8.3.1962, LG Frankfurt am Main, 4 Ks 2/63, Bd. 63, Bl. 11714–22.
KMW	*Konrad Morgen Waldeck Testimony.* Morgen's testimony in the trial *USA v. Josias Erbprinz zu Waldeck–Pyrmont*, trial 31 of War Criminals from Buchenwald Camp. US National Archives, Record Group 549, "Cases Tried," Josiahs Prinz zu Waldeck et al., Case 000-50-9, Boxes 425 to 464. Testimony of June 11–12, 1947, pp. 2736–2964.
KS	*Kurt Sachs.* Letter dated 26 February 1943 to Franz Breithaupt. Staatsarchiv München Spruchkammer-Akten 1482: Sachs, Kurt.
KWO	*Koch Weimar Opinion.* Translation of a document dated Weimar, September 11, 1944. Nuremberg document NO-2380. From NMT 01. Medical Case—*USA v. Karl Brandt et al.*, English Transcript: p. 9970 (24 June 1947). Harvard Law School Library. *Nuremberg Trials Project: A Digital Document Collection*, HLSL Item 2331.
LA	*Lauffs Affidavit.* Affidavit of Hans Lauffs, dated Ludwigsberg 26.7.45. Copy provided by Barbara Schwindt, who cites this (2005, p. 270, n. 381) as "Akten des 'Majdanek Prozesses,' Auschwitz-Dokumente, Bl. 25."
MCD	*"Ministries Case" Documents.* In *Trials of the War Criminals before the Nuernberg Military Tribunals* ("Blue Series"), vol. XIII. United States Military Tribunal IV, Case No. 11, *USA v. Ernst von Weizsaecker et al.*
MGI	*Grabner Interrogation.* Maximilian Grabner Report, DÖW Vienna (Documentation Centre of Austrian Resistance), File Number 23680/15. Copy of File of the Hessisches Staatsarchiv, Proceedings against Georg Reno, concerning Euthanasia (StA Frankfurt/Main 4 Js 444/59).
MHG	*Mitteilungen des Hauptamts SS-Gericht.* Published memoranda of the SS Judiciary Head Office, US National Archives, Record Group 242, microfilm T175A, roll 3.

NG-558   Letter from Otto Georg Thierack to Martin Bormann dated October 13, 1942. Harvard Law School Library. *Nuremberg Trials Project: A Digital Document Collection*, HLSL Item 4244.

NO-429   Affidavits by Waldemar Hoven. NMT 01. Medical Case—*USA v. Karl Brandt et al*. Harvard Law School Library. *Nuremberg Trials Project: A Digital Document Collection*, HLSL Item 154.

NO-434   Affidavit of Ferdinand Roemhild, former clerk to Waldemar Hoven. Harvard Law School Library. *Nuremberg Trials Project: A Digital Document Collection*, HLSL Item 612.

NO-630   Hitler's order to Bouhler and Brandt authorizing the "euthanasia" program. Harvard Law School Library. *Nuremberg Trials Project: A Digital Document Collection*, HLSL Items 2493 (original), 4814 (translation).

NO-1270   English translation of **NO 2187**. Report by Max Horn, director, on the Ostindustrie G.m.b.H. Harvard Law School Library. *Nuremberg Trials Project: A Digital Document Collection*, HLSL Item 3953.

NO-1875   Affidavit of Kurt Mittelstädt, SS Judge. Oberursel December 14, 1945. **HAW(1)**, Ermittlungsverfahren gegen Dr. Konrad Morgen 1970, p. 4.

NO-2366   Materials in Morgen's possession when he entered American custody. US National Archives ARC Identifier 597043 / MLR Number NM70 174.

NO-2380   Translation of a memo written by Morgen to the *ZbV*-court in Weimar, dated September 11, 1944. From the records of NMT 01. Medical Case—*USA v. Karl Brandt et al*., English Transcript: p. 9970 (24 June 1947). Harvard Law School Library. *Nuremberg Trials Project: A Digital Document Collection*, HLSL Item 2331.

NS7   Bundesarchiv Berlin-Lichterfelde, *Bestand NS7*. Files related to the SS Judiciary.

NS19   Bundesarchiv Berlin-Lichterfelde, *Bestand NS19*. Files related to the SS Judiciary.

ODD   *Oskar Dirlewanger Defense*. Documents in defense of Oskar Dirlewanger. Bundesarchiv Berlin-Lichterfelde R58-7633.

PAF   *Personalakte Alfred Fassbender*. Personnel file of Alfred Fassbender. Bundesarchiv Berlin-Lichterfelde BArch (ehem. BDC)/SSO/SS Fassbender, Alfred.

PAL   *Personalakte Arthur Liebehenschel*. SS Master file card for Arthur Liebehenschel. In *Archives of the Holocaust* Vol. 11, Part 2, ed. Henry Friedlander and Sybil Milton (Routledge, 1993), document 268, p. 52.

PCW   *Personalakte Christian Wirth*. Personnel file of Christian Wirth. Bundesarchiv Berlin-Lichterfelde, BArch (ehem. BDC)/SSO/SS/ Wirth, Christian.

PFL   *Personalakte Hermann Florstedt.* Personnel file of Hermann Florstedt. Bundesarchiv Berlin-Lichterfelde, BArch (ehem. BDC)/ SSO/SS/ Florstedt, Hermann.

PGS   *Personalakte Georg von Sauberzweig.* SS personnel file of Georg von Sauberzweig. Bundesarchiv Berlin-Lichterfelde. BArch (ehem. BDC)/ SSO/SS/ Sauberzweig, Georg von.

PHB   *Akte Horst Bender.* File on Horst Bender, Staatsarchiv Ludwigsburg EL 317/III, Bü 965.

PHF   *Personalakte Hermann Fegelein.* Personnel file of Hermann Fegelein. Bundesarchiv Berlin-Lichterfelde BArch (ehem. BDC)/SSO/SS/ Fegelein, Otto Hermann.

PKM   *Personalakte Dr. Konrad Morgen.* Pesonnel file of Konrad Morgen. Bundesarchiv Berlin-Lichterfelde, BArch (ehem. BDC)/SSO/SS/ Morgen, Konrad.

POG   *Personalakte Odilo Globocnik.* Personnel file of Odilo Globocnik. Bundesarchiv Berlin-Lichterfelde, BArch (ehem. BDC)/SSO/SS Globocnik, Odilo.

PS-1919   Himmler's Posen Speech of October 4, 1943. Harvard Law School Library. *Nuremberg Trials Project: A Digital Document Collection,* HLSL Item 3791.

RSS   *Reichsführer-SS.* Records of the Reich Leader of the SS and Chief of the German Police. US Archives, Record Group 242, microfilm T-175, rolls 3, 53, 248.

SF   *Strafsache Fellenz.* Trial of Fellenz, Bundesarchiv Ludwigsburg AKT B 162/1349 AR-Z 28/70 Band VIII, pp. 52–3.

SKV   *Spruchkammerverfahren.* Morgen's denazification proceedings in Ludwigsburg. Staatsarchiv Ludwigsburg EWL903/3, Bü2196; EWL 905/4; Bü1933.

SR   *Sporrenberg Report.* Published in *Historische Mitteilungen* 6 (1993): 250–77. With commentary and notes by Robert Bohn.

WHI   *Waldemar Hoven Interrogation.* Interrogations dated October 22, 23, 1946. Nuremberg Documents NO-4068, 4069. Harvard Law School Library. *Nuremberg Trials Project: A Digital Document Collection,* HLSL Items 221, 222.

WHM   *Werner Hansen Frankfurt Mitschrift.* Judge's notes on the testimony of Werner Hansen. Day 116 of the Frankfurt Auschwitz-Prozess (27.11.1964), Fritz Bauer Institut, *Der Auschwitz-Prozess: Tonbandmitschnitte, Protokolle, Dokumente.* 116. Verhandlungstag, 27.11.1964, pp. 25987–26049 (Berlin: Direct Media Publishing, 2004), pp. 26050–8.

WHT   *Werner Hansen Frankfurt Testimony.* Day 116 of the Frankfurt Auschwitz-Prozess (27.11.1964), Fritz Bauer Institut, *Der*

Auschwitz-Prozess: Tonbandmitschnitte, Protokolle, Dokumente. 116. Verhandlungstag, 27.11.1964 (Berlin: Direct Media Publishing, 2004), pp. 25987–26049.

WPA   *Werner Paulmann Affidavit.* Affidavit to the IMT by Werner Paulmann, July 11, 1946, document SS-64, "Blue Series" vol. XLII, pp. 543–51.

WRA   *Wilhelm Ruppert Affidavit.* Affidavit of Friedrich Wilhelm Ruppert, August 6, 1945. Nuremberg Document **NO-1903**, US National Archives. In English translation. An extract from Ruppert's affidavit, dealing with the Erntefest massacre, appears in *Die Ermordung der europäischen Juden: Eine umfassende Dokumentation des Holocaust 1941–1945*, ed. Peter Longerich and Dieter Pohl (Munich: Piper, 1989), pp. 227–8.

WTR   *Walter Többens Report.* Report by Walter Többens, "Bericht ueber Warschau und Werke von Poniatowa," dated Bremen September 15, 1945, "z.Zt. Detention Camp." YIVO Institute for Jewish Research, New York.

Published Sources

Aly, Götz. "The Planning Intelligentsia and the 'Final Solution'," *The Holocaust: Origins, Implementation, Aftermath*, ed. Omer Bartov (London: Routledge, 2000), 92–105.

Aly, Götz, and Susanne Heim. *Architects of Annihilation: Auschwitz and the Logic of Destruction*, trans. A.G. Blunden (Princeton University Press, 2002).

Anscombe, G. E. M. *Intention*, 2nd edition (Cambridge, MA: Harvard University Press, 2002).

Arad, Yitzhak. *Belzec, Sobibor, Treblinka: The Operation Reinhard Death Camps* (Bloomington, IN: Indiana University Press, 1987).

Arendt, Hannah. *Eichmann in Jerusalem* (New York: Penguin Classics, 2006).

Der Auschwitz-Prozess: Tonbandmitschnitte, Protokolle und Dokumente, ed. Fritz Bauer Institut and the State Museum Auschwitz-Birkenau in Zusammenarbeit mit der Stiftung Deutsches Rundfunkarchiv und dem Hessischen Hauptstaatsarchiv Wiesbaden, 2nd durchgesehene und verbesserte Auflage (Berlin: Directmedia Publishing, 2007).

Bahro, Berno. "Der Sport und seine Rolle in der nationalsozialistischen Elitetruppe SS," *Historical Social Research* 32 (2007): 78–91.

Bein, Alex. *The Jewish Question: Biography of a World Problem*, trans. Harry Zohn (Rutherford, NJ: Fairleigh Dickenson University Press, 1990).

Best, Werner. "Die Geheime Staatspolizei," *Deutsches Recht* 6 (1936): 125–8.

Browning, Christopher R. *Ordinary Men: Reserve Police Battalion 101 and the "Final Solution" in Poland* (New York: HarperCollins, 1998).

Browning, Chistopher R. *The Origins of the Final Solution: The Evolution of Nazi Jewish Policy, September 1939–March 1942* (Lincoln, NB: University of Nebraska Press, 2004).

Buchenwald Concentration Camp 1937–1945: A Guide to the Permanent Historical Exhibition, compiled by Harry Stein, ed. Gedenkstätte Buchenwald, trans. Judith Rosenthal (Frankfurt am Main: Wallstein Verlag, 2004).

The Buchenwald Report, ed. and trans. David A. Hackett (San Francisco: Westview Press, 1995).

Buchheim, Hans. *Die SS: Das Herrschaftsinstrument Befehl und Gehorsam* (Olten und Freiburg im Breisgau: Walther Verlag, 1965).

Buchheim, Hans. "The SS—Instrument of Domination," in *Anatomy of the SS-State*, ed. Helmut Krausnick, Hans Buchheim, Martin Broszat, and Hans-Adolf Jacobsen (New York: Walker and Company, 1968), 143–66.

Büchler, Yehoshua R. "'Unworthy Behavior': The Case of SS Officer Max Täubner," *Holocaust and Genocide Studies* 17 (2003): 409–29.

Cesarani, David. *Becoming Eichmann: Rethinking the Life, Crimes, and Trial of a "Desk Murderer"* (Cambridge, MA: Da Capo Press, 2004).

Dachau Liberated: The Official Report by the U.S. Seventh Army, ed. Michael W. Perry (Seattle: Inkling Books, 2000).

Dahm, Georg. "Das Ermessen des Richters im nationalsozialistischen Strafrecht," in *Deutsches Strafrecht: Strafrecht, Strafrechtspolitik, Strafprozeß, Zeitschrift der Akademie für Deutsches Recht*, Neue Folge, 1. Band, ed. Roland Freisler (Berlin: R.v. Decker's Verlag, G. Schenck, 1934a), 87–96.

Dahm, Georg. "Die Erneuerung der Ehrenstrafe," *Deutsche Juristen-Zeitung* 39 (1934b): 821–32.

Dahm, Georg. "Verbrechen und Tatbestand," in *Grundfragen der Neuen Rechtswissenschaft*, Georg Dahm, Ernst Rudolf Huber, Karl Larenz, Karl Michaelis, Friedrich Schaffstein, and Wolfgang Siebert (Berlin: Junker und Dünnhaupt Verlag, 1935), 62–107.

Dahm, Georg. "Gerechtigkeit und Zweckmäßigkeit im Strafrecht der Gegenwart," in *Probleme der Strafrechtserneuerung* mit Beiträgen von Paul Bockelmann, Georg Dahm et al. (Berlin: Walter de Gruyter & Co., 1944), 1–23.

Das kommende deutsche Strafrecht: Allgemeiner Teil: Bericht über die Arbeit der amtlichen Strafrechtskommission, 2. Auflage, nach den Ergebnissen der zweiten Lesung neu bearbeitet, ed. Franz Gürtner (Berlin: Verlag Franz Vahlen, 1935).

Das kommende deutsche Strafrecht: Besonderer Teil: Bericht über die Arbeit der amtlichen Strafrechtskommission, 2. Auflage, nach den Ergebnissen der zweiten Lesung neu bearbeitet, ed. Franz Gürtner (Berlin: Verlag Franz Vahlen 1936).

Deutsches Strafrecht: Strafrecht, Strafrechtspolitik, Strafprozeß, Zeitschrift der Akademie für Deutsches Recht, Neue Folge, 1. Band, ed. Roland Freisler (Berlin: R.v. Decker's Verlag, G. Schenck, 1934).

Dieckmann, Christoph. "The War and the Killing of the Lithuanian Jews," in *National Socialist Extermination Policies: Contemporary German Perspectives and Controversies*, ed. Ulrich Herbert (New York: Berghahn Books, 2000), 240–75.

Dworkin, Ronald. *Law's Empire* (Oxford: Hart, 1998).

Dyzenhaus, David. "The Grudge Informer Case Revisited," *New York University Law Review* 83 (2008): 1000–34.

Erntefest, 3–4 listopada 1943: Zapomniany epizod Zagłady, ed. Wojciech Lenarczyk and Dariusz Libionka (Lublin: Państwowe Muzeum na Majdanku, 2009).

Fest, Joachim. *Albert Speer: Conversations with Hitler's Architect*, trans. Patrick Camiller (Cambridge, MA: Polity Press, 2007).

Forsthoff, Ernst. *Der Totale Staat* (Hamburg: Hanseatische Verlagsanstalt, 1933).

Freisler, Roland. "Willensstrafrecht: Versuch und Vollendung," in Franz Gürtner (ed.) *Das kommende deutsche Strafrecht: Allgemeiner Teil: Bericht über die Arbeit der amtlichen Strafrechtskommission*, 2. Auflage (nach den Ergebnissen der 2. Lesung neu bearbeitet) (Berlin: Verlag FranzVahlen, 1935), 5–48.

Freisler, Roland. *Nationalsozialistisches Recht und Rechtsdenken* (Berlin: Spaeth & Linde, 1938).

Friedlander, Henry. *The Origins of Nazi Genocide: From Euthanasia to the Final Solution* (Chapel Hill: University of North Carolina Press, 1995).

Fuller, Lon L. "Positivism and Fidelity to Law: A Reply to Professor Hart," *Harvard Law Review* 71 (1958): 630–72.

Gleispach, Wenzel v. "Willensstrafrecht," in *Handwörterbuch der Kriminologie und der anderen strafrechtlichen Hilfswissenschaften*, ed. Alexander Elster and Heinrich Lingemann, vol. II (Berlin and Leipzig: Verlag von Walter de Gruyter & Co., 1936), 1067–79.

Greene, Joshua M. *Justice at Dachau: The Trials of an American Prosecutor* (Westminster, MD: Broadway Books, 2003).

Gross, Raphael. "Die Ethik eines wahrheitsuchenden Richters: Konrad Morgen, SS-Richter und Korruptionsspezialist," in *Moralität des Bösen: Ethik und Nationalsozialistische Verbrechen*, ed. Werner Konitzer and Raphael Gross (Frankfurt am Main: Campus Verlag, 2009), 243–64.

Gruchmann, Lothar. *Justiz im Dritten Reich 1933–1940: Anpassung und Unterwerfung in der Ära Gürtner* (München: R. Oldenbourg Verlag, 1988).

Günther, Hans F. K. *Rassenkunde des deutschen Volkes* (München: J.F. Lehmann, 1933).

Hambrock, Matthias. "Dialektik der 'verfolgenden Unschuld'. Überlegungen zu Mentalität und Funktion der SS," in *Die SS, Himmler und die Wewelsburg*, ed. Jan Erik Schulte (Paderborn, München, Wien, Zürich: Ferdinand Schöningh, 2009), 79–101.

Harman, Gilbert. "Moral Relativism Defended," *The Philosophical Review* 84 (1975): 3–22.

Hart, H. L. A. "Positivism and the Separation of Law and Morals," *Harvard Law Review* 71 (1958): 593–629.

Hartl, Benedikt. *Das nationalsozialistische Willensstrafrecht* (Berlin: Weißensee-Verlag, 2000).

Herbert, Ulrich. *Biographische Studien über Radikalismus, Weltanschauung und Vernunft 1903–1989* (Bonn: Dietz, 2001).

Herf, Jeffrey. *The Jewish Enemy: Nazi Propaganda during World War II and the Holocaust* (Cambridge, MA: Harvard University Press, 2006).

Herman, Barbara. "The Practice of Moral Judgment," in *The Practice of Moral Judgment* (Cambridge, MA: Harvard University Press, Cambridge 1993), 73–93.

Herman, Barbara. "A Cosmopolitan Kingdom of Ends," in *Moral Literacy* (Cambridge, MA: Harvard University Press, 2007), 51–78.

Herzl, Theodor. *Der Judenstaat: Versuch einer modernen Lösung der Judenfrage; Text und Materialen 1986 bis heute*, ed. Ernst Piper (Berlin: Philo, 2004).

Himmler, Heinrich. *Geheimreden 1933 bis 1945 und andere Ansprachen*, ed. Bradley F. Smith and Agnes F. Peterson, introd. Joachim C. Fest (Propyläen Verlag, 1974).

Huber, Ernst Rudolf. *Verfassungsrecht des Großdeutschen Reiches*, zweite, stark erweiterte Auflage der "Verfassung" (Hamburg: Hanseatische Verlagsanstalt, 1939).

Jünger, Ernst. *Auf den Marmorklippen* (Hamburg: Hanseatische Verlagsanstalt, 1939).

Keller, Ernst. "Ernst Jüngers Auf den Marmorklippen—Eine Erzählung und ihre Kritiker," in *Unravelling the Labyrinth. Decoding Text and Language. Festschrift for Eric Lawson Marson*, ed. Kerry Dunne and Ian R. Campbell (Frankfurt am Main: Peter Lang 1997), 19–35.

Kendrick, Gregory M. "A Question of Justice: Konrad Morgen and the Final Solution." MA thesis, San Francisco State University (November, 1988).

Kershaw, Ian. *Hitler 1889–1936: Hubris* (New York: W.W. Norton & Company, 1998).

Kershaw, Ian. *Hitler 1936–1945: Nemesis* (New York: W.W. Norton & Company, 2000).

Klee, Ernst, Willi Dressen, and Volker Riess (eds). *The Good Old Days. The Holocaust Seen by Its Perpetrators and Bystanders* (Old Saybrook, CT: Konecky & Konecky, 1991).

Klemperer, Victor. *The Language of the Third Reich: LTI—Lingua Tertii Imperii*, trans. Martin Brady (New York: Continuum, 2000).

Koehl, Robert Lewis. *The Black Corps: The Structure and Power Struggles of the Nazi SS* (Madison, WI: University of Wisconsin Press, 1983).

Koellreutter, Otto. *Deutsches Verfassungsrecht: Ein Grundriss*, 3. durchgesehene und erweiterte Auflage (Berlin: Junker und Dünnhaupt Verlag, 1938).

Kogon, Eugen. *The Theory and Practice of Hell: The German Concentration Camps and the System Behind Them* (New York: Farrar, Straus and Giroux, 2006).

Krug, Karl. "Drei Grundprobleme des kommenden Strafrechts," *Zeitschrift der Akademie für Deutsches Recht*, 2. Jahrgang (1935): 98–102.

Kuwalek, Robert. "Das kurze Leben 'im Osten': Jüdische Deutsche im Distrikt Lublin aus polnisch-jüdischer Sicht," in *Die Deportation der Juden aus Deutschland: Pläne—Praxis—Reaktionen 1938–1945, Beiträge zur Geschichte des Nationalsozialismus* Band 20, ed. Birthe Kundrus and Beate Meyer (Göttingen: Wallstein Verlag, 2004), 112–34.

Lindner, Peter. *Hermann Florstedt: SS-Führer und KZ Lagerkommandant: Ein Lebensbild im Horizont der Familie* (Halle/Saale: Verlag André Gursky, 1997).

Longerich, Peter. *Heinrich Himmler: Biographie* (München: Siedler Verlag, 2008).

Martus, Steffen. *Ernst Jünger* (Stuttgart, Weimar: Verlag J.B. Metzler, 2001).

Messerschmidt, Manfred. *Die Wehrmacht im NS-Staat: Zeit der Indoktrination* (Hamburg: Decker Schenck, 1969).

Mezger, Edmund. *Deutsches Strafrecht: Ein Leitfaden* (Berlin: Junker und Dünnhaupt, 1936).

Mezger, Edmund. *Deutsches Strafrecht: Ein Grundriss* (Berlin: Junker und Dünnhaupt, 1938).

Mommsen, Hans. *Beamtentum im Dritten Reich: Mit ausgewählten Quellen zur nationalsozialistischen Beamtenpolitik* (Stuttgart: Deutsche Verlags-Anstalt, 1966).

National Socialist Guidelines for a New German Criminal Law, ed. the Reich Legal Office of the Nazi Party. Nationalsozialistische Leitsätze für ein neues deutsches Strafrecht, 1. Teil, ed. Reichsrechtsamt der NSDAP. Reichsleiter Dr. Hans Frank, 4th edition (Berlin: Deutscher Rechts-Verlag 1935).

Nazi Conspiracy and Aggresssion ("Red Series"), Supplement B, Office of United States Chief of Counsel for Prosecution of Axis Criminality (Washington, D.C.: 1948).

"Notes of Eastern Territories Commander, Johannes Blaskowitz," *The Good Old Days: The Holocaust as Seen by Its Perpetrators and Bystanders*, ed. Ernst Klee, Willi Dressen, and Volker Riess (New York: The Free Press, 1991).

O'Donnell, James P. *The Bunker: The History of the Reich Chancellery Group* (Boston: Houghton Mifflin, 1978).

Orth, Karin. *Die Konzentrationslager-SS: Sozialstrukturelle Analysen und biographische Studien* (München: Wallstein Verlag, 2000).

Pauer-Studer, Herlinde, and J. David Velleman. "Distortions of Normativity," *Ethical Theory and Moral Practice* 14 (2011): 329–56.

Petropoulos, Jonathan. *Royals and the Reich: The Princes of Hessen in Nazi Germany* (New York: Oxford University Press, 2006).

Reichsführer! Briefe an und von Himmler, ed. Helmut Heiber (Munich: Deutscher Taschenbuch Verlag, 1970).

Reinicke, Wolfgang. *Instrumentalisierung von Geschichte durch Heinrich Himmler und die SS* (Neuried: ars et unitas Verlagsgesellschaft, 2003).

Reitlinger, Gerald. *The SS: Alibi of a Nation 1922–1945* (New York: Viking Press, 1957).

Rhodes, Richard. *Masters of Death: The SS-Einsatzgruppen and the Invention of the Holocaust* (New York: Random House, 2002).

Riess, Volker. "Hermann Fegelein: Parvenu ohne Skrupel," in *Die SS: Elite unter dem Totenkopf: 30 Lebensläufe*, 2. durchgesehene und aktualisierte Auflage, ed. Ronald Smelser and Enrico Syring (Darmstadt: Wissenschaftliche Buchgesellschaft, 2003), 160–72.

Riess, Volker. "Christian Wirth—der Inspekteur der Vernichtungslager," in *Karrieren der Gewalt. Nationalsozialistische Täterbiographien*, ed. Klaus-Michael Mallmann und Gerhard Paul, 2. Auflage (Darmstadt: Wissenschaftliche Buchgesellschaft, 2011), 239–51.

Sauer, Wilhelm. "Die Ethisierung des Strafrechts: Über die Prinzipien der Strafrechtserneuerung und ihre praktische Auswirkung," in *Deutsches Strafrecht. Strafrecht, Strafrechtspolitik, Strafprozeß*, Zeitschrift der Akademie für Deutsches Recht, Neue Folge, 1. Band. Ed. Roland Freisler (Berlin: R.v. Decker's Verlag, G. Schenck, 1934), 177–90.

Schäfer, Karl. "Nullum crimen sine poena. (Das Recht als Grundlage der Bestrafung. Zeitliche Geltung der Strafgesetze)," in *Das kommende deutsche Strafrecht. Allgemeiner Teil*. Bericht über die Arbeit der amtlichen Strafrechtskommission (Berlin: Verlag Franz Vahlen, 1935), 200–18.

Schaffstein, Friedrich. "Ehrenstrafe und Freiheitsstrafe in ihrer Bedeutung für das neue Strafrecht," in *Deutsches Strafrecht. Strafrecht, Strafrechtspolitik, Strafprozeß*, Zeitschrift der Akademie für Deutsches Recht, Neue Folge, 1. Band. Ed. Roland Freisler (Berlin: R.v. Decker's Verlag, G. Schenck,1934), 273–82.

Schenk, Dieter. *Krakauer Burg: Die Machtzentrale des Generalgouverneurs Hans Frank 1939–1945* (Berlin: Ch. Links Verlag, 2010).

Schmerbach, Folker. *Das "Gemeinschaftslager Hanns Kerrl" für Referendare in Jüterbog 1933–1939* (Tübingen: Mohr Siebeck, 2008).

Schmitt, Carl. "Der Führer schützt das Recht. Zur Reichstagsrede von Adolf Hitler vom 13. Juli 1934" ("The Führer Protects the Law"), in *Deutsche Juristen-Zeitung* 39 (1934): 945–50.

Schulte, Jan Erik. "Zur Geschichte der SS. Erzähltraditionen und Forschungsstand," in *Die SS, Himmler und die Wewelsburg*, ed. Jan Erik Schulte (Paderborn: Ferdinand Schöningh, 2009), xi–xxxv.

Schwilk, Heimo. *Ernst Jünger. Ein Jahrhundertleben. Die Biografie* (München, Zürich: Piper, 2007).

Schwindt, Barbara. *Das Konzentrations- und Vernichtungslager Majdanek: Funktionswandel im Kontext der "Endlösung"* (Würzburg: Königshausen & Neumann, 2005).

Sereny, Gitta. *Into That Darkness: An Examination of Conscience* (New York: Vintage Books, 1983).

Sheperd, Ben. "The Clean Wehrmacht, the War of Extermination, and Beyond," *The Historical Journal* 52 (2009): 455–73.

Siegert, Karl. "Nulla poena sine lege. Kritische Bemerkungen zu den Vorschlägen der amtlichen Strafrechtskommission," in *Deutsches Strafrecht. Strafrecht, Strafrechtspolitik, Strafprozeß*, Zeitschrift der Akademie für Deutsches Recht, Neue Folge, 1. Band. Ed. Roland Freisler (Berlin: R.v. Decker's Verlag, G. Schenck, 1934), 376–86.

Smelser, Ronald, and Enrico Syring. "Annäherungen an die 'Elite unter dem Totenkopf,'" in *Die SS: Elite unter dem Totenkopf: 30 Lebensläufe*, 2. durchgesehene und aktualisierte Auflage, ed. Ronald Smelser and Enrico Syring (Darmstadt: Wissenschaftliche Buchgesellschaft, 2003), 9–27.

Stuckart, Wilhelm, and Hans Globke. *Kommentare zur deutschen Rassengesetzgebung*, Band 1 (München und Berlin: C.H. Beck'sche Verlagsbuchhandlung, 1936).

Theel, Christopher, "'Parzifal unter den Gangstern?' Die SS- und Polizeigerichtsbarkeit in Polen 1939–1945," in *Die Waffen SS. Neue Forschungen*, ed. Jan Erik Schulte, Peter Lieb, and Bernd Wegner (Paderborn: Ferdinand Schöningh, 2014), 61–79.

Toland, John. *Adolf Hitler* (New York: Anchor Books, 1992).

The Trial of Adolf Eichmann: Record of the Proceedings in the District Court of Jerusalem (Israel: Ministry of Justice, 1992).

Vieregge, Bianca. *Die Gerichtsbarkeit einer "Elite": Nationalsozialistische Rechtsprechung am Beispiel der SS- und Polizei-Gerichtsbarkeit* (Baden-Baden: Nomos Verlagsgesellschaft, 2002).

Wegner, Bernd. *Hitlers Politische Soldaten: Die Waffen-SS 1933–1945: Leitbild, Struktur und Funktion einer nationalsozialistischen Elite*, 9. Auflage (Paderborn: Ferdinand Schöningh, 2010).

Weingartner, James J. "Law and Justice in the Nazi SS: The Case of Konrad Morgen," *Central European History* 16 (1983): 276–94.

Wette, Wolfram. *The Wehrmacht: History, Myth, Reality*, trans. Deborah Lucas Schneider (Cambridge, MA: Harvard University Press, 2006).

Wildt, Michael. *An Uncompromising Generation: The Nazi Leadership of the Reich Security Main Office*, trans. Tom Lampert (Madison: University of Wisconsin Press, 2009).

INDEX OF SUBJECTS

INDEX OF NAMES

CPI Antony Rowe
Chippenham, UK
2018-02-01 21:37